ABOUT TH

MW00390133

Shirley Smith is a psychotherapist, a highly recognised presenter and a best-selling author of three books, including *Set Yourself Free* and *Behind Closed Doors*. With degrees in philosophy; divinity; a background in psychology and behavioural science, Shirley draws on over 25 years experience in human functioning to help people identify and change behaviour patterns which block success and disrupt relationships. Her style is 'down to earth' and 'tell-it-like-it-is'.

Originally from the USA, Shirley was brought to Australia 21 years ago to train psychologists, doctors, counsellors and health professionals in the treatment of co-dependency, addictive behaviour and family of origin issues. Not only is Shirley recognised as one of Australia's leading specialists in this field, she is also a Certified Trainer and Facilitator in the educational applications of Neuro-Linguistic Programming and Generative Learning. In addition, Shirley is a certified hypnotherapist, an accredited Myers Briggs practitioner and an Executive Coach.

Shirley's work has been featured in nearly every mainstream Australian publication. As *New Woman* magazine's choice of Executive Coach, Shirley wrote a monthly column for their readers and has appeared on a number of television shows, as well as being featured on talkback radio programs Australia-wide.

After moving to Australia in 1988, Shirley became an Australian citizen in 1994, making her home in Sydney. She loves theatre, film, dance, new adventures and enjoys spending time with her grandchildren, good friends and playing with her little dog, "Sassy".

To book Shirley as a speaker, for a corporate training program, an executive coaching session, or enrol in one of The Radiant Group's Programs, Events or Seminars, or to contact Shirley Smith:

The Radiant Group Pty. Ltd.
PO Box 1605, Neutral Bay NSW Australia, 2089
Tel: +61 (0)2 9953 7000
Fax: +61 (0)2 9953 7100
E-mail: info@TheRadiantGroup.com.au
Websites: www.SetYourselfFree.com.au
          www.TheRadiantGroup.com.au
          www.ShirleySmith.com

WHAT PEOPLE ARE SAYING ABOUT
SET YOURSELF FREE AND SHIRLEY SMITH

In my medical and counselling practice, I have found Set Yourself Free *to be extremely useful for my clients. People from all walks of life and with a vast array of experiences find they can relate to much of what they read. The book moves, surprises and enlightens. It is full of wisdom yet simply written, making the information within eminently accessible. It is a useful tool for anyone wishing to explore further their journey in life.*

Dr. Leonie Aitken, Medical Practitioner

Set Yourself Free *is a powerful affirmation of the creative spiritual potential that resides within each of us. Shirley Smith has a sensitive but no-nonsense way of helping us see who we are, encouraging us to accept responsibility, and then gives us the clear steps to help us move out of our comfort zone to serenity, sanity and success.*

Jay R. Bacik, Author, Broadcaster and Minister.

Set Yourself Free *enlightened me and gave me the courage to heal the 'unfinished business' from my past. I can say with all confidence that many of my referred coaching clients have also been able to achieve healthy, balanced emotional lives and go on to realise their dreams diligently working through the processes described in Shirley Smith's book.*

A. McGuinness, Lifecoach.

This book provided clear, vital and readily accessible information to me. Personally it has helped 'set me free' from harmful habits and emotional baggage. Professionally it gave me a source of confident referral to help so many of my patients in my general practice.

Dr. Chris Roberts. MB,BS Medical Practitioner.

Until I found Shirley's book Set Yourself Free, *I felt completely alone and trapped in a miserable world of my own making. The information presented in the book was revolutionary to me, and provided the catalyst for a remarkable transformation in my own life that went beyond anything I could have previously imagined! I highly recommend* Set Yourself Free *to anyone with a genuine desire for change.*

Cherie Kellahan, Business Owner

Being the man, father and husband that I wanted to be was a far off fantasy. I really believed that joy and choice belonged to other people. Shirley's enthusiasm, knowledge and empathy encouraged me to challenge these beliefs and to explore all that life has to offer. Today, in my private practice, I often suggest Set Yourself Free *to clients who are seeking relief from conflict, emotional turmoil and a deeper meaning to life's journey and answer's to life's questions.*

Geoffrey Carthy, C.A.C

Shirley Smith offers a vivid and accurate description of the accelerating addictive malice which threatens the health and well being, of not only our own generation, but the very lives of our children, and grandchildren as well. This book provides accessible, compassionate and powerful step-by-step instructions on how to turn that future around. Reading this book was the wakeup call I needed to become fully alive, conscious and happy.

Nicola Lambert, Life and Business Coach

My immediate reaction after reading Set Yourself Free *is that it ought to be required reading for everyone. Read it and you'll discover why. Don't be fooled by the ease and accessibility of Shirley's writing.* Set Yourself Free *is a book of great depth and insight.*

Paula Forrest, Actor

Set Yourself Free *reflects Shirley's deep understanding of the recovery process and her ability to guide other's through it. It resonates with truth and hope. I frequently refer back to this book for further insight and to monitor my own progress.*

Anna Brennan

Having had no relationship with myself, this book speaks to me in a thousand ways of one important message: To learn about 'love addiction' which has been running my life for the last 30 years. NOW it is time to change it and step back into my journey.

Michelle Ling

Having been involved for over twenty years, in the US and Australia, with the evolution in the field of recovery from addictive behavioural patterns, I have no hesitation in declaring Set Yourself Free *as the best of best.*

The Reverend Grace Merrick, Unity Minister.

DEDICATION

I dedicate this book to my late Father and Mother,
John and Laura Smith,
who have always loved me and done the very best they could.

Set Yourself Free - Revised Anniversary Edition
Break the cycle of co-dependency and compulsive addictive behaviour

Published by:
The Radiant Group Pty Ltd
PO Box 1605, Neutral Bay NSW 2089, Australia
info@TheRadiantGroup.com.au
Copyright © Shirley Smith 1990-2010

First Published in Australia in 1990 by Bantam.
Reprinted 1990
Reprinted 1991 (twice)
Reprinted 1992 (twice)
Reprinted 1993, 1994, 1995, 1997, 1999.

Set Yourself Free - Revised Anniversary Edition
Break the cycle of co-dependency and compulsive addictive behaviour
ISBN 978-1479353408
Printed 2003
Reprinted 2006
Reprinted 2007
Reprinted 2010

Cover Design by Dolores Knox - Union Street Studio Pty Ltd, NSW Australia
Photography by Frank Jordan, contact frankjordan@primus.com.au

Distributed in Australia by:
The Scribo Group
18 Rodborough Road
Frenchs Forest, NSW 2086, Australia
Phone: +61 3 9761 5535
Phone: 1300 727 426
Email: orders@scribo.com.au
www.scribo.com.au

Layout & Design by Dolores Knox, Union Street Studio Pty Ltd, NSW Australia
Printed in China by 1010 Printing International Limited

SET YOURSELF FREE

Break the cycle of co-dependency and compulsive addictive behaviour

SHIRLEY SMITH

CONTENTS

ACKNOWLEDGEMENTS..I

AUTHOR'S NOTE TO THE REVISED,
ANNIVERSARY EDITION...III

PART ONE - 'THE PROBLEM'

CHAPTER 1 - BON VOYAGE...1
Setting Sail - How My Journey Began..1
Co-dependency Recovery Begins in Australia........................6
What happened?...7
Enough is Enough!..8
What About the Future?..9

CHAPTER 2 - ARE YOU REALLY FREE?........................11
What is Freedom?...11
Giving Up Labels Can Be Sticky!..14
Freedom Has A Price...15
Leaving Port - Where to Begin...16

CHAPTER 3 - DO YOU KNOW WHO YOU REALLY ARE?..19
Co-dependency - Australia's most common
and unrecognised disease..19
Where it All Begins - The Formative Years.........................20
Adapting Starts Early...22
Adapting Through Roles..23
The Hero...24
The Lost Child..25
The Caretaker...25
The Mascot..25
The Scapegoat...25
The Surrogate Spouse..26
Dave's Story - A Client's Personal Voyage..........................26

Changing Times, Changing Roles..................................28
Simone's Story - A Client's Personal Voyage..........................29
Recognising Child Abuse.....................................37
Physical Abuse...39
Sexual Abuse..39
Emotional Abuse...40
Abandonment...41
Intellectual Abuse...43
Spiritual Abuse..43
Moving From Victim to Victory...............................44
Some Characteristics of Co-Dependents.......................45
1. Self-esteem Issues.......................................45
2. Boundary Issues...46
3. Reality Issues...46
4. Dependency Issues.......................................46
5. Moderation Issues.......................................47
Dis-ease of Immaturity.....................................47

CHAPTER 4 - ARE YOU TRAPPED
BY DISTORTED REALITY?.....................................49
Denial..50
Intellectual Reality..51
Feeling Reality..54
How Are You Feeling?.......................................54
Adult Feeling Reality.......................................55
Carried Feeling Reality......................................55
Adult to Adult Feeling Exchange.............................56
Child Feeling Reality.......................................57
Spiritual Reality...58
Spiritual Bankruptcy..58
Is It Shame or Is It Guilt?...................................59
The Tall Poppy-Shame Connection............................60
Clever Cover-ups for Shame..................................61
Humility vs Humiliation.....................................61
Robert's Story - A Client's Personal Voyage....................62
Physical Reality - The Power of Addictions....................65
Defining Addiction...66

Alcoholism/Drug Addiction...69
Eating Disorders...70
Rageaholism...73
Workaholism...74
Compulsive Gambling..75
Religious Addiction..76
Thinking/Feeling/Doing Addictions.................................78
Sex/Love/Relationship Addictions....................................78
Alice's Story - A Client's Personal Voyage.......................79
The Good News...81
Releasing Addictions...82
Hang In There...82

CHAPTER 5 - CO-ADDICTIVE RELATIONSHIPS.............83
Mary's Story - A Client's Personal Voyage........................83
What Is Love?...88
You Might as Well Face It You're Addicted to Love................90
The Addictive Love Dance...92
Enmeshment...93
Escapes From Intimacy...93
Romance Addiction..94
Sex Addiction...96
Relationship Addiction...98
Are You In Ritual Or Are You in Relationship?.....................99
Examples of Unhealthy, Dependent Attitudes and Behaviour......102
Pin-pointing Your 'Payoffs'...104
Karen's Story - A Client's Personal Voyage.....................106
The Root of Dependency...110
Physical Abandonment...111
Abandonment Through Abuse...111
Emotional Abandonment..112
The Fantasy Bond..112
Grief - The Key to Healing Our Abandonment.................113
A Quick Re-Capitulation...114

TAKE A DEEP BREATH AND... FEAR FORWARD!.............116

PART TWO - 'THE SOLUTION'

CHAPTER 6 - KEYS TO KNOWING
AND HEALING YOURSELF.................................... 119
Finding Your True Colours.................................. 119
Needs, Wants and Desires.................................. 121
Needs..122
Wants... 124
What's Stopping You?....................................... 125
Desires.. 126
Shame Binds... 128
Summing it Up.. 129
Going Within - Recovery Starts with Discovery...................... 129
Your Inner Family... 131
The Child.. 131
The Adolescent..132
The Parent... 134
Inner Dysfunctional Parents.............................. 135
The Adult...136
Summary..138
Peter's Story - A Client's Personal Voyage.............139
How To find Your Inner Family..........................141
Regular Family Meetings.................................... 143
Developing Cooperation and Balance.................. 143
The Magic of Purpose.. 145

CHAPTER 7 - YOU DON'T HAVE TO
BE A JUGGLER TO BALANCE YOUR LIFE........................ 149
Creating Balance..152
Thought is Creative... 153
Vision - A Bridge To Our Bright Future.................156
Write It Down..156
You Can If You Will...157
When It's Time To Commit.................................157
Persistence Pays Off...157
What Are You Waiting For?.................................158
The Litmus Test for Your True Vision..................158

Ignite Your Vision.. 158
The Gifts of Feelings... 159
Make Friends With Your Feelings............................161
Embracing Your Fear.. 163
Let's Get Physical... 168
Which Lizard Are You?..171
Movin' and Choosin'...171
Beauty Restores Balance... 172
Recovering Your Spirituality.................................... 173
Discovering Your Higher Power.............................. 173
Forming a Partnership with Your Higher Power...................... 175
Natural Creativity... 175
The Days Of Wine and Roses.................................. 176
Handling Your Reality in a Balanced Way................178
Don't Medicate - Meditate..................................... 179

CHAPTER 8 - DON'T QUIT... SURRENDER....................181
The Trouble With Surrendering..............................182
Betty's Story - A Client's Personal Voyage................183
The Cycle of Control and Release............................186
The Benefits of Surrender.......................................188
Shelagh's Story - A Client's Personal Voyage.............. 188
How I Found the Twelve Step Program.....................192
What is The Twelve Step Program............................193
The Twelve Steps to Freedom................................. 196
A Word About Therapy...204

CHAPTER 9 - BUILDING HEALTHY RELATIONSHIPS..... 207
To open a new door close the old one.......................208
Completing Relationships Process 209
Treating Love Addiction.. 210
Stages of Withdrawal... 212
Writing an Inventory... 213
Boundaries, The Key to Self-Protection...................215
Zara's Story - A Client's Personal Voyage.................217
Types of Boundaries.. 220
How To Set Boundaries... 221

Physical Boundaries...221
Sexual Boundaries.. 221
Emotional and Intellectual Boundaries.........................222
Keys to Interdependency...222
Guidelines for Couples in Recovery............................ 224
Seven Steps to Build Healthy Relationships 226
One Meal You Can Do Without................................ 230
Family Meetings... A Means to Co-operation.................. 231
Guidelines For Functional Families............................. 231
Beyond Coping... A New Way of Relating..................... 232
Rules For Fair fighting..233
A Cup of Tea, A Bex and A Good Lie Down!.................. 234

CHAPTER 10 - TOWARDS FORGIVENESS
THE BALANCED APPLICATION OF LOVE......................235
Moving Through Recovery - What Can I Expect?..............237
Stages of Recovery.. 239
Grief, the Crucial Step Towards Forgiveness................... 240
Stages of Grief.. 242
Stage One - Shock, Fear and Depression.......................242
Stage Two - Denial...243
Stage Three - Anger..244
Stage Four - Hurt, Sadness and Pain...........................245
Stage five - Remorse...246
Stage Six- Toxic Shame.. 246
Stage Seven - Loneliness... 247
Stage Eight - Joy...248
Self Care During The Grieving Process.........................248
Grief and Recovery...250
Opening The Doors to Forgiveness..............................251
What Is Forgiveness..252
Forgiveness As the Relinquishing of Judgement................252
Forgiveness - Exercising our Capacity to Give................. 253
Forgiveness - Expanding Our Capacity to Love................254

AFTERWORD..257

BIBLIOGRAPHY AND SUGGESTED READING................ 259

ACKNOWLEDGEMENTS

As I reviewed the material that makes up this book - information gathered, lessons learned and memories recalled - I realised there were many people to thank and acknowledge, all of whom have contributed not only to my book, but also to my life.

I first wish to thank and acknowledge the many clients I've worked with in Australia over the last 14 years. Your courage and willingness to free yourselves to live happy, healthy and fulfilling lives continues to inspire me.

I am grateful for the many teachers who have contributed to me. Of these people, I especially would like to acknowledge Sharon Huffman, for encouraging me and giving me permission to write my first book; Terry Cole-Whittaker, the first voice of truth I heard; Chuck and Geri Little, for being the vehicles for my greatest teachings on balance and love; Becky Jackson, for her pioneering work on eating disorders; John Bradshaw, for his easily understood presentation on shame and family system theories as they relate to dysfunctional and addictive families; Anne Wilson Schaef for her groundbreaking work on romance and relationship addiction. Her work helped me to understand that addiction exists on a societal level. A special thanks to Pia Mellody, who gave me a clear and simple, yet complete understanding of co-dependency and love addiction and how to treat them. I am indebted to her for her pioneering work on the five primary symptoms of co-dependency and her material on child abuse, boundaries, feeling realities and the stages of recovery.

My colleagues, Dr Chris Roberts and Dr Leonie Aitken, from The Wholistic Medical Centre in New South Wales, are a constant source of referral and make great contributions to the recovering community through their excellent work.

I also wish to thank my first publisher, Judith Curr, for believing in this book and convincing me that I had a special ability to present information about co-dependency and addictive behaviour in a simple, accessible manner.

Anne Allanson saw and shared with me the vision of recovery in Australia. She was enormously generous, caring and supportive of me during the trials and tribulations of immigrating and getting started in a new country.

Nicola Lambert for her help with editing the client's personal stories, as well as her nurturing support.

To Dolores Knox for her artistic gifts with the cover design and book layout.

My assistant, Nicole Helich for her flexibility, competence and commitment to our work. I appreciate your wit and positive attitude - especially when we are tired.

I especially want to thank and acknowledge Fiona Toy at Virtual Admin Solutions. Fiona and I have worked together on many different projects for several years. For this book, Fiona's sharp editing skills; her willingness to be a sounding board and researcher for all aspects of its production and her flexible timeline is the reason this book is in your hands now. Fiona, I admire your professionalism and expertise and I treasure you greatly.

Respecting their anonymity, I offer heart felt thanks to the story writers for this Anniversary Edition, who candidly and generously shared their experience, strength and hope with you, so that you may be inspired to set yourself free.

A heart felt thank you to each of my 'soul sisters' Cherie, Shelagh, Audrey, Leonie, Michelle, Sharan and Nicola, for the honest, loving and supportive relationship you share with me.

I appreciate and acknowledge the tremendous love and support given to me by my late parents, John and Laura Smith and my sister, Sharon Johnson - even when they didn't understand or agree with me.

Finally, I want to acknowledge and give deep, loving thanks to my Higher Power who I call God. It is through God's guidance and loving direction (especially when I got myself out of the way) that this book came together.

AUTHOR'S NOTE
FOR THE REVISED,
ANNIVERSARY EDITION

Success happens by choice, not by chance.
Without choice there is no freedom.

You've heard the wisdom, "to thine own self be true" or "the truth will set you free." Like a boomerang, the opportunity to make choices from our truth returns to us many times in our life.

I never set a goal to write a book about co-dependency. In 1988 the topic became 'hot' in mainstream USA and in 1989, Bantam Australia asked me to write *Set Yourself Free* as the first Australian book on co-dependency, with Australian case histories. I'd been in the country for a year seeing clients privately, running programs and training health professionals for the treatment of co-dependency, addictive behaviour and family of origin issues. At the time, I was writing another book about spiritual freedom and wasn't interested in writing a book on co-dependency, especially since there had been many springing up in America since the mid eighties. After listening to a presentation I'd given on co-dependency, my publisher, Judith Curr, convinced me that I had a clear, yet simple way of getting across this seemingly complicated information.

Set Yourself Free's release in October 1990 started me on yet, another, personal voyage that I could write a book about - and maybe someday I will. Professionally, the book and its accompanying work has been a bit of a boomerang in my life. Let me explain.

By the end of 1994, I was tired. Tired of an enormous workload - tired of working with co-dependents and addictive types - and tired of people coming to work with me because they were in pain. I wanted to work with people who were passionate to 'move towards' something rather than 'move away' from something that was unpleasant. I closed my organisation, *Recovery Resources* and started working with companies, assisting them with vision, cultural change, leadership, communicating and teambuilding - in essence, the interaction of human dynamics. While I was loving my new work, I decided to continue to run one small co-dependency group to keep my hand in.

That small group of ten people quickly grew and before I knew it, I was boomeranged into another organisation which looked like *Recovery Resources*. Determined I wasn't going to get stuck with the label of the 'Co-dependency Queen', I simply called my company *Shirley Smith & Associates*. Just a 'temporary name until I knew what I wanted to do next'.

In 1997 I expanded my services to include executive coaching. I began attracting clients who had no idea about the 'recovery' field I worked in, yet, strangely enough, it wasn't long before they began discussing their relationship problems or the fact that they didn't call their mother after 5:00pm because of her drinking. I couldn't believe it! Was everyone co-dependent?

I then started offering *Empowering Communication* Programs for the general public, initially focusing on presentation skills. It didn't take long before the public speaking aspect was secondary to participants getting over the fear and shame of expressing their true self. It didn't matter if I worked with men or women, a group of lawyers, accountants, business executives, actors, sales professionals or mums who hadn't worked outside the home, my clients seemed to come up against personal barricades (mostly deep fear and shame) to their self-expression. In fact, I even had one course participant, a lawyer attending to enhance his business presentations, share with me that he woke at 3.00am crying from a childhood memory and proceeded to cry all night. He told me it was a most profound experience and after it, he felt better than he had in years!

Although highly skill based, the program has since morphed into a communication program which takes people through the fear of their authentic selves being seen and contributes to them having an identity shift. Meanwhile, the family of origin programs were doubling in size. No matter what I did, it seemed like I was destined to work with people on their personal, foundational issues. Every time I gave this work away - like a boomerang, it came back.

As time went on, I felt an inner calling and I just knew there was something **else** I was supposed to do in my work. Tired of trying to figure it out, I decided to take a sabbatical and went to live in the Blue Mountains midway through 2000. I would write that book on spiritual freedom I'd started many years ago; I'd be still and listen to the voice within, letting a direct inner knowing be the driving force for my work.

After a year, I suddenly felt it was time to pack up and return to Sydney. I hadn't finished the spiritual book yet, but I **did** know what I was supposed to do. I was guided to set up an organisation which publishes and provides books, programs and other resources to give people permission to shine - in their careers, their relationships, their businesses and personally. I was told (from within) to predominantly focus on the neglected spiritual and emotional aspects of people's lives - particularly the areas where they felt unfulfilled. The new organisation's name is *The Radiant Group* and it provides *resources to enrich individuals - relationships - business.*

I was also told to publish and promote other professionals' work, as well as mine. My previous experience in publishing was only from being an author, with a very large, mainstream publisher. During my mountain sabbatical the rights from my first two books had reverted back to me and I had a few remaining cartons of *Set Yourself Free*. I didn't know **how** I was going to do this - only that I would. With my new vision and books in hand, I returned to Sydney.

Without any promotion on my part, the phone began ringing, with people saying things like, "I just finished reading *Set Yourself Free* which was loaned to me by a friend" - or "I purchased *Set Yourself Free* at a school fete and just finished it" - or "*Set Yourself Free* has been on my bookshelf for years, and I suddenly started to read it." The requests were to either speak to me, or for referrals to counsellors and programs where they could attend. In a short time I found myself sitting in my lounge room, facilitating another family of origin/ co-dependency group. Boomerang! I couldn't believe it - was I destined to work with co-dependents and addicts for the rest of my life?

Perhaps you've heard the saying:

> *"If you love something, set it free.*
> *If it comes back to you it is yours,*
> *If it doesn't, it never was".*

At last, I found the missing piece - and 'my truth'. It had been there right under my nose the whole time. **The foundation to realise dreams; to have healthy intimacy relationships; to create a rich and rewarding life; to evolve spiritually; to feel successful - must be built on a solid, personal foundation.** Without this foundation, dreams turn to dust in the wind; things tend to fall apart just before a success is realised and we feel spiritually and emotionally bankrupt. I had witnessed this happening frequently with my coaching clients - capable, talented, creative people, frustrated from unfulfilled goals and dreams. They didn't have to be co-dependent or addicts to have holes in their foundation or to be living a lie through adapted roles they were carrying from childhood (see chapter 3). Having said that, many of my past clients who came for coaching, did discover they were, in fact, co-dependent or suffering harmful consequences from addictive behaviour.

To start my new business voyage, I had to go back and begin at the beginning. I felt it was more important than ever to expand and strengthen the foundation for the body of work I was about to create. Hence, you have the Revised, Anniversary Edition of *Set Yourself Free* in your hands.

From my experience of working with a wide diversity of people over the past twenty years, I can honestly say I believe this revised edition is more relevant today than when first published over a decade ago. Co-dependency and addictive behaviour is a costly and pervasive element of Australian society; increasing significantly since the book was originally released (note the updated statistics on addictions and disruptive relationships in this edition). I know people are tired of misery and disappointments - especially in their relationships. This book, and the follow-on work required to gain significant benefits, is not for those looking for another self-help, quick fix. It is for those who are looking for real answers to real life problems and are ready to take responsibility to make positive changes in their lives.

'Recovery' work is not the same as 'self-help' or other 'personal development' programs. Although recovery work 'helps' people to develop personally, it is specifically for those who have cracks in their personal foundations and are either interacting with addictive people or are addictive themselves. Denial and lack of education can prohibit people from realising they need to do this work, or life will inevitably deliver situations that force them to address these issues.

While I have plans to publish others' work in the future, as well as my own, the first people I am publishing are anonymous - the past clients who have so graciously shared their personal journeys with you in this revised edition. Although I've added a great deal of new information in this edition, I feel the personal stories are the most inspiring. I know they will enhance your life.

I am proud to offer you this new edition and will be using it as a foundation to the other resources I provide. I'll leave you at the beginning: *"Success happens by choice, not by chance. Without choice there is no freedom."* Because this book has found its way into your life, perhaps it's a catalyst for your new beginning. Happy sailing!

Shirley Smith
Sydney, Australia
October 2003

PART 1
'THE PROBLEM'

CHAPTER 1

BON VOYAGE

I believe we have the ability to choose a dream or at the very least, know what we want. In order to experience personal freedom as well as have our dreams realised, what's required is the development of emotional balance, mental clarity, physical vitality and a spiritual connection. Recovery from co-dependency and its attendant addictive behaviours will allow you to know what you want, choose a dream and develop what's necessary to achieve it.

I was born in California in the era of the Beach Boys so when I voyaged to Australian in my adult life, it was natural that I ended up right in the middle of Sydney Harbour. Because I've always had an affinity with the ocean and everything associated with it, I've decided to use sailing to freedom as a metaphor for the journey I took... and perhaps the journey you will take.

SETTING SAIL - HOW MY JOURNEY BEGAN

I first became interested in the concept of personal freedom at a time when it appeared, outwardly, that I was experiencing it in abundance.

It was the late 1970's and I was married with two young children in good schools. I had a successful career and a beautiful home in a prestigious suburb in California... all the things that signify modern middle-class 'success'. And I was young (27) with the promise of a wonderful life ahead of me. Yet inside I felt empty and trapped and I was totally confused about the source of my unhappiness.

One morning after my husband left early for work and the children were in school, I sat on the couch in my newly decorated living room drinking my third cup of coffee, smoking my sixth cigarette, unable to mobilise myself for work.

"What's wrong with you Shirley?" nagged a voice in my head.

"You've got all the things that should make you feel happy and free". Yet I felt unaccountably trapped, locked up deep inside. There was no apparent explanation for this state I was in - and that made me feel even worse. If I'd been a depressive or in debt or if my husband was having an affair or my children were delinquent, it would have made identification of my problem easy.

No, it didn't look as if I had a problem. Everything appeared to be under control yet I knew that deep down something was seriously wrong.

As time progressed, certain stark problems began to manifest, and then escalate. I became obsessed with controlling everyone and every thing, becoming addicted to being constantly busy, if not frantic. I was using coffee and cigarettes to pep me up and other chemicals to help me to sleep and relax. I was working in wine sales at the time and I started to drink regularly. I tried to convince myself it was part of the job and in an effort to avert my mounting desperation, I also kidded myself that if I had to drink, at least I was enjoying classy vintages.

Meanwhile, my husband's drinking increased to a level intolerable for us both. We decided he would attend a treatment centre for his drinking and I would participate in a program for family members. It was during that program that I began to uncover the true source of my pain and emotional bondage - which, to my amazement, started long before I met my husband. Although the condition wasn't named at that time, today it's known as 'co-dependency'.

The nature and causes of co-dependency are explained at length in Chapter 3, but I'll define it briefly here.

Co-dependency is a state of dis-ease that originates from the denial of the 'true self' in order to survive within a dysfunctional family, societal, educational or religious system during one's formative years of life. Co-dependents are so focused on and affected by someone else's behaviour, that they do not have much of a relationship with themselves. So, co-dependents don't know their true inner self, they have learned to keep it hidden so that a sense of their innate personal value, self-esteem and connection to others is distorted. As adults, co-dependents are either attracted to addictive types or have an addictive personality.

Co-dependency is a progressive disease that causes ever-increasing stress, misery, disruptive relationships, controlling behaviour and physical illness. If left untreated, co-dependency can lead to addictions such as alcoholism, drug dependency, eating disorders, work addiction, compulsive gambling or spending, sex addiction and love addicted relationships.

When the therapists in the centre we attended drew some diagrams on the wall illustrating a dysfunctional family system, I was shocked to see that it applied not only to our immediate family (my husband, myself and my children), but to the family I grew up in. At first I had trouble recognising this because my parents were not drinkers. Their marriage appeared 'solid'. My father was 'a good provider', my mother was a dedicated homemaker and I had an older sister I admired. We lived in a nice neighbourhood, we went to fine schools, wore good clothes, owned a lovely house with a dog and a bird and we took a holiday together every year. We represented the standard, happy middle-class picture.

But when I began to describe my family background, the personalities involved and how we related to one another, it was clear that the emotional dynamics were the same as those in families with much more overt problems. Although there was no alcoholism in my family of origin, I began to realise that my cherished mental pictures of our 'happy' family life were distorted and that I, too, had come from a dysfunctional family. With this new awareness, I also realised that many of the choices I'd made in my life - such as the type of men I was attracted to, my career, my lifestyle - weren't really choices at all. They were unconscious knee-jerk reactions. Gradually, it became clear to me that I had created my own prison and continued to be my own jailer.

When I looked at those diagrams on the board with this new understanding, at first I was furious. I questioned why someone hadn't told me this before or why no one had taught me this at school. How had I managed to get to adulthood with two children of my own without learning how functional families operate or how adults can negotiate without hostility?

After these initial realisations, I went through a phase of feeling desperately trapped in a situation I now saw was of my own making. I could see that I'd made my bed and felt that I now had to lie in it. I could see no solution, no reprieve, and no way out! Everything inside me was screaming to get out, run away. But I loved my children and couldn't imagine my life without them. I also wanted to do whatever was necessary to make my marriage work. Mercifully, the counsellors at the treatment centre convinced me that there was light at the end of the tunnel. But they explained that my husband and I had some work to do and a way to go before we'd be out of the darkness and into the light. They suggested we attend some type of therapy or counselling and insisted we attend Twelve Step programs* my husband, Alcoholics Anonymous and Al-Anon for myself.

As I began to participate in a program of recovery, I had more insights, began to come out of denial and understood that my husband's alcoholism was not our only problem. I had plenty of problems, too. I thought: 'Oh my God, am I a sick cookie! Boy do I have a lot of work to do on myself!' Of all the realisations I'd had to this point, this latter one flattened and overwhelmed me. My head spun with thoughts such as:' It's too hard', 'I can't do it', 'It'll take me years to recover', 'I've been so stupid, it serves me right', etc.

But armed now with all this new information and insight, there was no way I could go back - there was only one way for me to go and that was forward. Once I surrendered and accepted this, I began to feel relieved. I also felt grateful for the help I'd been given. Now all I had to do was follow the good suggestions I'd been given and take the steps - a day at a time - along the recovery path.

Since that time, many fine therapists have worked in the field of addictions, family recovery and what has now come to be known as co-dependency. Many of these experts (including the late Virginia Satir) believe that in our western society more than 96% of us grows up in environments that are less than nurturing and dysfunctional to varying degrees. And the problem is passed on through the generations. This doesn't mean we can assign blame for our adult problems on our parents, teachers or other major caregivers. They too grew up in dysfunctional environments. Neither should we condemn ourselves for the mistakes we've made in raising our own children. We are all fallible and as a spiritual adviser once taught me: "Mistakes are the newness of creation". We make mistakes so that we can learn from them and grow.

I won't pretend that recovery has always been easy or that it is over for me yet, but in considering the personal gains that I've made, the

---

*The Twelve Steps were originally formulated by Bill W, a co-founder of Alcoholics Anonymous in 1938. They were first published in 'Alcoholics Anonymous' in 1939. Today there are many different Twelve Step groups which meet regularly and focus on a single problem, such as overeating, co-dependency, gambling, drug addiction, sex and love addiction, etc. The only requirement for membership is the desire to abstain from the compulsive behaviour.

way my life has flourished and the freedom of choice I have today, I could never go back - and I'd gladly do it all over again.

In this regard, I particularly admire and relate to Australians. I've found them to be courageously persistent in difficult times. Australians possess an admirable pioneering spirit, no doubt borne out of overcoming the horrific hardships of early settlement. I believe that in order to have true freedom, you have to question and challenge your beliefs, thoughts, feelings, personal values, choices and way of doing things. To do this, I think you have to be a pioneer in your own life.

The purpose of this book is to help you to set yourself free. I believe that the fundamental key to personal freedom lies in maintaining balance in life. En route to this coveted state are many exciting adventures, challenges and self-discoveries. As Helen Keller once said: "Life is a daring adventure or it's nothing." But I've learned that *the only way out is the way through*. Be aware that once you stop your outer distractions, the feelings you have suppressed and repressed will arise within you. Allow yourself to feel them all and especially, allow yourself to grieve over the pain of your lost childhood. As you move through this pain, you'll begin to experience an increasing sense of inner freedom and joy.

In Part One, I've presented a lot of information, much of it highly emotive, which will help you to understand how we all become trapped in the first place and how we prevent ourselves from experiencing freedom. Some of the topics covered include dysfunctional systems, false childhood roles, and types of child abuse, various addictions and co-addicted relationships.

If you feel overwhelmed by personal realisations when reading the material in Part One, don't despair. There is a lot of hope and support for co-dependents. Recovery *is* possible. However, any readers hoping for a self-help 'quick fix' should look elsewhere. Recovery is a process - not an event. As someone who is 'walking the walk', I appreciate the value of practical suggestions, so in part Two I've included several - in the form of instructions, techniques and written processes - which I've called 'keys' to freedom. These will help you to let go of destructive thoughts, feelings and behaviour patterns, determine and express your own reality and thereby discover who you really are.

Once you begin to have a real sense of self, then the process of attaining balance and self-love can begin. Through the experience of balance and self-love, you begin to feel confidence, security and serenity. When you have integrated these qualities, you will then be able to give yourself permission to do what you really want to do in life.

And that surely is the ultimate freedom.

It's been said by many people in recovery that we have to learn to be selfish rather than selfless. I think this idea was initiated because co-dependents don't have a mature sense of self and are such classic people-pleasers and caretakers. As adults in recovery, we need to learn to be 'selfing'. When we are selfing, we have learned to take care of ourselves and still care for others; we have learned how to graciously receive a compliment and that it is healthy to want acknowledgement. I feel the balanced way to practise recovery is to be selfing.

I am a therapist and much of the information presented in this book has been derived from my professional training and work, but I am also a person participating in my own recovery, so I've included some very candid, personal stories and realisations. Some of the most inspiring and beneficial information I've been given along the way came from teachers who spoke frankly and from the heart, sharing their experience, strength and hope. My sincere intention is for this book to serve you in the same manner.

The first edition of Set Yourself Free was released in 1990 and I am privileged to have witnessed thousands of Australians freeing themselves and living a happy, healthy, fulfilling life. I wasn't always like that and I would like to share with you what happened as my journey of recovery continued when I first came to Australia over 14 years ago.

CO-DEPENDENCY RECOVERY BEGINS IN AUSTRALIA

When I left America in 1988, co-dependency was becoming a household word and, in fact, it was almost chic to be recovering from some sort of addiction. When I arrived in Australia that same year however, I discovered that here the opposite was true. No one I spoke to had even heard of the term 'co-dependency', and as I combed the local bookstores I couldn't find a single book on the subject. As a recovering co-dependent, I understand the dilemma or black and white thinking, knowing only too well how to swing between the dichotomies of life. This was not the first time I had been faced with two extremes: on one side of the world there was typical American overkill, while on the other side (in Australia) we were sweeping our problems under the carpet, and the last thing we would do is talk about them.

Curiously enough, I found I related more to the tight-lipped Australians. Perhaps this was because when I started my personal recovery program in America in the late 1970's, and at that time, I can assure you it was far from chic to be recovering from an addiction, or to admit to alcoholism in your family. In fact it was advisable to only speak about such things privately to others who were in the same boat.

In a similar climate, when I first began giving educational seminars and media interviews in Australia, many assumed that co-dependency was a concept I had personally developed. Gradually I began to realise the huge task I had taken on. Consequently, on a personal level, I found this to be a very challenging time. Not only was I going through my own adjustment in immigrating, and settling in to a new country, but I also found myself without colleagues or friends who really understood co-dependency and addiction recovery, a lifestyle I had been living for more than a decade. So there I was embarking on yet another learning curve: sometimes very painful and frightening, yet a new, exciting adventure. Or in other words, here we grow again!

WHAT HAPPENED?

A mainstream publisher, Bantam Australia, commissioned me to write a book on co-dependency for Australians, using case histories and language from Australia. Before my book was released, it was very obvious to me that people would need a place to go and begin the process of debriefing their childhood pain. Because I knew that some people might not be able to afford counselling or therapeutic programs, I gave starter packets for Co-Dependents Anonymous (CODA) meetings to the clients I was working with, emphasising the need for them to form their own self-help support groups as part of their recovery program. By 1989 CODA meetings had begun cropping up in the major Australian cities.

By 1990, several books from America on co-dependency began to appear in bookstores and many journalists were tagging the topic as a new 'flavour of the month psycho babble' from America. Having personally witnessed the pain, self-sabotage, confusion and destruction of relationships caused by co-dependency and addictive diseases in the lives of perfectly intelligent, well meaning Australian people, I was extremely disheartened by the cynical flogging of co-dependency by some of the Australian media.

In all fairness, it wasn't only the Australian media who misinterpreted co-dependency recovery. Unfortunately, many (though not all) co-dependents themselves fell into the trap of using the label of 'co-dependent' to wallow in their childhood pain and remain victims, instead of taking the steps to actually deal with their co-dependency and then face and recover from their addictions as well. Although it is extremely important to grieve childhood pain and identify co-dependent symptoms, many people are stagnating because they deny their addictions. Several of my clients have mentioned to me that they now recognise people in denial of their alcoholism, eating disorder or other addictions, who use CODA as a place to hide.

Emotional pain can either be recycled, leaving one stuck, or embraced so that one may get on with living. The initial stages of co-dependency recovery can bring about much relief and clarity, and can open many doors. After a time however, if one does not face one's addictions and seek treatment for them, many doors will shut abruptly and lasting change will not occur.

Addictions are processes of decreasing choice. Initially addictions give us the illusion of consistency, but as they progress, the roller coaster ride begins. One of the strongest symptoms of co-dependency is the attempt to control (everyone and every thing). Addictions enforce that by creating the illusion of being in control.

Denial lets us cope for a time, but eventually the false protection of denial fails and we lose control of our lives.

ENOUGH IS ENOUGH!

Today, co-dependency is fast becoming a household word in Australia. Nonetheless, it's a sad fact that Australia, more than ten years since the first edition of this book is still trailing the rest of the world in the recognition of alcoholism as a disease. That lack of recognition is apparent not only in the medical and mental health professions, but within the community itself. Conversely, where I once had few like-minded colleagues in Australia, I'm pleased to find there are now more and more health professionals and members of the community who not only accept but understand co-dependency, addictive diseases, and the need for specialised treatment.

There also seems to be a collective consciousness in the air, that says either, 'I've had enough', or 'Is this all there is to life?' Even people who have never heard of co-dependency or have no understanding of addictions are more willing to voice their frustration with unresolved pain and do something different to take charge of their lives.

After completing the first edition of Set Yourself Free, I had attended a graduation ceremony for people training to be professional presenters. The participants were a mixture of business people, health care professionals, teachers and academics, many of whom were parents as well. They were asked to give a five-minute presentation, a signature piece. It was to be something they felt very passionate about, something causing a profound impact on their life.

As each participant stepped onto the stage and gave their presentation, I became increasingly amazed by the incidents shared and the stories I heard. Many spoke of dysfunctional relationships with their parents. Others shared incidents of rape, child abuse, absentee fathers, alcoholism and the lack of expressed emotion and physical nurturing in their families.

This to me is only another example of the change I'd been witnessing that is taking place in Australia. Destructive symptoms from addictions; co-dependency; family of origin issues and unresolved issues from our formative years are finally surfacing and touching people in a most profound way. All over Australia, people seem to be letting the family skeletons out of the closet, and therefore freeing themselves from the shame and multi-generational re-enactments.

Recovering from co-dependency and addictive behaviour is allowing people to rise, like the phoenix, from the ashes of their past and fly with precision, having acquired the ability to directionalise their future.

WHAT ABOUT THE FUTURE?

Indeed, the path to freedom from co-dependency begins and continues with education and that is one of the reasons I wrote this book. It was only through education at that treatment centre over two decades ago that I began to become aware of the problems in my family of origin. With this knowledge and the help of therapy and Twelve Step programs, I began to walk on a path of recovery towards true personal freedom. I also wrote this book with the intention of making it part of my amends to my daughter Julie and my son Brian, in the hope of passing on recovery and functional behaviour to others, rather than passing on dis-eased and abusive behaviour.

Education and awareness act as interventions, dissipating denial - rather than painful life circumstances jolting one out of it. Considering the expanded awareness regarding co-dependency in the past few years, perhaps this revised edition is more relevant today than when I first wrote it.

I feel strongly that this is an opportune time to emphasise three very important points. Although education and awareness are the first steps towards recovery, by themselves they will do nothing to effectively change your life. First, one needs to be committed - even if you're not sure what to do, the commitment will take you there. Second, you must consistently participate - becoming involved and clearly observing what you are doing. Third, you have to be willing to feel your unexpressed feelings from childhood, as well as some of your adult life. This does not mean that you have to re-live it, however you need to release the pent up pressure and understand it so you can finally have resolution and move on with your life. This is what's needed to make lasting changes.

Most people seek out recovery to alleviate pain and frustration. I feel the essence of recovery is about living - truly living your dreams. Once we alleviate the pain from our past and become more balanced, we then have the freedom to expand our imagination, creativity, talents and skills. We also gain the ability to join with others and create true intimacy.

Walking on the path of recovery can at times become a bit of a balancing act - like walking on a tightrope. It is important to come out of denial, recognise destructive behavioural patterns and pay attention to our pain, without wallowing in it. On the other hand, we want to place our focus on what we want and who we are becoming. And, it is possible to acknowledge where you're at - while simultaneously looking at where you want to go.

It's been said that 'the path to hell is paved with good intentions' and 'we have to wait to get to heaven'. I believe we don't have to wait to experience heaven - and we need more than good intentions. Intention, taking action, and faith in a power greater than yourself will not only open the gates to many heavenly experiences, but give you the ability to move from a state of powerlessness to reclaim your personal power.

I invite you to join me now in the on-going journey of personal freedom. One day at a time, 'together we can'.

CHAPTER 2

ARE YOU
REALLY FREE?

WHAT IS FREEDOM?

I learned years ago that in order to be *free from* anything you must be *free in* it.

There are many misperceptions about freedom. Often, when you think you desire freedom, what you're really pursuing is escape. You fantasise 'If I could just get out of this job', 'if only I hadn't had children', 'If I could just move to another town', 'If only I could find a new lover', 'If only I could go on a holiday'.

How many times have you started the next relationship or job only to find the same problems recurring? I used to change jobs every year in the illusory pursuit of freedom, but after the first few months in a new position, once the excitement of the new people and environment wore off, I went back to feeling stagnant, bored and in similar situations that I'd be in before. Later, I realised that I had chosen the wrong profession for me in the first place.

What I was creating was a mosaic of freedom and success, but in truth I was not getting anywhere.

In Australia, I frequently hear people talking about how they would like to create more leisure time and holidays. They say: 'Oh, wouldn't it be wonderful if I could take holidays more often?' Holidays are fine, but they're not the panacea. Actually, I don't think that holidays are what Australians are really after. The national preoccupation with holidays and leisure time, I believe, mask a deeper need. I think people want the experience of freedom, the feeling of being free within their current situation.

I'll give you a couple of examples to explain this in the context of relationships:

Joan wanted to leave her husband, Tom, because she was very unhappy in their marriage. Tom spent little time with her, showed little interest in her and seemed much more involved with his mates at the pub or watching sport on television. Joan had put up with this for years and finally decided she'd had enough. She felt trapped and enslaved doing the cooking, laundry and being both mother *and* father to their children. She longed to be free, so she gathered up her courage and the children and left Tom. A couple of years later she remarried, Jeffrey. But within a few years of marriage to him, she found herself facing very similar problems.

Why? Because she didn't learn how to be *free in* her relationship. She didn't learn how to ask for what she wanted from him. She became so bitter and resentful, she didn't notice what she was getting. She had no skills in negotiating how to get her adult dependency needs met.

For a woman like Joan there will be no true freedom because she's trying to escape from a situation rather than learn how to be free in it.

Peter had a wife, Jennifer and two children, a respectable suburban home and a steady job, but he felt isolated and unappreciated. He was supposed to be strong, fearless, the family protector and provider. If he eased up in life, everyone else would suffer. The pressure of his responsibilities was too much for Peter. He felt trapped and longed to be free, yet he had too much guilt and fear to leave the marriage. He dreamt of an adventurous free wheeling life, sailing around the world on a sleek white yacht. The pressure on him continued to build and to relieve it, he escaped by taking more interstate business trips, drinking more and starting an affair with a younger woman, Anne. He perceived that Anne wanted and appreciated him without trying to make demands on him. In time, he did leave Jennifer for Anne whom he married a few years later. They had two children and five years down the track, Peter found himself back in the same boat - not the one sailing the Greek Islands!

Peter needed to learn to acknowledge that he had needs, that he wasn't a tower of strength and that he was never meant to be, that it was OK for him to reach out to his partner and to ask for help. In acknowledging his partner's strength and intelligence, he would have created a lot of freedom in the relationship -freedom from feeling that he had to carry the whole load.

Learning how to be **free from** something is only part of the process needed to attain real freedom. Another crucial part involves being **free** - to give ourselves permission to do what we really want to do. In other words, freedom to choose. The problem is that most people reverse this process, trying to be **free to** as the first step - and it doesn't work that way.

The thing about choice is that many people think they are choosing when actually they are *unconsciously* reacting to a person or situation.

As a teenager, I looked at the balance of power in my parents' relationship and it appeared to me that my father was the master and my mother was the slave. I decided therefore, that I had no desire to be a housewife or mother. Yet, a few years later, I woke up at with a husband and two children and asked myself: 'How the hell did I get here?' I did not understand that I had not truly chosen my own personal direction. Rather I had chosen what I did *not* want to be - and look where it got me.

To be **free to** do what you want to do, first you have to know what it is you want to do. You'd be amazed at how many people don't have a clue. Often when a new client comes to see me for counselling, there is an urgency about them.

They've usually been motivated by emotional pain or discomfort and they think that I'll have the answers that will set them on their path to freedom.

But when I ask them: "Why are you here and what do *you* want to get out of the session?" - they almost invariably don't know. They just know that what they've got in their life isn't what they want.

At this point, I ask them to answer a simple set of questions such as: Do you feel free to....

- Tell someone close to you what you really want to do, when you know they won't approve?

- Spend an extended period of time with one or both of your parents, without being angry or reactive?

- Say 'no' to sex, without being afraid of losing your partner?

- Spend Christmas Day somewhere other than with your family of origin, without feeling guilty?

- Accept and feel comfortable with your body, without getting fanatical about diet or exercise?

- Take a holiday from work or home duties, without constantly worrying what will happen in your absence?

Few clients can answer 'yes' to these types of questions. They are still reacting rather than choosing. Attaining true freedom requires you to attend to all three of the following aspects:

Become **free in...** Can you have what you want without escaping?

Become **free from...** Is there something or someone from whom you specifically want to be free?

Then become **free to...** Are you making conscious choices without reacting?

GIVING UP LABELS CAN BE STICKY!

We are all born free, but we start becoming entrapped from an early age. Through dysfunctional family, educational, societal and religious systems; the family roles we adopt and child abuse (which are all explained in Chapter 3), we unconsciously begin as very young children to adapt to these environments in order to get our needs met.

Thus we set up the lifelong tyranny of labelling ourselves in certain ways. As adults we think our biggest job is to keep those early labels intact, no matter what the personal cost. And, we do this unconsciously.

Many people are totally unaware that they're living in these unconscious limitations and that they're caught up in addictive behaviours that keep them on the swift, safe whirligig of denial. They drink excessively, use recreational drugs, take pills to relax and to medicate emotional pain, smoke, gamble, overeat, starve themselves, over-work, exercise fanatically, spend beyond their means or become obsessed with sex - either having it or avoiding it. Any distraction, rather than being still long enough to notice the pain of their current reality or examine its original source.

That's where I was when I was back there sitting on the couch. I was imprisoned and I didn't even know it; imprisoned in my own labels. I was a 'good daughter', 'loving and sexy wife', 'devoted mother', 'successful career woman', 'loving sister', and the 'entertainment committee' for my husband and kids. I looked at all those labels and it hit me that underneath I didn't know who I was. I was afraid to let the labels go because there might be nothing underneath them. I felt the terror of my identity becoming unglued. So I had to control myself to stay safely bound to my labels.

Since change is the only constant, you are only truly free when every aspect of your life is in movement. If you don't feel safe enough to remove or change your labels, then you are probably stuck.

The glue that keeps your labels stuck on you is made of the *"have to's," "ought to's"* or *shoulds*. Many people spend decades unconsciously living their lives in a way that they perceive other people (parents, spouses, friends, colleagues) expect of them. I frequently tell my clients: "Don't 'should' on yourself!"

These expectations originate in our families and are perpetuated through our entire society. As small children we are told: 'Do this!' 'Don't do that!' 'You should... be good, be quiet', 'hold still', 'try harder!' 'Don't cry!' etc.

So we've incorporated the voices of those authority figures inside our heads and often we allow these voices to rule and label us for years. As adults, we are still not free from those voices. Real freedom is recognising when to follow your own inner voice and when to say 'no' to those authority voices.

FREEDOM HAS A PRICE

Years ago I had a boss who was always saying, "Shirley, there ain't no free lunch." That aphorism used to irritate me, but as time went by, I realised that he was right. Attaining inner freedom has its price, I began to realise that in order to have the things I wanted, I had to let go of the things that were in the way. It was a bit like personal spring cleaning, throwing out the old to make space for the new.

I often use the following analogy to explain this. Imagine yourself as a bucket. In the bottom is some mud and the rest is filled with water. The mud represents the unresolved pain, shame, fear, guilt, and confusion of your childhood and the negative beliefs you developed about yourself then and still retain. The water represents the real you, your truth and many possibilities for full self expression.

As you set sail on your voyage to personal freedom, you begin to take in new truths, which is like pouring clear water into your bucket. And what happens? The mud is stirred up and your life initially appears more confusing and uncomfortable. If you stop pouring the water at this point the mud can turn to quicksand. It may feel as if it could swallow you up. But this needn't happen. The muddy water will clear up sooner than you expect, *if you keep going*. I call this process 'emptying your bucket' and I what I mean by this, is that you have to let go of the faults (mud) in order to realise your truth (the clear water).

In order to be, do and have what we want, we must start and continue to empty our buckets.

LEAVING PORT - WHERE TO BEGIN

Although freedom is a personal inner experience, you can't discover it alone. The key to unlocking your personal freedom is through a relationship with a Higher Power of your own understanding.

By building a feeling of rapport with your own Higher Power, you develop a centeredness, a sense of power within yourself. This will give you the inner strength to make the choices and changes that will improve your life. You can rely on your Higher Power for your cues - rather than relying on those whose approval you seek.

People come to me for counselling and coaching, thinking there's some complex, secret formula to getting life 'right' and they want me to tell them what it is. Although I have expertise in my field, I quickly let them know that I'm not God, or any other authority figure they may be tempted to place upon a pedestal. You must realise that YOU are the one who keeps yourself in bondage and YOU, with the help of your Higher Power and the guidance of a professional, are the only one that can set yourself free, I explain.

Developing a relationship with your own concept of a power greater than yourself is the key to tapping in to your own internal information system. If you can't tap into that, you will be eternally indebted to others for your answers and keep yourself in a dependency role.

Finally, I tell people they can do a very simple thing which has powerful consequences if done from the heart. And that is: you *set your intention* on what it is you want. You don't know how you are going to get there, that will become apparent in the process. Just be willing for it to happen and surrender the process and timing to your Higher Power. If you're sincere, and willing to participate, your intention is more than enough to start for the process of change and growth to begin. I can't tell you how it happens, but if done sincerely, I know it works because I've tried it often.

A powerful demonstration of this happened to me when I tried for the umpteenth time, to quit smoking. At one time I had quite for two years, but I'd taken it up again. Then I learnt the concept: 'Don't quit, surrender' (see Chapter 8). I set my intention to be a non-smoker. I knew that I had exhausted every resource and technique on the planet and I'd spent a few thousand dollars in the process. I had run out of all my good ideas and need help. I asked my Higher Power to do for me what I couldn't do for myself. And then after a series of rapid, unexpected events, and at a time when I least expected it, the cigarettes gave me up. In order to stay free from them, I relied on a support group for experience, strength and hope to continue to be a non-smoker, a day at a time.

With my intention, my willingness to participate and do something different and the help of my Higher Power, I became free from this powerful addiction. This was a significant step along my path to freedom.

It may sound too simple to be true, but I've seen it work miracles in many people's lives. I invite you to try it.

CHAPTER 3

DO YOU KNOW
WHO YOU
REALLY ARE?

CO-DEPENDENCY - AUSTRALIA'S MOST COMMON AND UNRECOGNISED DISEASE

One of the major stumbling blocks to freedom that I've encountered in my life and with my clients is the disease of co-dependency.

I won't begin with a textbook definition of co-dependency because you may initially reject it as being irrelevant to you. Instead, I'd first like to explain the background to how co-dependency became recognised and categorised. Then I'll outline the causes and characteristics of the disease and how you can treat it.

Co-dependency, no doubt, has existed since time immemorial, but it was first 'discovered' in the mid-1970's in the United States. Doctors, mental health professionals and counsellors treating alcoholism and chemical dependency realised that these addictions seriously affected all the family members. As family members participated in the alcoholic's or addict's treatment, practitioners observed that the whole family was 'sick' and exhibiting as many behavioural disorders and disturbances as the identified patient. The family dynamics in almost every case had clearly enabled the patient's addiction.

But co-dependency as a dis-ease is not confined to the extreme case of alcoholism and drug addiction. As professionals worked on understanding and defining co-dependency, they found that it was the source of many other addictive disorders including work addiction; eating disorders such as anorexia, bulimia, compulsive overeating; gambling, debting, or compulsive spending; sex addiction and co-addictive relationships.

They also found that it extends across all socio-economic groups, that about 96% of the population grow up in families which are, to some degree dysfunctional as well as less than nurturing and that the disease is multi-generational.

Co-dependency has a powerful impact on the broad spectrum of our society. 50% of Australian marriages now end in divorce; domestic violence, child abuse and crimes against the elderly are shockingly prevalent, all kinds of addictive behaviours are rampant and the incidence of cancer, heart disease and stress related illness is increasing. All of these serious problems have some foundation in co-dependency.

Several books about co-dependency and addictions have been published in the United States in the past decade. In Australia, support groups and specialised treatment programs are now available (see www.theradiantgroup.com.au/resources.html for listings of contact numbers) and there are thousands of co-dependents in active recovery. Many consistently attend Twelve Step support groups such as Co-dependents Anonymous (CODA); they are working the steps with the help of 'sponsors' (another member who has already worked the Twelve Steps) and are learning to practice the principles of recovery in their lives. Many are also working with health professionals and counsellors specially trained in the areas of addictions, compulsive behaviour and co-dependency recovery.

Unfortunately, there is massive denial in our society of the factors, which cause co-dependency - they are: dysfunctional family, educational, societal and religious systems; child abuse and the roles we've taken on in our formative years in order to get our needs met.

WHERE IT ALL BEGINS - THE FORMATIVE YEARS

If you are a parent, I would ask that as you read the following information you focus on *your* childhood and major caregivers, not on yourself as a caregiver. If you focus your attention on yourself as a parent rather than on how you were parented, you will not be able to see clearly your own incidences of childhood abuse. This will hinder your recovery, making it more difficult to rectify the mistakes you've made with your children.

I am a mother and a grandmother. I went into recovery from co-dependency when my children were ten and seven. A year later, after separating from my husband, I found myself a single parent. Like everyone else, I loved my children deeply and I tried to be the best parent I could. Inevitably, over the years, I made plenty of mistakes. As I've walked the path of recovery, I've grown and changed and been able to make amends with my children for my past dysfunctional behaviour as a parent. I've been able to model to them more balanced and mature behaviour. I wanted them to grow up like that, but in recovery I learned that first I had to exhibit those characteristics myself. In other words, you can't give what you don't have. First things first. Focus on yourself!

Over the years, many parents have come to me feeling incredible guilt for their past mistakes and want to right them. They can see the character defects in their grown children and as a parent, feel totally responsible for these flaws. From the experience of the intimate work I've done with so many people and their families, I have come to believe that each soul has a purpose and a theme, and as parents we do not have to assume total responsibility for the challenges or unpleasant things that happen to our children. However, this does not give any of us the right to be abusive to others, yet, in the bigger picture, we as parents can make amends by changing our behaviour now and as a survivor of abuse ourselves, we don't have to remain victims.

We all have choices and reading the following information will give you many options to free yourself from guilt and being a victim. To gain this freedom, you have to work for it. It's that simple. And sometimes you have to let go of others when they don't want to change - for some of you, this might even mean letting go of your adult children.

To understand the dynamics of a family, or any group of people, think of it as a system. A system is comprised of different elements interacting with each other. The principle of all systems is that the whole is greater than the sum of the parts.

To illustrate, I'll use the analogy of internationally recognised family therapist, the late Virginia Satir, who was also known as the 'mother of family therapy'. Picture a set of wind chimes: notice that the separate pieces hang in balance with each other, yet each has its own size, shape, sound, beauty and function (just like individual family members). Each chime seems separate, but is connected to all of the other chimes by wire or string. If one chime moves in the breeze, it affects the 21 movement of all the other chimes, albeit, sometimes subtly and almost invisibly. Once the movement stops, each chime in the system returns to its original place.

The wind chime system, like the family system, is defined by the interaction of its individual parts, rather than by their sum total. In a family, it could be said: I am an individual and a group simultaneously. Each person in the family system plays various 'parts' or roles.

The foundation of the family system is the *relationship* between mum and dad. This relationship is born out of the relationship each partner has with himself or herself and the degree to which their relationship is healthy is the degree to which the family system will have a good foundation and function well.

If mum and dad have good self-esteem, are comfortable within themselves and know how to take care of their individual needs, then they come together as two whole, balanced people. This energy allows them to expand themselves and have more to offer their children. This constitutes a functional family system.

However, what happens in many relationships is that mum and dad come together, each feeling like half a person. They gravitate together because each hopes the other will fulfil the qualities he or she lacks. Our society even has an expression for this. How often have you heard someone introduce or refer to their partner as 'my better half?' In this situation, the parents are still trying to satisfy their childhood needs through each other and if that fails, then through their children. In psychological terms, the emotional dynamics between two such 'half' people, reduces their healthy functionality as parents to even less - or arithmetically, a half times a half equals a quarter.

ADAPTING STARTS EARLY

In a dysfunctional family, one in which mum and dad are sick, addictive, immature, or their relationship has a weak foundation, children begin adapting to fill in the gaps and balance the system. They start to act out, unconsciously, what is repressed or unexpressed by their parents and they take on various roles and labels.

Research has shown us there are really no secrets in families, so even if problems, rifts, tensions and other forms of imbalance are not spoken of, children will sense this and react in a manner designed to restore balance. This is why you so often see extreme differences between siblings - each unconsciously takes on a very different role to balance the family system.

For example, if a father has a lot of repressed fear, yet seems totally fearless in his actions, one of the children may become paranoid or frightened or have asthma as a way of acting out this emotion. Or if a mother is a rigid disciplinarian and very controlling, her daughter may become anorexic because to her this seems to be the only way she can gain control.

If mum or dad are sexually repressed or have a dysfunctional sexual relationship, one of the children will usually act out to the other extreme by becoming very promiscuous. Another may carry the shame the parents have around their own unfulfilled sexual relationship. This child may unconsciously choose a mode of behaviour such as overeating and becoming overweight, designed to avoid sexual contact.

A young child who throws tantrums or behaves antisocially towards siblings or other children at school may be acting out the unexpressed anger of one or both parents. This child becomes the 'problem', thereby relieving the frustration in the family.

ADAPTING THROUGH ROLES

Understanding and eliminating the 'roles' you took on in your formative years is one of the most important things you can do to free yourself from stress, misery, physical illness and disruptive relationships. This is easier said than done because we have unconsciously linked our roles to our identity - and have used them to feel that we are valuable.

Each family role has negative and positive aspects. It is because of the positive aspects that it is difficult to identify that you have adopted a 'role'. The dominant positive aspect will usually be something that you naturally value. For example, caring people who love to give become the *Caretakers*. High achievers and those who like responsibility become *Hero's*. *Lost Children* are great with fantasy and imagination and know how to get out of the way, avoiding conflict. *Mascots* are good at relieving tension, making others feel good and are great at defusing emotional explosions. *Scapegoats* keep the family or group together by taking the brunt of disapproval and attention away from any dysfunction and a *Surrogate Spouse* is a good listener and excellent advisor. These are great qualities and values that most of us admire.

Whenever you are in the process of shedding a childhood role, you will seem like you are losing your sense of value and you may feel worth less than you did before. If you persist giving up the role, you will eventually feel relief and a sense of being the 'real you' for the first time in your life. You can also expect to feel incredible energy and clarity around what you'd like to do in any given situation. In the many years since I have been working with this issue, I can't tell you the depth of positive, significant changes that I have observed happening for people. At the end of this section, there is a very powerful story from one of my past clients which will show you the benefits of giving up those false roles. But first, let me briefly explain about the roles.

In a dysfunctional family system, each member unconsciously plays out different roles, thereby giving up his or her own, unique, authentic self. It's important to remember that the whole family is dis-eased (not just the apparent trouble-maker or addict) and each member plays their role to meet the needs of the system. Individual needs do not get identified and remain unmet. One of the most difficult tasks, for most of the people I've worked with over the years, is to identify and meet their needs. When it comes to needs, for some there are big blanks, confusion for others and most feel embarrassed or are highly critical of their needs.

Keeping the family together at all costs is imperative. This is a closed system and in this dynamic, it is more important for the system to survive than an individual to thrive. The late Virginia Satir also identified patterns of behaviour, ones used under stress, which are known as 'The Satir Categories'. One of her students, Sharon Wegscheider-Cruse, developed the family roles in her early work with children of alcoholic families, which has since been expanded upon over time by other professionals.

Let's take a further look at some of the common dysfunctional family roles:

THE HERO

This child scores high marks in school, excelling in sports, winning honour and dignity for the family and ensuring they personally get lots of emotional strokes for such effort. As an adult, the Hero may be a super-achiever, but secretly he or she feels guilty because they have a brother on the dole and a sister struggling with four children and an unhappy marriage. The price paid in terms of the Hero's well-being is high, because they are usually driven, workaholics, perfectionists and incredibly lonely. As this dis-eased behaviour progresses, Heroes feel increasingly inadequate and try harder to cover this up by isolating themselves, thus becoming even more lonely.

THE LOST CHILD

Parents may say of this child: 'Oh, Betty is such a good girl. She never causes any trouble. She's so quiet, always doing her own thing in her bedroom, never bothering anyone.' And no wonder, this child, sensitive to the tense emotional waves in a family, feels a deep loneliness and escapes from the external scene through private fantasy. Where the Hero brings dignity to the family, the Lost Child fulfils the need of the family system for separateness and autonomy. This child is invisible and spends a lot of time alone, but it is not a healthy aloneness. When grown, it is the 'lost child' who is forgettable, and often aren't even seen or missed at a function.

THE CARETAKER

The Caretakers role in the family system is to provide a sense of caring. Addicts or immature parents are often self-centred, leaving the other family members missing out on vital care. Caretakers primary goal is to avoid conflict. They crave peace at any price. They fear abandonment and feel that other family members cannot take care of themselves. They have an inordinate need to be needed as this gives them their sense of worth. Caretakers often work in the helping professions; are found managing teams or running a small business. On the outside they seem loving and caring for others. They sigh a lot and can be martyrs. Although Caretakers never tell you, on the inside they are usually seething - waiting for others to give to them what they give to others.

THE MASCOT

This child is the comedian, the family entertainer, making everyone laugh and thereby bringing a sense of fun and playfulness to the system. Mascot's are especially good at sensing the unexpressed pain in the family. They can pick it up like radar. Trapped behind a clown's mask, the Mascot is unable to express their real feelings of pain and isolation. This will emotionally handicap them in adult relationships.

THE SCAPEGOAT

The Scapegoat takes the blame for the family by acting out the unexpressed conflicts. They almost always get caught stealing, fighting or misbehaving and by doing this, they take the focus off the dysfunctional dynamics in the family. This lets the family (or mum and dad) band together to 'help' the scapegoat and ensures that the family will stay together. The Scapegoat may become drug addicted, alcoholic or have a series of illnesses. If the family has unexpressed anger or pain, the Scapegoat will act this out for them as a release valve. The price the Scapegoat pays is evident.

THE SURROGATE SPOUSE

The Surrogate Spouse is the one who mum or dad downloads their problems to, often complaining about each other. This can also be the favourite or special child who is privy to information the other children aren't. Surrogate Spouse children have the most problems in their adult spousal relationships - many remain single and don't understand why. They have difficulty with intimacy and often feel engulfed when close to another. The Surrogate Spouse role often sets up a love/hate relationship with the parent when they become adults. This type of adult/child relationship is not only confusing to the child, it is emotional incest. One of my former clients, Dave learned the value of identifying and giving up this role.

DAVE'S STORY
A CLIENT'S PERSONAL VOYAGE

For many years I invested a lot of effort in helping people. Everyone thought I was a really nice guy. If you wanted advice, I was there for you. Need help laying that new driveway? No problem. A short-term loan? The only question was how much!

In relationships I would do anything for my partner. I'd even anticipate her needs before she had thought of them herself. I thought that if I looked after others they would take care of me. Boy, was I angry when that didn't happen. Of course it never occurred to me to let people know what I wanted, they were supposed to work it out like I did for them. No matter how hard I tried to do 'the right thing', my relationships never seemed to work out.

Nevertheless, I always had the best looking girlfriend and life seemed pretty good. As one of my teachers was later to say: "I was looking good and going nowhere".

Then my friends started getting married and having babies. Basically, they were growing up and getting on with their lives.

But not me - I was looking around for people to play with. I soon learnt to fill the gaps between relationships with drugs, alcohol and gambling; not consciously, just when I was at a 'loose end'. Besides, they were only 'recreational' drugs and as time went on, I found drugs to be a lot more reliable than people, after all, they don't leave you!

I became 'socially anorexic'. Why bother with all the 'drama' of life when I could be cosy and safe at home. I was in the most reliable relationship I'd ever had and her name was marijuana.

This is the way I lived for the next 10 years, in denial. I didn't take this journey deliberately, I just woke up one day wondering how I had got here.

Looking back, I now know that I was literally dying by inches, which wasn't easy to detect: I ran a very successful company earning me $500,000 a year; my health was still intact and I had plenty of women around - unavailable women that needed taking care of.

*Eventually I found my way to Shirley thanks to a friend who simply suggested I take a look at her work. I didn't need any help, of course, but it might be fun and I might learn some things. I read **Set Yourself Free** and participated in some of her programs.*

Slowly at first, Shirley was able to show me a different perspective on life. I came to see the unmanageability of my life. I came to see that many of my behaviours were designed to hide my true feelings of anxiety, pain and grief from the world and myself. In fact, I think I 'came to'!

I had a difficult time and at first it seemed impossible to change. Can you imagine how horrified I felt when I discovered that ever since adolescence, I had been my mother's surrogate spouse, enabling and carrying my mother's pain for most of my life. After the pain passed from that realisation, so many things made sense about my life and intimacy issues with women. No wonder I had such a love/hate relationship with women, attracting unavailable and needy women who only wanted to get something from me! When I wasn't getting my need to be needed fulfilled, then I was avoidant, not allowing anyone to get close.

I also realised I had carried other 'negative' feelings for years, many since childhood and that my personality and how 27

I related in the world was set up a long time ago.

When this all came to the surface, I didn't particularly like feeling exposed. The last thing I wanted was to show the world what a mess I had made of my life. I had gained such enormous value in looking good and helping others. I had to become willing to give that 'high' up too!

Once I admitted to myself that I couldn't do it alone, I met others who understood my dilemma. I found that a lot of things weren't my fault and that the way I felt was not unique. I received heaps of support and felt great relief.

My life has changed a lot since then. Instead of trying to please everyone, I'm living my own life, I make choices based on what I want not on what I think is expected. I say no to people and things when I choose to; I choose my friends; I make choices and accept the consequences. I love to feel, even pain, because when it passes, it gives me great insights.

Most importantly, I stopped getting my value from care-taking people and I no longer enable needy women or save damsels in distress! Instead, I, along with my business partner have been instrumental in building a very successful company. Yes, financially successful, however, I define the true success of my company by the great synergistic team we have. Today, I know how to have healthy relationships.

I have more passion and curiosity about life at 55 years old than I did as a young man. I run my company part time because I started a three-year graduate diploma course in counselling this year.

I am truly a happy and free man, just like Shirley promised!

CHANGING TIMES, CHANGING ROLES

Children may assume two or three different roles, with each role being given prominence at different times in their lives. For example, if an elder child leaves the household, the system becomes unbalanced. To restore balance, another member must take on that child's role. This happened to me in my family. My sister, who is six years older, had the Hero and Lost Child roles, whereas I was the Caretaker and Scapegoat. At seven, I began to get migraine headaches regularly. I also suffered a series of rashes and allergies. I was often in trouble and was punished more frequently than my sister.

When I was 12, my sister married and left the household. At that point, I became a diligent student and even took on a part-time job, working hard at school, becoming an achiever, trying to make Mum and Dad proud, as well as get me out of the house and away from the constant bickering and tension between my parents. I had effectively added my sister's hero mantle, as well as becoming a surrogate to my mother. It took me ten years of counselling and then recovery to finally understand that my deeper issues where not with my Dad (he was the strict, raging, 'squeaky wheel'), but with my 'saint' mother.

In a functional family system, the parents are there to meet the needs of the children. In a dysfunctional family system, the children's purpose is to meet the needs of the parents. Having our needs neglected takes away our feelings of worth, whether we are conscious of this or not. Taking on adapted roles, gives us the illusion of being valuable and therefore worthy.

As we have seen, in the dysfunctional family system, children adapt from their authentic selves in various ways in order to balance the system and make the parents comfortable. Yet, the parents are also uncomfortable because as children, *their* needs were not met either. Now, as adults, they unconsciously recreate the same patterns in the families they form. Thus, the dysfunctional patterns are repeated through the generations.

This is a serious form of child abuse, yet our society is dangerously oblivious to it. I think the most important thing an individual can do is to free themselves from their childhood roles. The following story from a former client will show you the dire consequences of these roles in our adult lives.

SIMONE'S STORY
A CLIENT'S PERSONAL VOYAGE

I have always valued freedom. As a child, freedom meant the ability to follow my own rules, in my own time, and leave all of the 'have to's' behind!

If you are reading this book, then you will have some understanding of dysfunctional family systems and the adapted 'roles' children unconsciously assume in order to bring a sense of balance and control to their environment. This information and the healing work I have done in this area of my life, have 29 *given me the freedom I've always dreamed about. I gained the courage to express my true self and to walk out of a 10-year corporate career, which had enslaved and degraded me to the core of my essence.*

Looking back, I can see how I took the template of my childhood roles and re-enacted them precisely in my adult life - especially in my career.

Through the healing work I did to recover from my childhood, I learned one of life's secret laws is that you will keep re-enacting the same patterns and behaviours in your life, even if they are very destructive, until you are ready to change. And, even when you make the choice to change, you will usually be required to re-enact that behaviour pattern at least one more time. Only this time, you are looking through the lens of consciousness and you get to correct the error - and do it differently. This breaks the pattern, giving you lasting change. That's when you know you are truly free.

In this chapter, Shirley has described the most common family roles, and if you are like me, you have probably already identified with at least one, if not several!

If you played the part of the Hero, you are most likely a very high achiever with the equivalent of a mantle full of trophies and a lonely heart; if you identify with the Caretaker, you are probably driven to 'care for' and 'be there' for everyone in your life, but find it extremely difficult to receive, and painful to realise that no one ever seems to care for you the way you do for them! As a Lost Child, you are invisible much of the time and often when someone is missing, people don't remember it is you! Or perhaps you were emotionally incested by becoming the sounding board for one of your parents as they downloaded their woes to you? If the Scapegoat is a better fit, you know that causing trouble or being 'the problem' means that everyone is always looking at you fingers pointed, and a disappointed look in their eye... but at least they are not looking at what is wrong with the family! And finally, if you have chosen to be the Mascot, you will know better than most the emotional climate in a situation and feel compelled to distract and make everyone feel better.

The foundation for my adult behaviour patterns was cemented in my childhood. Like many people, I have parents who love me, care about me and want the best for me. And, like many people, I grew up in a violent, alcoholic home with a loud, raging father who sometimes pushed my mother around.

To the outside world, we looked like any typical, middle class, suburban family - mum, dad and two little girls who were 'spoilt' with all the toys and treats imaginable; but on the inside, it felt like we were living in a war zone. The constant tension and fear meant that it was not a safe place for a child to be.

I don't remember when or how I 'decided' to play out my first role, but being a cute, funny mascot just came naturally to me. Entertaining and making everyone laugh was something I truly enjoyed, until it became my 'job' and until I realised that if I didn't, I feared a giant, bloody, screaming punch up would erupt.

I was constantly surveying the interaction between the adults and if I caught so much as a 'dirty look' between Mum and Dad, I would instantly swing into 'movie star' mode and start singing and joking and entertaining the wild crowd in my living room. I'd do just about anything to ease the tension, and feel safe again.

When I was five, my little sister was born. I have to be honest; this was not a happy time for me. I felt that the attention that I had been getting for being 'cute and adorable' was being stolen. After all, the only thing that is cuter than a sweet, smiling, 5 year old, is a sweet, smiling, cuddly little baby! She became the new family mascot.

Still motivated by my need to keep the peace, win approval and get some attention from mum, I switched to the Caretaker role. I began to suck in all of the feelings in the family that were free floating throughout our home. I became hyper-vigilant to people's moods and feelings, developing a 'sixth sense'. My father would only have to swing his car into our driveway and I would 'know' if we would be 'eating' or 'wearing' our dinner that night.

I became obsessed that my mother or Nan was about to die. In preparation for my dream job as a successful reporter, I used to constantly walk around with a tape recorder in my hand, interviewing friends and family on an array of fascinating matters. *A couple of years ago, my aunt found one of those tapes and right there in audio digital was my voice, at the tender age of nine, instructing and counselling my grandmother to stop smoking! I had yet to master the art of verbal sophistication and simply and earnestly told her that "I'd rather you be on the booze than the fags Nan!" As you may have guessed, my Nan is an alcoholic as well (my mother married her mother without realising it).*

As a teenager the violence at home escalated and it became apparent that no one was going to save us. It was a terrifying time, as most nights for me were spent lying awake in bed terrified and on a razor's edge, wondering if someone would be killed before the sun came up.

Adding to my repertoire of roles, I became the self-appointed troublemaker (Scapegoat) and physical protector of Mum and my sister. I suppose somehow I had decided that someone needed to be strong enough to stand up to Dad, the most terrifying bully I had ever known, or we may all end up dead or committed.

My appearance changed as I developed a tough, hard exterior to match the resilience and internal fortitude I felt was required. I piled on weight and became angry and rebellious. Without provocation, I started to be bullied by other teenagers - one night at the ice skating rink, a girl I didn't even know started swinging at me, only to later discover that I wasn't who she thought I was! Only when I became an adult and sought some counselling, did I understand why I piled on the weight. It gave me a sense of feeling bigger and stronger, as well as providing a cushion to protect my vulnerability.

At home each evening I would stand guard waiting for the inevitable explosion of rage that would come as dad covered up his feelings of shame, fear and inadequacy. Night after night of terror, torture and torment continued for many years. I would like to tell you that a miraculous healing occurred; that some turning point came for our family. The truth is that it did not. Somehow my sister and I survived and moved on with our lives, focusing on our careers.

After completing university, I felt a sense of hope to start my own life and leave the pain and confusion of my childhood behind. What I didn't understand is that even though I left home, I took my family roles with me! I discovered dysfunctional 'family' systems are not contained to 'families', any group or organisation can be dysfunctional to varying degrees and, of course, are filled with people acting out their preferred family roles. Therefore, the same dynamics that play out between family members can also appear at work.

When we are ready to heal or change, we unconsciously attract the people, places and opportunities to help us. Often times, these 'opportunities' will be disguised as horrible events and nasty people, and things may not always be as they first appear. For example, a work environment may look like a place where people go to make money and progress their careers, but it can also be the perfect place to find healing. I did!

As a young, 'starry eyed' 22 year old, an absolute 'dream job' in one of the largest multi-national 'family branded' companies in the world was literally handed to me on a silver platter.

I could hardly believe my luck. I had seemingly fallen right into it and secretly felt a mixture of fear and delight. Delight because I felt as though I was the luckiest girl in the world and fear because I was afraid that they would wake up and realise that I really wasn't that good after all. I was afraid that they would see right through me and see me as the impostor I felt I was!

My need to prove myself, coupled with my desperate longing for attention, propelled me headlong into my first re-enactment of a family role - THE HERO!

I had not assumed the Hero role within my family because it had been reserved for my little sister in our teen years. In retrospect, I can see that I saw this as my big opportunity to steal the limelight and take my turn as the 'star'. I had always viewed the Hero role as more exciting and revered, yet a little out of my league! I felt more comfortable swinging between being the troublemaker and the caring one. So, you can see how seductive my newfound career really was!

In an attempt to ensure that I was valuable, I worked tirelessly to devise new and exciting ideas and programs that would knock the socks off everyone. It worked!! I was celebrated and rewarded for my effort, dedication and commitment to the cause. For a while, I was the proverbial golden child and it felt good. Very good. The more praise and attention I got, the more

I wanted! On the inside I was afraid that all of the attention would stop. I felt compelled to keep pushing and driving myself to out do my past achievements.

I was starting to wear out when my worst fear presented itself, so I really didn't see it coming at all. With a promise of a promotion and a department change, I somehow ended up stuck in a position, which gave me no room to shine. My new job was mundane, boring and lacked the glitz, glamour and challenge of my former position - which was now filled by someone else. How on earth did this happen?

Confined in a role that didn't suit me, I felt desperately trapped; obsessed constantly about leaving; and yet I couldn't, the fear was too great.

Set Yourself Free *seemed to leap off the department store bookshelf into my hands. I took it home and read it in one sitting. Mind you, I had quite a selection of self-help books, yet I had not related to any book like I did to this one. I seemed to find myself on just about every page and felt moved to write a letter to Shirley, thanking her and telling her about myself. I was surprised when someone from her office called me - I made an appointment for a counselling session and before I knew it, I was talking about my childhood, and more importantly, the immense pain and frustration I was feeling about my work.*

I told her I just couldn't take it anymore and wanted to resign, but felt terrified. Shirley talked about surrender, and how challenging that concept was for an ACA (adult child from an alcoholic home). Understanding these dynamics somehow gave me the courage to resign. I will always remember my first lesson in letting go. In a fine example of being 'rescued', one of the very senior managers who had been my mentor since day one, refused to accept my resignation and got me a fantastic new position in a different department - and I was given a $10,000 pay rise with a new company car to boot! I was so thankful and awestruck that I threw myself into outperforming all over again. Once again it worked and I was back in the comfortable position of being adored and celebrated! I learned later that one of the unspoken rules in the company was that favourite 'family members' never leave the family!

After a few years and a couple of demanding bosses had passed, I secretly started to resent the pressure placed upon me to shine. Around this time my department was restructured and I took over the responsibility of managing a medium size team of people providing me with the perfect opportunity to be relieved of the 'Hero' and re-enact 'The Caretaker'.

As a chronic caretaker manager, I felt it was my responsibility to protect and shield my staff from the harsh 'bullying' authority figures. I saw myself as the strong one, the one who could 'take it'. I spoilt them; budgeted for extra training to advance them in their careers; covered for them and bent over backwards to be the most understanding manager in the company. No department in the company would have a team like mine! In return for this 'sacrifice', I secretly expected their undying loyalty and gratitude - and of course I didn't get it from them.

I was starting to seethe with resentment when the 3rd and most painful pattern emerged - the 'Scapegoat'. This lethal combination of the scapegoat and caretaker led me to one of the most painful experiences I have ever lived through, and provided me with the impetus to make one of the biggest decisions of my entire life.

The conditions that enabled this pattern to surface were simple - a new, overly empowered, autocratic boss who severely lacked people skills. His 'persecutor' role hooked right into my 'victim' DNA, causing him to believe that if there was a problem, somehow, someway I must have caused it. Bingo. Perfect match of a persecutor and victim - it was like being right back home with Dad.

Sandwiched between my over-indulged team and my raging boss, I was stuck in the middle of an out-of-control situation. I had a team of whinging kids who I had allowed to abdicate adult responsibility, and a self centred, mean spirited boss who was more interested in finding someone to blame than some way to solve a problem.

One day, quite unexpectedly, I was called into a meeting with the head of employee relations, my boss and a senior operations manager. It seemed I was under some kind of investigation. Apparently, my entire team had gone to my boss and raised some very serious complaints about me, and the lack of support I gave them! I couldn't believe my ears! Some of my team accused me *of misappropriating funds, paying for personal items and allocating them to other categories. Later I discovered this little witch-hunt was spearheaded by my assistant manager (the one on the team I had given the most to, grooming her to someday take my place).*

You could feel the delight emanating from my boss. Here was his chance to get rid of me, and it was only a few months before my 10-year long service leave! I was dumbfounded when he then told me that I wasn't allowed to speak with any on my team about any of this because they all said they were terribly afraid of me.

The situation reached a crisis point, culminating in the need for me to seek external legal support, as I became the scapegoat. Because I was so overwhelmed with fear, the objectivity of my lawyer was extremely helpful and incredibly validating. With the help of my lawyer, Shirley and some very supportive friends, I walked through every step of this horrible situation - consciously doing it differently. I calmly provided all details of my expenditures. Using every communication skill I've ever learnt, I carried on with business as usual with my team - only I stopped care-taking them and did everything within my power not to be scapegoated by anyone. In the end, I was completely vindicated, with some of the team secretly coming to me to apologise.

The pain some of us will allow in our lives before we find the courage to let go and make some significant changes is mind boggling. Symbolically this was a deep spiritual experience for me, as it represented betrayal by the family at the deepest level possible. There I was, experiencing the same feelings I had as a teenager. I hadn't escaped the game - I had simply changed the players! I learned that I was unconsciously acting out a pattern, to try to resolve what I didn't get a chance to when growing up. Almost 9 months after this event occurred, and after more than 10 years of service, I finally had the courage to resign.

As shocking as it was, in retrospect I am grateful this experience occurred. I can see clearly now that the only way 'out' of a situation you don't want, is 'through' and I am convinced that had I left this company five years earlier, I would have found my way to a similar company and a similar set of circumstances.

A magical transformation occurs when you are no longer being driven by unconscious, unresolved feelings and patterns. It's called FREEDOM. You can't describe it totally, but you certainly know it when you have it. Not only have I left this company, I have left behind the deep, unconscious roles that once defined and ruled me. I feel that I have worked through all of these patterns and roles and have resolved them on a very deep level. I am no longer driven to play a part that isn't really me. I am a free woman.

My life is immeasurably different today. I thought I would feel lost, uneasy and empty after leaving my corporate position. I was surprised, in fact, at how good I did feel. My health returned, the weight came off, my confidence emerged and people tell me I look radiant. I received many consulting offers and came up with a great business idea that is so simply successful.

Today, as I write this story, I delight in my newfound freedom and independence. I follow my own rules and all of the 'have to's' in my life have been changed to 'get to's'! I 'get to' do things in my own time - like writing a story on a Monday morning! I can't stop repeating "Life just doesn't get much better than this!"

RECOGNISING CHILD ABUSE

There is widespread denial and lack of understanding about the extent and nature of child abuse that exists in our society.

I agree with Pia Mellody's definition of child abuse: "Anything that is less-than-nurturing or shaming". The dictionary says that to nurture is "to educate, to feed, to nourish and to help grow or develop".

Before I give specific examples of the different forms of abuse, I want to explain that all of these forms can be expressed in different ways. They can be either *overt* or *covert, empowering or disempowering* to the child. Often, abuse is disguised as discipline.

Overt Abuse is clearly visible to everyone, whether it be physical, verbal or behavioural.

Covert Abuse is indirect, passively aggressive and deviously manipulative. It also includes parental neglect, such as withholding love or emotional nurturing.

The harmful effects of this type of abuse are greatly underestimated, mainly because it is so hard to recognise. Here are some examples of covert abuse:

Debra has a high-powered career, a charming husband and a darling four year old daughter, Catherine. Debra is tired when she comes home from work. She rushes to collect Catherine who wants her mother's affection and attention, but instead is lovingly placed, night after night, in front of the television.

Catherine's emotional needs are being neglected. Catherine is a covertly abused child.

Kevin is divorced, wealthy and has a daughter and a son. His children have everything that money could buy. When they spend a weekend with him, Kevin spends his time reading the paper, cleaning the pool and watching sports on television. When he takes them out, it is to an event he is interested in. His son gets extra attention and approval when he excels at competitive school sports- the more trophies, the more admiration.

Kevin's children are being abandoned by him. On the outside, Kevin provides abundantly for them, but in emotional terms they are bankrupt. This is covert child abuse.

Joanne's friends and family regard her as a loving, caring mother and homemaker. She gives her affection, support and time freely to her children, except when they don't behave the way she wants them to. When they are naughty, she withdraws her love, support and approval, ignoring them until she gets her own way.

Joanne controls her children through emotional abandonment. Joanne's children are being covertly abused.

Abuse will either empower or disempower a child.

Disempowering Abuse is done in a manner which shames a child, making him or her feel less than others, as though they are not 'good enough'. It takes away the child's innate sense of value and power. A disempowered child will grow up to feel inadequate, insecure and a victim.

Empowering Abuse gives a child a false sense of power, making them feel more important and better than others. An empowered child will grow up to feel superior and become abusive or a victimiser.

Most of us have experienced both styles of abuse and subsequently vacillate between feeling better than or less than others; we alternate between being offensive with others and being victimised.

PHYSICAL ABUSE

When a child's physical body is not treated with respect or is ignored or attacked, this is physically abusive. This includes any type of physical hitting or belting, by hand or with an implement; face slapping; shaking a child; hair pulling; head banging; or holding a child down and tickling them. It also includes intrusive procedures such as enemas; insensitively poking or prodding at any orifice without general respect for the child. A child can also be physically abandoned by a parent or parents who are absent through death, divorce, desertion, illness or workaholism.

Some parents fail to give their children sufficient physical nurturing - cuddles, hugs, a loving touch; or they neglect the physical nurturing needs of a child. Some adults are more demonstrably affectionate to their animals than their children.

SEXUAL ABUSE

This includes intercourse, anal sex, oral sex, masturbation (the child touching the offender or the offender touching the child), sexual touching, hugging or kissing.

Covert Sexual Abuse

A disturbingly common from of covert sexual abuse, which causes very harmful consequences, is when a parent allows their child to sleep with them regularly. An example from my client files involves a single mother who complained that her small daughter would not sleep the whole night in her own bed. Using the excuse that she was too weary to discipline the child, she allowed the child to sleep with her. Through her therapy, we discovered that she was missing the warmth and comfort of a man in her life and the cuddling of her daughter was fulfilling part of that need. This is inappropriate bonding and will affect the child's sexuality in later years.

The failure by parents to give their children appropriate sexual education is also covert sexual abuse. Many of my women clients have painfully recalled the onset of their menstrual cycle - they had not been given any information on why they were menstruating or what to expect and were extremely frightened and embarrassed.

Overt Sexual Abuse

- **Voyeurism:** This might take the form of a parent looking at nude magazines or they may ogle their teenager as the child is dressing. Often, the way a child recognises this is that the parent's look gave them a 'sick' feeling.

- **Exhibitionism:** Parents dressing seductively or parading nude in front of their children. Whether the nudity is sexually abusive depends on whether the parent is being sexually stimulated by this behaviour.

- **Verbal sexual abuse:** Calling girls names such as 'a little tart', a 'whore', a 'slut', or being told 'you look cheap'. Also, I have had several men break down and cry in my office when recalling how their mothers ridiculed their burgeoning teenage sexuality.

As a form of self-protection, most men and women have completely blocked out any recollection of sexual abuse. They only seek help when they are having problems with their sexuality or sexual relationships. Through therapeutic processes, they are able to recall and deal with past incidences. This frees them to experience healthy, functional sexual relationships.

EMOTIONAL ABUSE

The most widespread form of child abuse, emotional abuse manifests in various ways.

Verbal Abuse

This occurs when a child is belittled, criticised, called names, ridiculed or yelled at. Hearing someone else being verbally abused is equally abusive because even though a child knows he or she is not at fault, they still suffer from the power of the onslaught. Many adults cannot handle anger or loud altercations because these remind them of the intense upset they felt as children when they heard their parents arguing.

Social Abuse

Children's friendships are extremely important for their social development. When parents interfere in the relationships their children have with their peers, either directly or indirectly, this is social abuse. Many children and teenagers feel they can't bring their friends home because of their parent's behaviour. There may be alcoholism; sickness or mental illness in the family or dad may fly into a rage at the drop of a hat. Perhaps mum nags dad to an embarrassing degree, or, maybe there is simply an ill-defined but cogent implication that the family has a terrible 'secret' which could be uncovered by visitors.

My school friend Rose had a father who was a rageaholic noted for ridiculing her in front of her friends. I remember a particular time when he humiliated her in front of her high school sweetheart. When her boyfriend didn't leave her after that mortifying incident, she said to me: "My God, I better hang on to him!" As soon as she turned 18, she married him to get away from the home.

Here is a list of some more emotionally abusive behaviours: criticising, patronising, withholding love, deceiving, inflicting guilt, dumping anger, shaming or degrading, betraying, teasing, ridiculing, bullying or intimidating, disapproving, breaking promises, making vague demands, misleading or raising hopes falsely, under-handed comments, humiliating, blaming, yelling, insulting, threatening, not taking seriously, being cruel, responding inconsistently or arbitrarily, mocking feelings, needs and wants.

ABANDONMENT

As a child is being abused, no one is really there for them. They are all alone. Hence, abuse IS abandonment. When parents abuse children, the abuse often stems from the parents' own unresolved issues, rather than what the child is doing or not doing.

Children depend on their parents for survival and to meet their dependency needs. Pia Mellody defines dependency needs as the need for food, clothing, shelter, medical/dental care, physical nurturing, emotional nurturing (time, attention and direction), sexual guidance and information, and financial guidance and information.

Emotional nurturing is fundamental to a healthy developing maturity. It also involves instructing children how to undertake the basic tasks of living. As children receive time, attention and direction from their parents, they learn who they are in a positive way. This gives them their sense of worth and value.

Neglect occurs when emotional dependency needs are only partially met. Abandonment occurs when these needs are not met at all.

Children who are dispatched to boarding school at a young age are emotionally abandoned even though this may not be the parents' intention.

In the first three years of our lives, we need to be admired and unconditionally loved and accepted for who we are. We also need our parents' physical presence and behaviour to reflect to us at any given moment this self-love and acceptance.

'Mirroring' needs to take place whether the child has a dirty nappy, is screaming, crying, ill, laughing or cooing, whether they're clean and quiet or dirty and noisy. This need for 'mirroring' is what Alice Miller, doctor and author, calls our 'narcissistic supplies' and a large portion of our adult population is deprived of this. This is despite the fact that their parents may have been encouraging, sensitive and caring.

It takes a highly emotionally mature adult to consistently 'mirror' back to his or her child a sense of their innate preciousness and value. Most adults are emotionally undeveloped because their emotional dependency needs were not met when they were children. These people are little children inside adults' bodies and are commonly referred to as 'adult children'. Our society is full of adult children trying to be good parents.

These immature parents *need* their children's approval and admiration, so they can finally get *their* narcissistic needs met. This syndrome is the basis of our society's obsession with super achievement. Many talented, highly successful people, who have been praised and admired for their talents and achievements, suffer from this form of emotional abandonment. These achieving types will say: 'My parents were always around and supportive, but I only ever felt loved when I was being admired and praised.' This type of person is a victim of emotional deprivation.

A dear friend of mine came to this realisation in her early thirties. As a young girl, the only time she had won her parents' interest and admiration was when she did well at school. As an adult, she was a workaholic, running her own successful business, a high earner, socially well connected and financially independent. She tired of the associated pressures and felt burned out, but was afraid to get off the achievement treadmill because she said she would feel like a 'totally unlovable nobody'. She desired marriage and children and felt her biological clock was ticking away. Because she did not want a mate who would be attracted to her only for her achievements, she courageously let go of her high-powered career and lifestyle in order to relax and be herself. During the next 12 months she concentrated on loving herself without all of her symbols of success, and as a result she attracted her current husband and is now expecting her first baby.

INTELLECTUAL ABUSE

Basically, intellectual abuse attacks or ridicules a child's thinking. When this abuse occurs in a family, there is no permission for children to have a different opinion from their parents. The unspoken message to the child is: 'You are stupid. And it's my right to tell you how to think.'

Teaching and guiding children towards solving their own problems is necessary for healthy, intellectual development. Ignoring children's problems or frequently stepping in and solving them for the children robs them of the opportunity to learn to problem-solve for themselves.

SPIRITUAL ABUSE

In spiritual abuse, the parental message to the child, whether spoken or implied is: 'I am the Higher Power in this family. I'm the one who decides what's right and wrong and I have the right to tell you what to believe!' In a functional family, the parents would admit to their children that they too sometimes have doubts about their own ideas and beliefs.

Many years ago, I attended a seminar about spirituality in which I was asked to write a letter to God, stating all the times I felt down, angry and distrustful of God. When I had completed my letter, I was asked which of my parents was the most dominant authority figure. For me, it was my father and I was told to change 'Dear God' to 'Dear Dad'. This exercise had a profound impact on me, for it graphically demonstrated that I was reacting to God in the same manner as I related to my father in childhood.

Virtually all abuse is spiritual abuse because at the moment of abuse, the offender has all the power and ipso facto, *is* the Higher Power.

Other less evident forms of spiritual abuse include:

- When a parent demands that a child be perfect, essentially they are asking them to be God-like. But humans are fallible and it is normal to make mistakes. Often, parents refuse to admit their own mistakes, implying to the child that they (the parents) are perfect.

• When a parent over-controls a child, it impedes the natural process of learning how to do things their own way. As a result of this, children grow up having difficulty making their own decisions and rely on advice from everyone else.

• When a family sets rigid, oppressive rules which are almost impossible for the child to keep and which are seldom kept by the parents either. How many of us relate to the adage: 'Don't do as I do, do as I say.'

• When parents are addicted to religion, they may neglect their children by making their religion their priority in terms of time and attention. Religious addicts may use the concept of a punitive God to threaten and control the children or to instil guilt. They believe that all their problems occur because of some fault in their relationship with God. Like all addicts, religious addicts are empty inside, devoid of any ability for self-reference. They don't know how to provide structure or problem solving skills needed to develop to maturity.

Such addicts do not understand about having a partnership with God. When they act as though helpless or like martyred victims, leaving total responsibility for their lives to God, the children grow up to be irresponsible. We need to have a balance - between learning to 'let go and let God', and taking action for ourselves.

As I explained in Chapter 3, the key to unlocking your personal freedom is through a relationship with a Higher Power of your own understanding. If you don't have a healthy sense of, and a loving partnership with a power greater than yourself and if you don't confront issues of spiritual abuse from your childhood, it will block your path to freedom.

MOVING FROM VICTIM TO VICTORY

After reading the preceding information about dysfunctional family systems and child abuse, you may be feeling very emotionally stirred up because of realisations or memories which are surfacing. This initial period of confronting such issues is a necessary step on your path towards freedom - and it will pass.

If we don't know our family histories, the roles we played and the type of abuse we experienced, we are likely to repeat them and never be free. Terry Kellogg, a pioneer in treating child abuse and co-dependency says: "In order to change anything, you have to make it real."

We have to come out of denial and look clearly at the reality of our histories. We have to give up our delusion and fantasy about our family pictures and images. And finally, we have to thaw out and have *our* feelings about our histories. In this way, we can set ourselves free to make the decisions in our adult lives that will give us the fulfilment we desire.

In recalling and resolving our childhood histories, it is imperative that we do *not* go through this process blaming our parents. Rather, we need to account for who offended us, what happened, how we felt about it then and how we feel about it now. Only by doing this can we begin to change the reactive behaviour patterns that adversely affect our adult lives.

As children, we were dependent on our major caregivers for our safety and survival and were unavoidably *victims* of their abusive behaviour. We need to face that, have our feelings about it and allow ourselves to grieve the losses of childhood. As adults, we need to relinquish the victim mentality we developed in our formative years, take responsibility for our lives now and thereby move from victim to victory.

SOME CHARACTERISTICS OF CO-DEPENDENTS

I've come to believe that most people are co-dependents to some degree and in treating this dis-ease I find it helps people to be able to identify and address their specific problem areas. The following check list will help you to find where you're not functioning in a healthy balanced way.

1. SELF-ESTEEM ISSUES

- I seldom feel on an equal par with people. I usually feel 'better than' or 'less than' those I am with.

- I worry about what others think on my close friends and family.

- I receive my value from being needed by others.

- I feel I ought to relieve another's pain.

- I feel responsible for protecting those I'm close to.
- I tend to 'love' people I can pity and rescue.
- I tend to criticise and nag.
- I am damagingly self-critical.
- I try to control and manipulate other people's behaviour for my own comfort.

2. BOUNDARY ISSUES

- I am unable to set realistic limits for myself.
- I think the embarrassing behaviour of someone close to me reflects on me.
- I tend to lose my own identity in intimate relationships.
- I often isolate myself socially and emotionally.
- I am often attracted to people who hurt me.

3. REALITY ISSUES

- I am a 'people pleaser' and I constantly seek approval from others.
- I avoid conflict and confrontation as much as possible and am frightened by angry people.
- I abandon my values if they differ from someone who is important to me.
- I have trouble distinguishing my own reality from others' realities.
- I can divulge to strangers intimate information I'd like to share with my partner, yet am unable to because I fear rejection.
- I feel guilty standing up for myself because I feel I don't have rights.
- I have distorted or non-existent spirituality.

4. DEPENDENCY ISSUES

- I have difficulty knowing and/or taking care of my own need and wants.

- I set aside my own interests to care for another.

- I try to solve others' problems.

- I depend on others to make me feel happy.

- I have a history of nervous attacks, allergies, rashes, headaches, depression, being frequently tired and non-specific illnesses.

- I create alliances with my children to get them on my side.

- I occasionally indulge in suicidal thoughts.

- I depend on alcohol, coffee, tea, sugary substances, prescribed and recreational drugs, food, work or sex to give me a lift or relieve my stress - and often become addicted to some of these.

5. MODERATION ISSUES

- I operate in extremes in my thinking, feelings and behaviour.

- I have little or no ability to maintain balance.

- I often swing from rage to resignation.

- I am hooked on excitement because it gives me a sense of aliveness.

- I am afraid of authority figures.

- I have difficult sharing who I am with others and hearing them share who they are with me.

DIS-EASE OF IMMATURITY

Now that you have some understanding of the causes and characteristics of co-dependency, I would like to give you my definition: Co-dependency is a state of dis-ease that originates from the abandonment of the authentic self in order to survive within a dysfunctional family, societal, educational or religious system during one's formative years of life. Co-dependents are so focused on and affected by someone else's behaviour that they have very little relationship with themselves.

So a co-dependent doesn't really know his or her true inner self. They have learned to keep it hidden so that a sense of their innate personal value, self-esteem and connection to others is distorted. As co-dependency progresses, it will result in stress, misery, disrupted relationships, controlling behaviour and physical illness. If left untreated, co-dependency can lead to addictions such as alcoholism, drug dependency, eating disorders, work addiction, compulsive gambling or spending, sex addiction and love addicted relationships.

Co-dependency is a dis-ease of immaturity. We were not allowed to mature to our full potential because we have been raised in dysfunctional environments and experienced child abuse.

As children, we are naturally egocentric and have boundless energy. We need both qualities to do the demanding work of growing up. When we have to use our energy to defend ourselves from abuse, no matter how subtle it may appear, the subsequent drain causes a diminished spontaneity and a lack of feeling valued. Because we don't feel valued, our development stages are impaired and ultimately we do not fully mature.

I often use a rose analogy to explain this syndrome. I've sometimes received roses where buds never opened, instead, they drooped at the ends. I later discovered these were grown rapidly, artificially and unnaturally in hot houses. Perhaps they didn't receive all the water, natural sunlight, fertiliser, time and attention they needed to mature and bloom naturally in their own good time. As a result, the buds didn't flourish to the maturity of an open flower. Co-dependents are like those roses. They didn't flourish or mature to their full potential and they often die without knowing or expressing who they really are.

So many people are in such pain and confusion today that it is hardly surprising that the information about co-dependency has spread rapidly, been accepted and acted upon so quickly and eagerly. People are tired of being in pain, trapped in outmoded, destructive behaviour patterns and longing to break free to a new way of living. I know from my own personal experience that with willingness, education and treatment, breaking free from co-dependency is possible.

CHAPTER 4

ARE YOU
TRAPPED BY
DISTORTED REALITY?

As human beings, we are made up of physical, emotional, intellectual and spiritual aspects. Together, these aspects constitute our sense of personal reality. They determine our individuality and sense of self. In a balanced person, these aspects function interdependently. For example, negative or fearful thoughts can stimulate overwhelming feelings, which in turn create stress that can contribute to physical disease. When we are dis-eased, or out of balance mentally, emotionally or physically, it affects our essence, which is our spirituality. It is important to our growth and maturity to utilise all the aspects of our reality. Doing this helps us to attain balance in our lives.

Reality is a matter of perception. No two people have the same reality because much of our reality is formed during our upbringing. Inevitably we have thoughts about everything we see in our physical environment - whether it is a church, a school, a full moon, a spider, an exhibitionist at a crowded train station or the neighbours arguing over the back fence. These thoughts, to which we assign personal meaning, also generate certain feelings. In turn, these feelings determine the type of behaviour we will or won't adopt.

Let's take the example of the exhibitionist at the train station. Imagine the scene: It is rush hour and several people of varying ages and backgrounds are waiting at the underground railway station for their train home. Suddenly, a man in a raincoat strolling along the edge of the platform, opens his coat, flashes his genitals at the crowd, then swiftly runs off. Each person on the platform may react differently to this incident. Their reactions will be filtered through the lens of their childhood experiences.

For example: A woman who was sexually abused as a child may exclaim: "Oh My God!" and flee the scene in fear. A man who, as a young boy, had witnessed his mother being bashed and subsequently had taken a protective role towards women, may shout: "You pervert!" and give chase to the flasher. A psychotherapist who is in the crowd, may say to themselves: "Oh, there's a level two sex addict. I know how to help that poor guy." A married couple within inches of the flasher may have dramatically different reactions. The wife, in panic, clutches her husband's arm, saying: "Darling, aren't you going to do something about that terrible man?" The husband, who has been conditioned since boyhood to repress his feelings, especially fear, denies that he even saw the flasher. "Who?" he replies, feigning ignorance and adding sarcastically: "What's your problem now?" Meanwhile, a voluptuous woman in a figure-hugging dress and heavy make-up, who in early adolescence was frequently esteemed by men for her prematurely large breasts, nudges her girlfriend and whispers: "Get a load of his equipment! Wonder what his telephone number is?"

As we grew up, we often got direct and/or indirect messages of what to think, how to feel and what to do or not do. We learned how to adopt the reality of our major caregivers. This is why co-dependents selectively alter who they are and what they think and feel in order to please others. They suffer two types of distorted realities. Either they don't know what they think, feel and want to do or they do know, but won't let on because they fear disapproval. The classic example is the chameleon type. This person changes or withholds their opinions and alters their behaviour according to the people he or she is with.

DENIAL

Before we go any further, it is important to understand the power of denial. Accepting something outside of the familiar is not only uncomfortable, for many, it is down right painful. Especially if we must accept something that goes against our beliefs and values, or something that triggers our repressed sadness, shame, fear anger or guilt. Of course our first instinct is to deny it in any way we can!

Denial is a self-defence mechanism to defend against pain, or the reality of situations that cause us pain. On the unconscious level, we have learned to use denial by witnessing others' behaviour in our formative years, particularly as we were learning to survive in the big world. Denial helps us to survive when we don't know how to handle overwhelming emotions, situations beyond our control, or we simply don't know another way to operate.

Denial diminishes as we process our past repressed feelings, come out of the trance of our childhood roles and start making conscious choices. The sooner you go into the pain, link it to its original source and identify the pattern, the sooner you will become free to choose from your true self. There is a wise saying, 'this too shall pass'. After years of working with people to resolve their past distorted realities, I have invented an evolved version of this saying, '*this too shall pass if you are willing to pass through it*'. This means that you fully participate with the healing process - not just 'grin and bare it'.

I celebrate you passing through your pain and distortions. Do what you can to be gentle and compassionate with yourself - but pass through it! As long as you remain trapped in distorted reality, attaining personal freedom is an impossibility.

Now let's separate each aspect of reality and look at some of the ways in which distorted reality manifests.

INTELLECTUAL REALITY

In a functional environment, children are supported in their ability to think. Even though a child has much to learn, they are encouraged to learn to think for themselves and taught methods of problem-solving. This type of system will allow a child to fully mature intellectually.

Distorted thinking, like other adaptive behaviour, is also learned in the formative years and can develop as a survival tool for living in a chaotic, unsafe environment. These thinking errors can become chronic, progressive and keep us from experiencing freedom. Since these distorted thinking patterns will limit us and prevent recovery, it is important to learn how we apply them in our daily lives.

Following is a list of some distorted thinking patterns:

1. Blaming
This is an excuse to not solve the problem and is used to build up a resentment towards someone else for 'causing' whatever happened. Blaming takes the focus off the one who is pointing the finger.

2. Justifying
This is a defensive form of explanation and keeps the focus on the justification of rather than the solution to a problem.

3. Analysing
This keeps us in our heads, thereby evading our feelings by intellectualising a problem.

4. Excuse-making
The purpose of excuse-making is to protect one's behaviour or the behaviour of others - i.e. family members and authority figures.

5. Super-optimism
This is a narrow-minded masquerade of positive thinking which permits a person to function according to how he or she wants rather than according to the facts of the situation.

6. Redefining
This shifts the focus of an issue to avoid solving a problem. It also is indicative of ineffective thinking in that it avoids dealing with the subject in question.

7. Vagueness
Being unclear and non-specific to avoid being pinned down or confronted on a particular issue.

8. Assuming
The co-dependent spends a great deal of time assuming what others think, feel and are doing. Usually these assumptions are egocentric and arise from childhood experiences. They reinforce one's distorted reality.

9. Minimising
When we minimise dysfunctional behaviour or circumstances, from our past or in our present, we can avoid facing it.

10. Grandiosity
This is minimising or maximising the significance of an issue and in doing so, justifies not solving it.

11. Ingratiating

When we overdo being nice to others and go out of our way to act interested in them, it is done to manipulate situations and people and to control the outcome of events.

12. Dishonesty

This is the most commonly known characteristic of co-dependency and shows up in different forms at different times. Dishonesty confuses, distorts and takes the focus off the behaviour of the co-dependent or the one he or she is trying to protect. A few types of dishonesty include:

- Making things up which are not true.

- Saying partly what is so, but omitting major sections.

- Pretending to agree with someone else or approving of another's ideas or plans in order to look good, when in fact one has no intention of going along with these or does not really agree.

13. Victim playing

The basic belief here is that: 'I am right and others are wrong.' Co-dependents who take the victim position passively-aggressively offend, which comes across as the co-dependent justifying their actions and makes the other party look like the offender. The victim player interacts with others to invite either criticism, rescue or enabling behaviour from those around him or her. The victim stance is sometimes difficult to recognise as this pattern of behaviour is usually unconscious and so, the victim may need the help of others to recognise his or her distorted beliefs.

14. Mental Obsession

Perhaps the most preferred way to defend against pain. Second nature to addictive types and co-dependents, we do it like breathing!

Most of these distorted thinking patterns are unconscious and we don't understand why we do them, so don't use the preceding information to beat yourself up for your particular thinking patterns. Rather, use it to help you to clarify where some of these may be restricting you.

FEELING REALITY

In our culture there is a general attitude that to feel at all is a sign of immaturity. If we show our feelings, even moderately, we are considered emotional types; and if we dare to express strong feelings, we may be regarded as 'over the top' when we're joyful or 'having a breakdown' (that once-ubiquitous Australian phrase) when we're sad or afraid.

The social codes of the western world dictate that men are not to be fearful, women are not to be angry and no one is to feel pain at all. If we have pain, either emotional or physical, we should medicate it as soon as possible. A woman who expresses her anger, especially at a man, is thought to be overbearing, unfeminine and sexually unattractive. A man expressing his anger, however, is seen as being powerful and forthright. Women are expected to be fearful so they can be protected by men, but men who show their fear are considered cowards or wimps. These attitudes are totally unrealistic, highly damaging and perpetuate a distorted feeling reality on a societal scale.

Instead of being trapped unawares by these detrimental attitudes, we need to understand how our feeling reality may be distorted. We also need to learn how to give appropriate expression to all our feelings and to understand that it is healthy and positive to do so. This is what happens in a functional family system.

For the co-dependent, the feeling reality is usually the most impaired. Without a healthy feeling reality available to us, we are operating as handicapped people. Feelings that are not talked about or given appropriate expression will *always* be acted out or projected on to others. Projection occurs when we unconsciously ascribe to others our own feelings, especially if we've judged our feelings as undesirable.

Unexpressed feelings are also muscle-bound as our bodies store emotions. This accounts for a lot of unexplained tension, soreness, and general aches and pains. People who've frozen their feelings over the years can be assisted to get in touch with them and release them through bodywork such as acupuncture, rolfing, shiatsu and deep tissue massage.

HOW ARE YOU FEELING?

For many of us, identifying our feelings can be quite perplexing. Often when I ask new clients how they are feeling, they tell me what they are thinking. Other common responses are 'I don't know', 'not bad', 'not good' or 'fine'. These responses are examples of people who are confused, frozen, out of touch with, overwhelmed by or denying their feelings.

When we're trapped in a distorted feeling reality, it is common to escape from our feelings rather than to learn how to use them. Unfortunately, most people only become willing to identify and express these true feelings when there has been some major problem in their lives (i.e. relationship break-up, mid-life crisis, losing a job, death of a loved one, panic attacks, or quitting an addiction).

To simplify this process, I like and use Pia Mellody's categorisation of the four feeling realities - adult feeling reality, carried feeling reality, adult-to-adult feeling exchange and child feeling reality.

ADULT FEELING REALITY

Our basic raw feelings are joy, fear, pain, loneliness and anger. Guilt, lust and shame are a combination of thinking and feeling realities, but they are so pervasive in our lives that, for our purposes, I've included them as basic raw feelings.

When we are operating in our adult feeling reality, we are able to identify and express our raw feelings in a mature, responsible way - without over-reacting to people or situations, even when others try to 'push our buttons'.

Being able to exercise positive self-control with our feelings will provide us with the energy, intuition, protection, growth and freedom that most of us are looking for.

CARRIED FEELING REALITY

All of our feelings are positive and give us special gifts. In childhood we learned to unconsciously take on and 'carry' the feelings of other people. Because of this, we may distort, become overwhelmed by or over-react when we express our feelings. This confusion has caused us to judge many of our feelings as negative.

We experience these overwhelmed, carried feelings as:

Hysteria	rather than	Joy
Panic or Paranoia	rather than	Fear
Hopelessness	rather than	Pain
Isolation	rather than	Loneliness
Rage	rather than	Anger
Immobility	rather than	Guilt
Greedy, Obsessive Desire	rather than	Lust
Worthlessness	rather than	Shame

Understanding and releasing carried feelings is a key to developing a healthy, balanced feeling reality. How did we learn to carry feelings in the first place?

When a major caregiver is *irresponsible with or in denial of* his or her feeling reality, the feelings being denied or handled irresponsibly will be unconsciously picked up and carried by the children in the vicinity. This happens especially when a child is being abused in any way. (Child Abuse is defined in Chapter 3). This is why children who've been sexually abused usually feel intensely dirty, ashamed and afraid to tell anyone about their assault.

I frequently identify glaring examples of carried feelings in my clients. One such person was Fiona, a 32-year-old who was inexplicably fear-ridden. In her therapy, we discovered that she had been carrying her father's fear since she was a little girl. She recalled one incidence when she was three and had been playing in the front yard with a ball. Her father, who was supposed to be supervising her while her mother was at the supermarket, was chatting over the fence with a neighbour. When her ball rolled onto the street, she ran to get it and was almost hit by a car. As her father heard the screech of brakes, fear and adrenalin coursed through him. But because his upbringing did not permit him to acknowledge and express his fear (*'real men aren't afraid'*), he had to suppress and deny his fear - even to himself!

He ran to his daughter and instead of comforting her, he belted her bottom and chastised her for having run onto the street without looking. Fiona's father acted irresponsibly with his anger and was in denial of his fear. As he was abusing her, she 'carried' his anger and his fear. We discovered several more instances in which Fiona had unconsciously carried her father's fear. This explained her fear-ridden state.

Most of the overwhelming feelings that surface when we stop suppressing them in one way or another aren't even ours! Through progressively releasing the carried feelings, expressing and embracing our adult feelings, we will begin to feel a greater sense of freedom in our lives.

ADULT TO ADULT FEELING EXCHANGE

It is possible to break the childhood pattern of carrying feelings for others by establishing emotional boundaries. (I'll explain how to do this in Chapter 9).

Most people have damaged emotional boundaries, which allow them to practise an 'adult-to-adult feeling exchange'. This is when we take on other people's feelings in the present. Usually, these feelings don't seem to fit the experience. They can make one feel embarrassed, overwhelmed and crazy.

We do this by unconsciously exchanging, carrying and often acting out the feelings of the adults to whom we are close. Often, this unconscious act is done in the same manner we carried feelings from our caregivers during childhood.

This syndrome is particularly identifiable in marriage/couple counselling. Many times when couples come in, the man is cool, collected and controlled and the woman is an angry, emotional basket case. He seems to think the problem is that his wife needs to pull herself together and has come to therapy primarily to support her to do that. Meanwhile, she's bought into the idea that she's the problem and begins to question her own sanity.

In probing beneath the superficial circumstances of this type of case, I often find that the man has refused to acknowledge and express his feelings and therefore the woman is carrying and acting out his unexpressed feelings. She will particularly do this for him in the same way that she did it for the parent he most resembles - e.g. mother was never angry, father was never sad and neither ever expressed shame.

On the other hand, we've all known women who profess that they don't get angry. They present an unfailingly jolly and optimistic face to the world and if you ask them how they are, will mostly respond: 'Fine, just fine.' Often such women have partners who are raging maniacs. They have unconsciously chosen men like this, so that they can get indirect relief from their repressed anger (as the man acts it out) while outwardly they remain a 'saint'.

CHILD FEELING REALITY

The child feeling reality is comprised of old unresolved feelings from our childhood. As we begin the process of going within to discover our feelings about our histories, many of us will be unable get in touch with certain feelings; some may feel nothing at all.

The degree to which our childhood feelings weren't expressed and validated is the degree to which they are locked inside of us and frozen. When we allow ourselves to recall and identify our 'child feeling reality', it feels as if we're thawing out. However, all of our frozen childhood feeling reality obviously will not thaw out overnight. It can be a slow process and is best taken a day at a time. It's important to remember that this is a time to be gentle with yourself, as these feelings are vulnerable and need to be acknowledged and purged.

Often, when we become aware of and begin to feel our frozen feelings, we childishly want to express them to our parents or siblings and demand that they acknowledge them. Doing this is usually disastrous because while it confronts the dysfunctionality in the family system, it also triggers more confusion, suppression and denial. Also, be aware that analysing our past and debating with our families is a defensive *mental* process which takes us out of our *feelings* and into our heads. And then we're right back where we started.

I would strongly recommend expressing your childhood feelings in a Twelve Step support group such as Co-dependents Anonymous or Al-Anon (See Chapter 8) or with a therapist (particularly in a group setting) or in another program which specialises in treating these issues.

SPIRITUAL REALITY

It is in the sharing of who we really are that we experience our spirituality and feel connected with all of life. As you share your authentic self with another - your imperfections and fallibility as well as your successes and talent - then you will feel a true connection.

It's our own 'healthy shame' that allows us to do this. 'Healthy shame' is the psychological foundation of humility and a normal feeling. Shame occurs when you notice your fallibility and allow others to know about it, whereas guilt arises as a feeling of regret when you operate outside of your own value system. When we experience our healthy shame, we feel mild embarrassment and are aware of our imperfections - but fundamentally we still feel that we're okay. Our healthy shame tells us that we are not God, that we need help, and that we can and will make mistakes.

SPIRITUAL BANKRUPTCY

There is, however, another kind of shame which is quite damaging. This is 'carried shame' or what John Bradshaw refers to as 'toxic shame'. The roots of toxic shame are in child abuse and child abuse is the root of co-dependency.

Every time a child is abused in any manner and to any degree, the offender is acting shamelessly. What I mean by this is that they are in denial of their shame at the time the abuse is taking place. As you would have deduced from the preceding material, most of us are carrying a lot of toxic shame. This has caused most of us to be 'shame-based' people. Toxic shame is an unbearable, painful feeling about one's self as a person and it *always necessitates a cover-up.*

Bradshaw says: "Shame as a healthy, human emotion can be transformed into shame as a (state of) being. As a state of being, shame takes over one's whole identity. To have shame as an identity is to believe that one's being is flawed, that one is defective as a human being. Once shame is transformed into an identity, it becomes toxic and dehumanising."

Our identity is based primarily on our sexuality. As individuals, we identify according to our gender and their associated roles. However, our spirituality is about our essence, our very beingness. It is who we are as human beings, beyond our labels, roles and gender. Therefore, when we are carrying toxic shame, we are spiritually bankrupt.

When we are spiritually bankrupt, we feel totally diminished and have an inner sense of being insufficient. We feel robbed of our dignity, exposed, inadequate, worthless and deserving of rejection.

IS IT SHAME OR IS IT GUILT?

Shame is commonly misidentified as guilt. How does one tell the difference? When we feel guilty, our conscience is troubled and we regret having behaved in a way that violates our personal values. Guilt does not reflect directly upon our identity, nor diminish our sense of personal worth. A person with guilt might say; 'I feel terribly sorry about the consequences of my behaviour'. In doing so, they reaffirm their personal values. With guilt, the possibility of repair exists and learning and growth are promoted. But shame is a painful feeling about one's self as a person. A shameful person sees no possibility of repair because shame pervades their very identity. No growth or learning is derived from the experience because it only confirms one's negative feelings about one's self. Guilt says: 'I made a mistake.' Shame says: 'I *am* a mistake.'

It is possible to feel guilt and shame at the same time when others know you've made a mistake. An instance of this might be a person phoning their office to say they have the flu and won't be in for the day, when actually they've been out partying until the wee hours and are hung over. They may feel guilty about having lied to their employer. But when the employer discovers what really happened and confronts the person, the employee would feel both guilt and shame.

THE TALL POPPY-SHAME CONNECTION

When I first came to Australia, many Australians told me of the 'Tall Poppy Syndrome'. I thought it odd and didn't understand why it occurred. While people were able to clearly identify the syndrome and were discomfited by it, they didn't seem to know why or how it had evolved. However, they were only too willing to issue frank warnings about the dangers of achieving too much success and prominence in this country. Only when I learned about the history of Australia did I start to understand the genesis of this phenomenon.

The foundation of this country was built on 'carried shame'. The convicts who were the first settlers were profoundly abused. The English Government acted shamelessly in deporting the convicts to a hostile and unchartered wilderness at the edge of the world, in many cases for 'crimes' of an extremely petty nature. Everything about this act totally devalued the people. They were rejected, abandoned, incarcerated and horrifically physically abused. Anyone who has read Marcus Clarke's classic novel *For The Term of His Natural Life* or Robert Hughes' best seller *The Fatal Shore* will be unable to deny the grim horror and unimaginable atrocities which took place both during the passage out and during the establishment of what amounted to a police state. There is no doubt that the founders of Australia were shamed!

Since abuse and distorted feelings and thinking are passed down through the generations, it is small wonder that contemporary Australians have trouble expressing themselves and believing they are good enough. The 'cultural cringe' which so plagued Australians in years gone by seems to me to have been inescapable given the history of the nation. Shame (the feeling that one is not good enough) permeates through the collective unconscious of Australians.

When our foundation is based on a belief and a feeling of not being good enough, we view ourselves as 'short poppies'. In other words, we didn't bloom to our full potential. Therefore, when we gaze across the field and see a vibrant tall poppy in full bloom, it is a painful confrontation of our own perceived inadequacies. Immobilised by shame, we find it simpler and less painful to cut down the tall poppy than to acknowledge and deal with the shame we are unconsciously carrying from our ancestors.

As long as one continues to think and behave as a short poppy, one remains, metaphorically speaking, imprisoned. Only through releasing the 'carried shame' can we begin to set ourselves free.

CLEVER COVER-UPS FOR SHAME

To put the Tall Poppy Syndrome into perspective, I would like to point out that many countries, cultures and races have had shaming experiences throughout their histories. Countless people throughout the world are shame-based.

Let's take for example the United States. Americans are renowned for being materialistic, success-oriented overachievers and perfectionists. It would appear that these types of people are confident, self-assured and capable. But for many of them, their 'I've-got-it-all-together' facade is an unconscious cover-up for shame.

In America, people are revered for rising to the dizzying heights of success, while in Australia, people are cut down for growing too tall. Both of these are extreme behaviours which arise from distorted thinking and feeling. Americans and Australians both have their roots in shame, but they act it out in different ways.

HUMILITY vs HUMILIATION

The foundation of true spirituality is humility. One of the reasons people struggle with their spirituality is that they confuse humility with humiliation. Since the ultimate in humiliation is the exposure of our painful, toxic shame, people unconsciously do almost anything to prevent this from happening. This is why people today are preoccupied with keeping busy. We have become more like human 'doings' than human 'beings'. This compulsive activity is fuelled by the need to distract ourselves in order to avoid confronting our toxic shame. Yet when we finally allow ourselves to stop, we have a stillness through which we can get in touch with who we really are.

While we continue to cling to our distorted realities, they will keep us feeling afraid, inadequate and continually chasing illusory 'fixes' to fill up the hole inside of us. In short, we'll remain spiritually bankrupt.

For a co-dependent, addict or someone from an addictive/dysfunctional system in their formative years, the emotional and spiritual realities are usually the most impaired. Because spirituality and repressed emotions are more covert than their overt cousins, intellectual and physical realities, they are more easily passed on through the generations. The following story from a former client is a good example of someone who didn't give up and was rewarded beyond his wildest dreams.

ROBERT'S STORY
A CLIENT'S PERSONAL VOYAGE

I had been living with my wife-to-be for 6 months, she was 3 months pregnant and I was starting to come down off the romantic high of new love. With the wedding only 3 months away everything was starting to unravel. In the beginning of the relationship I was full of confidence, Now, impending fatherhood was bringing feelings of being swamped and overwhelmed. We were starting to argue and when we weren't arguing we often weren't talking at all. To top it off I wasn't earning any money and I wasn't liked by my in-laws-to-be.

Being 6 years clean and sober and always on the lookout for an answer, one day I came across a self help book called **Set Yourself Free**. *As I scanned the pages I couldn't believe my luck -finally, here was the information I needed to fix my wife! I thought that if I could just get her to read it, we wouldn't have so much conflict. I even felt convinced it would help my mother-in-law too! Half way through the book I started to become disinterested and remember feeling puzzled as to why I had lost interest. With the birth of our first child nearing, I had lots on my mind, so I put the book down.*

After our son Connor was born we decided to shift up to the Kimberleys in the remote outback of Australia, the Kimberleys. As my young family grew so too did my feelings of being alone, angry, confused, and most of all being trapped. In the past I had the perfect solution to escape from uncomfortable feelings - I would take drugs. Now sober I was battling the emotional build up without them, and losing. When the dam burst I would spray everyone with my emotional torrents and pain-filled rages. I was scaring my wife and young family, and the worst of it was that I recognised that I was starting to mirror the actions of my father!

My father had been very critical of me, either pointing out a 'better' way to do something or showing his displeasure with my efforts. Eventually, after years of trying to 'do things right' I had come to accept myself as simply not 'good enough' to be worthy of his love. Extremely controlling, he was a torturous enforcer of rules- if broken he would hit out hard with his notorious leather strap. I had sworn I would never hit my children and here I was starting to smack my son. I hated myself for this and felt trapped inside my father's prison. To get some relief, I started to smoke some dope again and even took up drinking alcohol. My downward spiral continued. One day I accidentally came across the book **Set Yourself Free** *and started reading it again. This time as I read it I heard the words in the context of my own experiences. I noticed an excitement I hadn't felt in years. I wanted so much for my situation to change. The book opened my eyes again, and gave me insight into why I was doing some of the things I was doing. I wanted desperately to renew a loving relationship with my wife. I wanted so much to have a good, fatherly relationship with my son. Most importantly, I wanted my self-respect back. The book gave me the path I was looking for to stop feeling crazy and alone.*

It was so important to me, I moved my family back to Sydney from the other side of the country and I started attending Family of Origin Groups with Shirley's organisation. The early discussions about feelings alerted me to the fact that I didn't know what I was feeling. Most of the time I was numbing out my feelings until I couldn't keep them down anymore. People were talking about feelings like fear, sadness, joy and anger. They were also sharing about a feeling called shame. I remember realising that I didn't have a clue about it, yet somehow I knew that it was the big one for me. Over a number of weeks in group therapy, I was gently supported through the process of feeling, exploring and sharing my feelings.

One evening during group we were going around in a circle sharing how we felt. I could hardly hear as I was doing the usual rehearsing in my head about what I was going to say. I always had to get it just 'right'. It came my turn and with sweaty palms, 63

I shared to the best of my ability, feeling relieved when my turn was over. After it moved to the next participant, I suddenly had a strong surge go through my body and experienced the usual 'shit I could have said that' and, 'why didn't I share that' and 'I hope I made sense'. In the safety of that moment I recognised the feeling of shame and that I had been unconsciously feeling it ALL MY LIFE! I started laughing then crying then laughing again. This feeling of being a MISTAKE had been with me for as long as I could remember.

Most of my life I'd spent trying to make myself look so good (often at the expense of others, trying to make them look less) and taking drugs for years so as to not have to experience that horrible feeling. After all, it was only a bloody feeling, and didn't have anything to do with who I really was. Following the joy came pain as I started feeling the loneliness that had been associated with life long feelings of worthlessness.

Once the shame started to thaw, others feeling came. I felt so scared and never knew fear had been with me from my first waking breath in the morning to my last conscious breath at night. When ever I had told anyone in my family that I was scared I was always told not to be silly and that there was nothing to be scared of- I soon learnt to stop telling my family I was scared and pretended that everything was all right. Wonderful sensations like joy and laughter, returned as well and again I realised something from my childhood... I'd never felt that it was ok to be happy.

*Reading **Set Yourself Free** and attending group therapy helped me on my journey back from the shroud of shame that had cloaked me since childhood to my true self. I have learnt that feelings come, go and pass on through - as I am willing to pass through them.*

It is now possible for me to feel fear, shame, loneliness, anger, or joy, and experience all of my feelings positively. My children feel safe to come to me and tell me when they feel scared. They know that it's ok to feel whatever they are feeling. Today I have a new relationship with my anger. I can feel it and let it pass through me before I respond. I can actually choose what to do when I'm feeling angry and that awful urge to smack my children has completely left me.

Today, I am no longer lonely nor do I wake with a pit of fear in my stomach. I am so much lighter and my choices for responding to life only grows. My life is rich with increased confidence and I have a new career that I love and is right for me. I experience joy relating with my wife and I feel the freedom to love deeply.

I'm especially proud that I have broken the cycle of multi-generational abuse in my family. I love watching my children grow, and delight in their ability to express and create so freely and enthusiastically.

*I am grateful for coming across **Set Yourself Free** and for the love, care, safety and encouragement I received during my incredible journey of transformation. Thank you Shirley for helping to set my family free!*

PHYSICAL REALITY - THE POWER OF ADDICTIONS

In this context, when referring to physical reality, I am talking about behaviour. One of the most blatant ways in which distorted physical reality manifests is through addictions. Contrary to popular belief, addictions do not originate from bad habits, however, the physical/behavioural reality is where they are usually first uncovered.

Addictions, which are much more prevalent in our society than most people realise, diminish our freedom because they are ***processes of decreasing choice***. They distract us and take away our ability to focus and connect. At first, an addiction give us an illusion of consistency and a way to take care of ourselves. But eventually, we lose our ***apparent*** control and realise we do not know how to be consistent in our self-care. In fact, the addiction is usually masquerading an area of immaturity in our life. As an addiction progresses, it takes away our opportunity to develop, expand and mature. Addictions are sustained through denial, because for a time they allow us to cope and therefore give us the illusion that we've already developed and matured.

In fact, I agree with Dr Anne Wilson Schaef who, in her best-selling book *When Society Becomes An Addict*, contends that the addictive process operates routinely at organisational, societal and global levels.

There are two categories of addictions - ***substance addictions and process addictions***.

Substance addictions such as alcoholism, chemical dependency, (nicotine, caffeine, narcotics - whether they be prescription or recreational drugs), or eating disorders (overeating, anorexia, bulimia and fat/thin disorder) involve ingesting or injecting a substance into the body.

In *process addictions* people are engaged in ritualistic behaviours where the 'rush' or 'high' comes from the process of performing a series of actions. For example, the high that a compulsive gambler gets when his or her horse wins is only part of the payoff. The rest comes through the ritualistic 'process' of reading the form guide, phoning contacts for tips, selecting a bookmaker and placing the bet. Likewise, for the sex addict, the seduction process, as well as cruising, obsessing and fantasising, becomes as big a payoff as orgasm.

Other process addictions include compulsive spending and shopping, love addiction, religious addiction, work addiction, thinking addiction; or you may be addicted to rushing, raging (silent or explosive anger) or being busy. Sometimes a process and substance are components of the same addiction. For example, there are many rituals associated with eating and serving food in our society. In such cases, breaking the addiction is particularly difficult.

The above process addictions are ways that we can generate an adrenalin rush and excitement, thereby distracting ourselves from whatever we are feeling. Being hooked on our own adrenalin, I believe, is the basis of all addictions. The excitement it enables us to feel cuts through our emotional numbness and gives us an illusion of feeling really alive.

DEFINING ADDICTION

The word 'addiction' is used lightly and accepted colloquially. According to the dictionary, the root word 'addiciere' means to give one's self up, or to devote one's self to something in a habitual or obsessive manner.

It's been said that co-dependents have compulsive and addictive personalities. I'd like to briefly define the difference between compulsive and addictive behaviour. When we are being compulsive, we *feel* we are *in* control. When we are being addictive, we *know* we have lost control, but we are compelled to do it anyway. If our co-dependency is left untreated, we will become addicts of some sort. It is inevitable.

There is also a difference between abusing something and being addicted to it. Abuse takes the easy way out and looks for the softer way, providing a crutch to relieve pressure and put aside fears. *There is an element of laziness when we are abusing something.* In order to give up the crutch we must take steps to embrace our fears. *With addiction, there is frustration rather than laziness.* Addicts are addicted to their substance or process, because they don't see that there is another way to function.

John Bradshaw says: "Compulsive, addictive behaviours are not about being hungry, thirsty, horny or needing work. *They are about mood alteration.* Compulsive, addictive behaviours help us manage or keep a lid on our feelings. They distract us or alter the way we are feeling so we don't have to feel the loneliness and emptiness of our abandonment and shame."

Vernon Johnson, author of the book *I'll Quit Tomorrow* (which is considered to be the best available model for the treatment of the disease of alcoholism) has defined alcoholism and chemical dependency as "an addiction to mood altering chemicals. The most significant characteristics of the disease are: it is primary, predictable, progressive, chronic and fatal".

David Smith, from the Haight Ashbury Free Clinic in San Francisco California, defines an addict as: *"anyone who continues to use any substance or process in spite of adverse consequences."*

Terry Kellogg's criterion for addiction is:

- It's euphoric.
- It's readily available.
- It's fast acting.
- There are unclear cultural guidelines about its use.
- There are tolerance changes with its progression.

Pia Mellody in her book *Facing Codependence*, has defined an addiction as: "Any process which takes away intolerable reality." Addictive processes thus become a high priority, increasingly taking away time and attention from other priorities in our lives.

To be trapped in our co-dependency is to be in intolerable pain. While physical pain can be awful, one can obtain relief from it and there is usually the hope of a cure. But the pain and shame over the loss of your authentic self is chronic. There appears to be no relief from it or cure for it because the implication is that the whole person is defective. We opt for a mood-altering experience to alleviate this pain. But this is not a cure, only a 'quick fix'. Any way of mood-altering pain can become addictive. If it takes away relentless discomfort, it becomes a high priority and our most important relationship.

When you have a blinding headache, for example, it is hard to think of anything or anyone else. Obtaining medication to relieve the pain in your head becomes your over-riding priority. Other commitments go out the window until the pain is relieved.

We have many unconscious defences (such as minimising, delusion, suppression, repression and denial) with our compulsive behaviour and addictions, however there is one primary dysfunction at work - denial.

Addiction is sustained through denial and feels like survival. Denial always perpetuates 'acting out'. When we're in denial, we cannot see that what we are doing addictively is really harmful, either to ourselves or others.

Addictive behaviour is so socially integrated into our society that much of it goes unrecognised. Generally, people have multiple addictions which operate simultaneously. Some may be actively expressing one addiction, while having several others suppressed. Others have several addictions which they keep under strict control, doing a little bit of everything to avoid exposing themselves as an addict. Commonly, addictive personalities quit acting out one addiction only to supplant it with another from their latent repertoire. How often have you seen someone quit smoking only to put on several kilos of weight? That's why quitting or 'switching' keeps you on a merry-go-round of denial and doesn't give you the experience of freedom.

It is well documented that addictive diseases follow a predictable and progressive course. Left untreated, they are chronic and fatal. I cannot stress how important I feel it is to drop any petty, moral judgements regarding addictions. One addiction is not 'worse' than another and they can all be equally life-threatening. It is time we took a mature approach to understanding addictions by *educating* ourselves about their cause and treatment.

This certainly applied to my life several years ago when I entered the treatment centre. That education and intervention saved me from the inevitable descent into chronic alcoholism, lung cancer, financial ruin and self-hatred.

Education is the first step in coming out of denial. If you suspect that you have an addictive personality or you are in a relationship with an addictive type, then I suggest you seek treatment. For a time, addictions and compulsive behaviour may give you the illusion of consistency; survival or being in control - but in the end you and those with whom you are involved will always lose!

The following are brief descriptions of some of the obvious and some not-so-obvious life-threatening addictions:

ALCOHOLISM/DRUG ADDICTION

Alcohol is a drug, so I will refer to both alcoholism and drug addiction as 'chemical dependency'. Chemical dependency is a fatal disease - 100% fatal. In 1956 the American Medical Association formally recognised alcoholism as a disease. Before that time society viewed alcoholics or drug addicts as irresponsible or immoral people. This is a complete falsehood. In my experience, many chemically dependent people are highly responsible, with high moral values.

Alcoholism is characterised by addiction to a mood-altering chemical and the most significant characteristics of the disease are: it is primary, predictable, progressive, chronic and fatal.

- A *Bulletin* cover story claimed that: "For a country whose earliest white civilisation used alcohol as a currency and whose definition of manhood is: 'He holds his booze well', it is no surprise that Australians have a drink problem... and the highest rate of alcohol brain damage in the world." In 1997 the Australian National Council on Drugs reported that Australia "had the second highest per capita consumption of absolute alcohol of the English speaking nations (the United Kingdom was the highest)"

Another problem which I've encountered in Australia and which I believe is enormous is the addiction to prescription drugs. This is supported by the available statistics that show:

- One in three Australians has used tranquillisers at some time.

- An estimated 10 million prescriptions for minor tranquillisers (to counter anxiety and stress) are issued in Australia each year (these are prescribed twice as frequently for women as they are for men).

- Tranquilliser overdoses have resulted in 2995 admission to State hospitals from 1997 to 2002 and that the victims, again mostly female, cost the community $2.6 million.

- Over $21 million worth of tranquillisers are prescribed annually.

A persistent myth about drug addiction is that some drugs are addictive and others aren't. Many of my Australian clients have reported to me that their doctors advised them that Serapax and Valium are not addictive 'as long as you use them moderately'. The trouble with that notion is that I've yet to meet a co-dependent who knows how to practise moderation in their daily living. That's why they're in my office. And, by the time they're well into active recovery, they don't need Serapax anyway!

Nicotine and caffeine addiction are also chemical dependencies. Nicotine in the system causes the release of adrenalin and a rise in blood sugar. Within seven seconds after entering the system, endorphins are released from the brain, giving the nicotine addict a temporary sense of well-being.

And how many of us use tea, coffee or Cola as liquid speed?

EATING DISORDERS

Becky Jackson, a pioneer and expert in the treatment of eating disorders, claims that most expressions of eating disorders consist of a combination of a biological predisposition and a 'process' addiction. She says that eating disorders generally manifest themselves in three primary symptoms and three secondary symptoms.

The primary symptoms are:

- The obsession with eating or starving.
- The obsession with food.
- The obsession with body image.

The secondary symptoms are:

- The obsession with nutrition.
- The obsession with health.
- The obsession with exercise.

The secondary symptoms represent attempts at control.

Clinicians usually divide eating disorders into four categories:

Compulsive Overeating

Overeating is characterised by an unexplainable, driving need to eat. People often try to justify the fact that they are overweight by excuses such as 'I inherited this problem from my mother. She's fat, too'; 'I have glandular problems'; 'I just had a baby two years ago'; 'It's middle-aged spread'; 'I have to attend a lot of business lunches/dinners' and that old standby 'I have big bones'.

It is well-documented that among people who diet, 95% regain the weight they lost, within five years. A person who diets and loses weight has the illusion of being in control and able to 'fix' their problem.

National Health and Medical Research Council figures show that in 1990, 43% of men and 33% of women were overweight or obese. By 2003 these figures have risen to 65% (an increase of around 51%) and 45% (an increase of 36%) respectively, indicating an alarming trend.

Two-thirds of women and men now have a waistline greater than 80cm and 94cm respectively.

The levels of obesity in young children are also sky rocketing with the proportion of obese girls aged 7-15 increasing by 358% from 1.2% in 1980 to 5.5% in 1995. There has also been an increase in the number of obese boys aged 7-15, from 1.4% in 1980 to 4.7% in 1995 (a growth of 235%).

The *1999-2000 Australian Diabetes, Obesity and Lifestyle Study* estimated that 7.5 million Australians aged 25 years and over were overweight.

Excess weight is set to overtake smoking as the biggest cause of heart disease. Furthermore, it has become a public health crisis with treatment of illness associated with being seriously overweight ballooning to a huge 800 million dollars a year.

Anorexia Nervosa

Increasing numbers of women in our society are obsessed with being thin. It has been estimated that 40% of all women are involved in trying to change their diet or their exercise pattern to lose weight, at any one time. This obsession is constantly fuelled by the fashion, beauty and advertising industries and by the way women are portrayed in films and on television programs. 'Thin' has become synonymous with 'beautiful'.

Anorexics often come from families who assign great importance to self-image.

Characteristics in the family system of an anorexic include non-expression of feelings and perfectionism. One parent is often extremely tyrannical and rigid, while the other is obsessive and out of touch with their sadness and anger. For these partners, the foundation of their relationship is based on its looking good to outsiders. The anorexic is like a dry drunk - controlling, domineering, driven and usually overachieving. He or she is a reflection of the dysfunctionality of the family.

Bulimia

Bulimia is a cycle of binging (overeating) and purging (vomiting, diuretics, laxatives and over-exercise). People binge eat to anaesthetise their carried shame and 'stuff their feelings'. After the medicating effects wear off and the feeling of shame resurfaces, they then transfer their shame about themselves to shame about their secret binge eating. The same dynamic takes place in obesity.

In 2000-2001, there were 2417 and 3731 episodes respectively of care in public and private hospitals for eating disorders in Australia. The Australian *Burden of Disease and Injury Survey* found that eating disorders were the fourth leading cause of burden in females aged 15-24.

Males are as prone to bulimia as females. Many have an addiction to physical fitness and they purge in order to preserve their youthful bodies. The purging represents the bulimics' desires to cleanse their innate feelings of shame. By vomiting, they are literally throwing up their feelings.

Fat/Thin Disorder

In my experience, the fat/thin disorder is the most commonly untreated problem and the one which people most try to minimise. People with this disorder often have two sets of clothes - their fat clothes and their thin clothes. Mental obsession is at the heart of this disorder - obsession about food, body size and shape, dieting and counting calories. It is this mental preoccupation which provides the desired mood alteration in the addict.

Susan Paxton of The Centre of Adolescent Health, Victoria (1995) summarised the findings as follows:

- More than 70% of teenage girls want to be thinner, even those of low weight.

- Two-thirds of Victorian women want to lose weight while only one-third are actually overweight.

- On any given day, about 60% of Australian women are on some sort of diet.

- 13% of girls thought that smoking was a good way of dieting.

Figures from Australia's two largest weight loss centres show that in 2002 Australians spent 200 million dollars in the flourishing weight-loss industry. Membership of Weight Watchers exceeds 120,000 in Australia alone.

RAGEAHOLISM

Expressing healthy anger restores our sense of strength and power. But raging provides only an artificial sense of power. Although we perceive rageaholics to be very powerful, in fact they are not innately powerful. However, the fallout from a raging parent can have an impact on the family system which is as devastating as that caused by an alcoholic parent.

Raging is also a common addiction in itself. Just as rape is not about lust, raging is not about anger. It is a cover-up for pain, fear and shame or a combination of all three. Raging isolates and protects the rageaholic from the intimacy they fear because they are shame-based.

Raging takes different forms. Overt raging may involve yelling, screaming and exploding into physical violence. You can sense the progression of the raging process as the volume and speed of the rager's speaking escalates. Like alcoholics, rageaholics may actually have blackouts. Silent raging happens in our heads. How many times have you lain in bed at night unable to sleep because a scenario of an incident that has upset you is running over and over in your head? As you're silently ranting and raving, you're not allowing yourself to feel the probable underlying hurt, fear or shame.

I once had a boyfriend who was a tall, handsome, 'decent', clean cut, intelligent, loving and gentle man (a 'good catch'). After going out for several months, I felt that he was really not for me and I ended the relationship. This was done amicably and with mutual regard. A week later he kindly dropped off an invitation for me 'and friend' to attend a gala, social event. This made me furious and I stomped about my house, slamming doors and raging in my head about what this gesture implied. Being a recovering rageaholic, I realised I was over-reacting and decided to look at what was really going on for me. Through a therapeutic process, I discovered the source of my problem. In my head I could hear my mother's voice, as clear as a bell, whining: "You never like anyone *nice and clean cut*. You always pick the alcoholics and sick ones." My raging was covering up the shameful feelings I had about not living up to my mother's expectations.

The extent to which raging prevails as a common addiction in Australia is reflected in the escalating and horrifying figures on domestic violence. That domestic violence in Australia is endemic is amply and well-documented. In 1996, The Australian Bureau of Statistics surveyed 6,300 Australian women and found that:

- 23% of women who had ever been married or in a de-facto relationship had experienced physical or sexual assault (the study did not record emotional, social or financial abuse) at some time during the relationship.

- 50% of women experiencing violence from a current partner had experienced more than one incidence of violence. Injuries reported included bruises, cuts, stab and gun shot wounds.

- 38% of women experiencing violence from a current partner had reported that children had witnessed the violence.

The Australian Institute of Criminology analysed homicides in Australia between 1989 and 1999 and found that 20.8% of all homicides involved 'intimate partners' and that of these, 65.8% occurred between current partners whilst 22.6% occurred between separated/divorced partners.

WORKAHOLISM

Although workaholism carries nowhere near the social stigma of alcoholism or some of the other addictive diseases, it is nevertheless insidious and wreaks havoc in many lives.

For the workaholic, work is the drug of choice because excessive working medicates emotional pain and gives a false sense of self-esteem.

Workaholics rarely ever laugh or have fun. They don't have many close friends and often their primary relationships are falling apart. They develop physical symptoms such as chest pains, abdominal problems, headaches, allergies, rashes and chronic fatigue.

Although workaholics seem to be dedicated workers and good providers, it is a fallacy that they are overworking to provide for their families, to prove their loyalty to their companies or to make a contribution to society.

The truth is they work fanatically because they are obsessed and need to fill the void they feel inside. They are perfectionists and no matter how much they work, it never seems good enough. What they are seeking through their work is self-validation. They measure the value they place on themselves by the tangible results they achieve. 'How much' and 'how many' become the barometers of their success.

'Yuppies' (young urban professional people), especially, have made it fashionable to be workaholic. Imagine being at a party where someone refuses a cocktail, explaining that they're an alcoholic. This would create ripples of embarrassment and discomfort among those within earshot. But only metres away someone could boast that they are a workaholic and generate amused approval from the same guests.

COMPULSIVE GAMBLING

Compulsive gamblers are addicted to action. It gives them a high. Caught up in the thrill of this addictive process, they forget about all their problems and pressures. Gamblers Anonymous defines compulsive gambling as: "making a conscious choice regarding the outcome of an event, with or without wagering money or objects, when in reality it is uncertain or depends upon chance or skill". This definition makes it clear that gambling is not restricted to cards, dice, roulette wheels or horse races. Many who play the stock market are also compulsive gamblers.

For compulsive gamblers, money is the bridge to self-esteem. Nothing is more important or less important to them and they will do whatever is necessary to obtain it. Conversely, money isn't important to them when the mortgage is overdue, bills are stacked up and credit cards are way over their limit.

Because they have low self-esteem, compulsive gamblers develop false pride and grandiosity. I see the Melbourne Cup, an event of such reverential proportions that it stops an entire nation for half a day, as a metaphor for this syndrome. The Cup has many attendant addictive rituals - betting, getting drunk, office sweepstakes, overspending (on clothes and parties), the whole country standing still for those few minutes - anyone would think Phar Lap had died on the cross! It's not as if this day is Good Friday, Christmas Day or even Australia Day. It's a horse race!

They say Australians will bet on two flies crawling up the wall and statistics seem to support this. In the year 1999-2000, Australians had placed 11 billion dollars in bets with the TAB and other on/off-track betting facilities. In 1990 Australians spent 12 billion on gaming (poker) machines. By 1999-2000 this figure has jumped to a staggering 74 billion dollars. These two figures are just a sampling of the population's national predilection for gambling. Additionally, of course, gambling takes place in other areas, including SP betting, lotteries, art unions, Lotto, in casinos and in illegal gambling establishments. The overall annual figure is astronomical at 113 billion dollars.

Another way a compulsive gambler practices his or her addiction is by 'putting one over' someone. This is particularly evident in those types who always have some new deal cooking. Every time this type puts one over on someone, a voice inside tells them they've won.

RELIGIOUS ADDICTION

The rise in Spirituality and New Age consciousness is a mixed blessing for some people. According to the Australian Psychological Society, the number of Australians seeking the help of a psychologist for problems of anxiety and depression has leapt by 75% in just two years. This figure is expected to rise again this year. In our western culture we are experiencing an unparalleled awareness of our human failings. For many this conscious discomfort is turning people towards 'drugs' like religion as a means 'to take the pain away'.

Religious Addicts use religion, 'spirituality' or God like a drug to make them feel better or 'better than' and to control, themselves or others. They are extremely shame-based people who crave a sense of righteousness to alter their moods.

Like any addictive process, a pathological relationship with God or religion does temporarily relieve pain and may even appear to heal. Denial and delusion are especially strong around religious addiction. Indeed, John Bradshaw states: "Religious addiction may be the most pernicious of all addictions because it's so hard for a person to break his or her denial. How can anything be wrong with loving God and giving your life for good works and service to mankind?"

Religious addicts sometimes become religious workaholics who avoid their emotional responsibilities to their families by being unavailable when they are out crusading, saving souls, fanatically studying the Bible or other religious texts.

I encountered a most graphic example of the destructive consequences of religious addiction in one of my male Australian clients. He was one of eight children, his father was a minister and his mother was an educated woman with a teaching degree. The father, loved and admired by many, appeared to outsiders to be an extremely kind and generous man, doing all that he could to meet the needs of his congregation and the local community. In fact, the father was a fanatical religious addict, a workaholic and, in the privacy of his own home, a rageaholic (the son recalled his father giving his mother a black eye). He frequently abandoned his family in favour of puffing up his own self-righteous ego by saving souls and doing good deeds for others. Meanwhile, the family suffered emotional and financial hardship.

The mother, a good Christian martyr, was so overwhelmed by the burden of caring for eight children on a shoestring and mostly on her own that she was totally out of touch with her own angry emotions. As the household slid into dirty chaos, she 'numbed out' by watching television. My client recalled that his mother was so desperate to survive financially that they often picked the weevils out of their cereal and once he got a terrible fright when he crunched on glass fragments while eating the pie his mother had served for dinner. She had broken the neck of the tomato sauce bottle, but being a spendthrift, she poured the sauce on the pies anyway!

If this story sounds extreme to you, I can assure you that in my experience in treating clients from religiously addicted families, such shocking scenarios are commonplace. Shame has entered many lives through the door of religion. It's no wonder that masses of people are shame-based, fearful and feel like sinners considering the constant preaching, condemning, judging, guilt trips and misinterpreted Bible quotes they're received from righteous, religious addicts.

In America, we see overt, over-the-top instances of religious addiction in the incredible TV evangelism programs and their massive followings. In Australia, religious addiction appears to be more covertly expressed. Hundreds of my clients have had to overcome the abuse that happened to them in religious boarding schools. Such abuse has scarred their adult lives - adversely affecting their sexual relationships, their spirituality, their self-worth and their ability to relate to their partners and children. 77

The prestigious, religious boarding schools in this country boast of their ability to produce 'high achievers'. But how many of these achievers are neurotic, driven workaholics? This is a hidden, but huge problem in Australia.

Although many of us have experienced spiritual abuse to some degree, I would like to draw a distinction here. Being raised by a full-blown *religious addict* creates a family system which is as dysfunctional as one created by an alcoholic, workaholic, rageaholic, etc. It is particularly difficult for people to understand this, as religious addicts appear to be such saints.

THINKING/FEELING/DOING ADDICTIONS

When we live in distorted reality, we become addicted to different aspects of it. I've mentioned mental obsession several times. It is a pivotal part of the addictive cycle and is also addictive in itself. People constantly retreat into distorted thought processes to avoid painful feelings.

We can also become addicted to certain feelings. In a feeling addiction, one feeling is used to cover up other feelings that a person is afraid or ashamed to feel. For example, angry people often use sadness and self-pity to mood alter and avoid facing their healthy anger. This is the badge of honour of all martyred mothers.

Commonly we use activity and busyness to distract ourselves from our intolerable realities. This can be done by addictively going to movies, reading, watching sports on television, caring for pets and plants, exercising, spending, shopping or hoarding.

You can also be addicted to interruptions to your thought process. If you have many interruptions, it proves you are a busy person, so you must be needed. You will set up your entire life for interruptions, so you can feel needed. Or maybe you did not really want what would come if you succeeded at what you were doing. Fear of success afflicts many adults who come from dysfunctional families. If you have enough interruptions, then you have reasons not to succeed. This inability to stay focused is a common problem for co-dependents.

When people who have 'doing addictions' stop distracting themselves with busy activity, they begin to get in touch with their emptiness and loneliness. It's only when we can face and embrace the emptiness and loneliness that we can let them go and be free.

SEX/LOVE/RELATIONSHIP ADDICTIONS

These addictions are so inter-related and so prevalent in our society today and they cause so much pain and confusion, that I've devoted a chapter to them. Please refer to Chapter 5, *Co-addictive Relationships*.

The following story from one of my former clients, Alice, is very inspiring to me. It is a good example of someone from an addictive family who developed an eating disorder and then switched addictions to a co-addictive, abusive relationship.

ALICE'S STORY
A CLIENT'S PERSONAL VOYAGE

I had cause recently to write an 'ideal scene' for my life. The exercise was part of a workshop I was putting together for final year Life Transformation students at the college where I teach. Before long, I realised I was writing the scene just as I was living it today.

How quickly things can change. Not that long ago, the only thing 'ideal' about my life was the façade of it. I virtually had what I now describe as a lease on life, and my line of credit was running out, fast. It hit hard when it happened. At the time, no one would have guessed that I was in so much pain I contemplated not going on with my life. You see, the outward appearances of my life were very deceptive. My husband and I ran a high powered company and we were living in a beautiful, waterfront house on Sydney Harbour. I had a precious new-born baby in my arms and I had created a nest of creature comforts to die for. And die I nearly did. Behind the fickle façade, I was crippled with trust issues, fear, anxiety and low self-esteem. Everything about myself and my life felt inadequate. My relationship was shallow and shrivelling. The house of cards came crashing in: the business, the charade I was living and I were all bankrupt, red-inked emotionally, physically and spiritually.

As it would happen a dear friend reached out with a helping hand just when I needed it most. She introduced me to a self-help community called 'recovery'. Inside that community I found my way to Shirley's book **Set Yourself Free**, *and then to Shirley herself. I began attending her programs and doing the exercises in the book from that time onwards my life changed forever.*

Even though I had a University degree and loved learning, what I received in those programs was an education I had never 79 *been exposed to. I learned what it meant to build and live with a stable foundation, I learned what was missing from my life and how to replace high drama with conscious asset building. Learning, not too late, that I was my most important asset of all! Not flash cash or even bricks and mortar. My educational process was accompanied by nurturing, kindness and support, necessary ingredients that had eluded me in my childhood as the bright, 'she'll- be-right' first-born, with a handicapped sibling.*

The biggest surprise of all was discovering the impact growing up in an alcoholic home had made to my adult life. My eyes were opened to how many normal healthy childhood needs of mine just hadn't been met. At last the links were drawn to explain my suffering with the illness of bulimia nervosa during my teens and twenties. Finally I understood why my eating disorder seemed to miraculously fall away without treatment when I met my emotionally-needy, adrenalin-fuelled husband. My missing parts were filled by our mutual co-dependent enmeshment. I had simply switched one obsession, for another - the bingeing and purging of food for the bingeing and purging of 'love'. I lunged between a ribald romance and a ruthless reality. The years I had spent alone as the 'lost child' fantasising in my bedroom, facilitated an easy transition from my eating disorder to the love addictive fantasy I carried about my marriage.

My eating/love addiction disorder had left me with the emotional maturity of a young teenager. I only knew how to binge or starve my feelings away, swinging between the 'good-girl' or the hidden 'little-girl' (very little). In Shirley's programs I learnt all about the nature of feelings and how I had buried mine under the banner of needing to look good. I began to be released from the private torture chamber of my inadequacy hell, where I would whip myself black and blue. With Shirley's guidance, I learned to own my feelings, understand their important messages, express them, and deal with them appropriately.

Finally the extent of my 'pretending over the discomfort and insecurities' became clear to me. It is not a common choice but I decided to leave my husband and go out on my own. I wanted the chance to 'grow my self up'- all over again. I wanted to learn for myself the realities of life, and to stop pretending. With the amazing support of professionals, the recovery-community and the friends I had made within it, I found a courage I never knew I had. I determined then and there that I was prepared to do what ever it took to become a fully functioning adult, with a manageable adult feeling-reality. And above all, to bring love, and all its wonderful feelings, back into my life.

It was quite a challenge, but looking back the most important thing I've done in my entire life. I had a small child in tow, an old protection racquet and a grandiose 'big-house-on-the-hill' illusion to dismantle. I re-joined the workforce and humbly met myself anew in the fresh relationships that developed around me.

Skinning a few shins in the early days only helped to grow my confidence. I began to take on things that had been impossible for me in the past. With some coaching support, I found myself negotiating pay rises, new jobs, the buying and selling of properties, new relationships with men and even a new career.

Today, I am constantly learning and re-learning how to come out of hiding and present myself honestly to the world, with no smoke screen. I don't make promises that I can't or am not willing to follow through on - something I used to do quite often.

I wouldn't say I have got it right now, because well, I just wouldn't say that anymore. What I would say is that today I have the ability to right myself after any strong wave or even storm, just like a buoy bobbing on the ocean. I can quickly make contact with an inner peace, strength, and guidance, sometimes with the help of a friend, but always at my own instigation.

I feel very grateful for the gifts I have in my life today; the ability to cause myself love; serenity; integrity and growth, being among the most precious. I take this opportunity as a soul mission, not just to thank Shirley for the incredible work that she does and has inspired me to do, but as a gesture of encouragement to those who are in pain or those who stay where they are unhappy, or those who go on living in pretence. What I urge of you is to take on the community and consciousness of change and REALLY GO FOR IT. For some of you dramatic change like mine may be the way, for others the path may be more gradual. What I do know, is that without jumping from the protective 'nest' I had created, I may never have discovered I had 'wings', nor that there was WIND beneath them.

THE GOOD NEWS

Unlikely as it seems, addictions do have a positive function - they medicate the pain of our guilt and shame. When we are having a shame attack, we are frozen and immobilised. We cannot create or produce much of anything; neither can we experience physical or emotional satisfaction. We are contributing and achieving nothing!

Every addiction that we have serves a purpose. Alcoholics and drug addicts whom I've treated in therapy have said: "I would have died without my alcoholism/drug addiction." Their untreated co-dependency probably would have been lethal for them had they not sought relief through their addictions.

Because addictions in their early stages sometimes 'save' our lives, we need to bless them for the wisdom they bring us and release them. If we don't, they will progress and take away our life force.

RELEASING ADDICTIONS

You cannot resolve an addiction in an intellectual manner. The resolution lies beyond the realms of the intellect. It exists in a primal place within you. No addiction can be given up. The most you can hope for is that an addiction wears out. You can wear an addiction out in a moment by giving up the belief that it enables you to survive. How you do this is simple: you find another way to survive that looks more satisfying and pleasurable than the addiction.

Initially, all addictions enable us to 'escape', giving us the *illusion* of freedom, but steadily they trap us and rob us of true freedom. Addiction is a process and symptom of spiritual bankruptcy. This is why we need a spiritual recovery. (See Chapter 8).

HANG IN THERE

By now I'm sure most of you have identified those areas in which your reality may be distorted. If you're feeling overwhelmed by the extent to which you are trapped in distorted reality, don't despair. In Part Two, I will share with you some practical steps ('keys') designed to help you attain more personal freedom. This process constitutes what Jung says is our fundamental spiritual purpose in life - i.e. to learn to progressively become more of who we really are.

CHAPTER 5

CO-ADDICTIVE
RELATIONSHIPS

If you turned straight to this chapter, you're probably very ***other focused*** - particularly when it comes to a 'significant other'. You might be thinking that if you could just learn how to create the 'right' romantic relationship, you'd be happy and most of your problems would be solved. You long for intimacy: more time and attention from your partner; good companionship and fulfilling sex. Or perhaps you're tired of your partner nagging, criticising, needing something from you that you can't or won't give?

The good news is: you really ***can*** create fulfilling, happy relationships. It's actually simple, although not always easy. Mary's story is testament to this. When she first became my client, Mary had been single most of her life. She'd had a few sexual affairs and fewer dates. Like many single, professional women, Mary longed for intimacy and a partner to share her life with. Her story is an inspiration to me.

MARY'S STORY
A CLIENT'S PERSONAL VOYAGE

> *Today I found myself dreaming again.*
> *In this familiar dream I'm walking along a glorious beach, hand in hand with my partner, feeling happier than I've ever been and totally at one with myself and the world. I know that I can have anything my heart and mind wants, and I'm tingling*

83

with the joy of being alive. Then, the shock of my true reality hits when I always wake to find myself alone, with my doubts and fears, wondering how and when things will ever change.

Today however, was different. This time I realised I was already awake, and the dream had become a reality. I found myself thinking back on my journey to this place.

My name is Mary and I grew up in a seemingly ordinary and normal middle class family. My Dad had a 9:00 to 5:00, Monday to Friday office job and hid behind the papers at night. Mum was a secretary, who stopped work when she married, had me and, five years later, my little brother Freddie. We lived in a suburban house with our cat, and had beach holidays every year. We didn't have a lavish lifestyle, but it was a comfortable one.

I adopted the family roles of 'surrogate spouse' and 'caretaker', always listening to my mother's complaints (usually about my Dad), trying to 'fix' her problems, and never holding an opinion or expressing an emotion contrary to that of hers. (If I did, I was quickly told that I was 'wrong' to think or feel that way.) I did this so well and for so many years, that I eventually lost touch with what I really felt or thought most of the time. Is it any wonder that I became a lawyer to prove myself in the world, yet, hiding the fact I felt terribly inadequate in my personal relationships - especially my love life.

I continued these roles of 'caretaker' and 'surrogate spouse' in my personal relationships, and to some extent in my work as a lawyer with legal aid. Often I would find myself with men who had lots of problems, who would put me down or try to control me. I found it increasingly impossible to be relaxed and confident, and wore myself out trying to guess what I 'should' be thinking, feeling or doing to win others' approval. What I felt, what I thought, and what I wanted were a mystery to me. Relationships were either short-lived or non-existent. At the ripe old of age of 36, I realised I was more comfortable and probably better off on my own.

Just when I was about to give up, someone gave me the book **Set Yourself Free**, by Shirley Smith and invited me to one of her lectures on co-dependency and addictive relationships. Although I really didn't think it was for me, it was my loneliness, frustration and yes, desperation that led me to go. Besides, *everything else I had tried hadn't worked - and believe me, I'd read many books, attended other courses and had even seen a couple of counsellors.*

Because there are no obvious addictions such as alcoholism or gambling in my family or in my own history, it was initially hard for me to see how this model could apply to me, but it was via this path that I finally made the breakthroughs I had wanted so much. I started to identify some of the patterns that had developed in my life that were holding me back from being truly myself and from having long term intimacy with a man.

By participating in different programs I started to become alive again, feeling the full depth and breadth of my feelings that had been buried and frozen for so long. Anger was an unacceptable emotion in our home, and it was a long time before I could unleash it onto innocent and uncomplaining pillows and mattresses. The relief that afforded me in easing various chronic bodily aches and pains was astonishing. There were times when I had to summon up more courage than I ever dreamt I had, to face and embrace crippling fear and shame. Without the education and emotional support of the programmes I did with Shirley, I don't believe I could have done it.

There were many wonderful surprises along the way, such as how quickly I could release deep grief and be joyous and light-hearted minutes later. I discovered a sense of humour that had been hidden, as it was my brother who had been considered the funny one (mascot) of the family. My playful, creative aspects began to blossom when released from their old bonds of shame and doubt. At the end of it, I found a new and wonderful 'me' and have felt comfortable with anyone in any situation ever since.

As a caretaker I had only felt secure when in 'control' (although that's always an illusion), so letting go and trusting the process was difficult and scary. One of the big changes was that I started taking more risks, having always played it safe before. I spoke up more boldly, ventured more daringly, dressed more sensuously, and played more frivolously. I got involved with a couple of men that still weren't 'right', but sensed it sooner and left before too much pain and drama ensued.

Then I met my current partner.

From our first meeting there was an openness, honesty, and 85 *ease between us. We have been able to develop an intimacy that I used to dream about, through sharing our feelings (especially the so-called 'bad' ones that our society tends to shy away from - anger, fear, shame, pain) and being willing to really hear each other, even when it was uncomfortable to do so. I have had to apply many of the skills I learned in those programs, especially refraining from trying to control or 'fix' my partner, which at times takes a tremendous effort and lots of support from others.*

By reducing caretaking at work, I've actually been more effective at assisting my clients, and less drained. I have a more comfortable relationship with my parents, and can accept them for who they are, and can be more my true self in their presence. I've learned how to communicate appropriately in my inner personal relationships and I'm more willing to confront others when there is a conflict between us, and can more readily hear others when they are upset with me.

The mask I used to wear, and the wall around my heart, have melted away to allow the real me to be seen, my true voice to be heard, and my soul to sing. My dream of someday becoming a radiant bride will come true this year, and I never would have believed it was all an inside job!

In the first edition of this book, I titled this chapter *Love Addicted Relationships*, making many references to 'love addicts'. The last thirteen years since publication and working with many couples has taught me a great deal more about the dynamics of relating. When examining couples' interactions, especially if one or both are either overly dependent or anti-dependent, I have found that they are both hooked into an addictive pattern of relating. I call this pattern of relating **'the co-addictive love dance'**.

When a couple comes in for counselling, one partner usually appears to be more needy and desperate (the puppy dog one), while the other seems to have things under control. In the past, we would have identified the needy 'love addict' as the one with the most significant problem. Counselling couples for several years has shown me that both partners are equally involved in the addictive dynamics.

Although co-addictive dynamics play out in all different types of relationships, it is usually the romantic/spousal ones where the most intense pain is felt. Why? Because these relationships trigger the deepest unresolved childhood issues of abandonment, engulfment and the fear of intimacy in adults. Additionally, people have too many fantasies, unrealistic expectations, and have either withholding or defensive behaviours that play out in their love relationships.

Symptoms of painful, love relationships are the most popular reason counsellors and self-help book publishers are in business. I can't tell you the hundreds of times that I have asked an audience I was presenting to, to raise their hand if they have tried marriage/couple counselling and to put their hand down if it worked. You guessed it, the only thing that drops is their faces!

I believe this is because many couples are co-engaged in an intense addictive pattern. This can be played out as an emotional roller coaster ride or be devastatingly disappointing when the relationship goes flat and feels empty. Either way, you become exhausted trying to cover up the hole inside or disillusioned when you can't.

Because of these dynamics, marriage/couple counselling is ineffective for co-addicts if treatment for addictive behaviour is not firstly administered.

In this chapter it is my intention to educate you about the dynamics of co-addictive relationships, so you can pull your head out of the sand and begin to identify debilitating behaviours that are keeping you trapped in frustration and preventing you from creating intimacy.

Having healthy, happy relationships takes work. There are no shortcuts to romantic nirvana. There's no 'quick fix' to fill that hole inside of you. If you skipped the preceding chapters and are now about to flick across to the chapter on building happy relationships, you probably won't get to the source of the problem. This type of behaviour is symptomatic of why you have relationship problems in the first place. In fact when unresolved issues from your formative years are ignored, it almost always progresses to some form of addictive relationship pattern, especially in sexual, romantic or spousal relationships.

The more an individual experiences rejection or deprivation in their formative years, the more a person seeks security and a sense of wholeness (to fill the perceived hole inside) in their love relationships. Although these relationships are initially euphoric, they eventually develop into an addictive attachment. This pattern of coupling can only be interrupted when each individual focuses on their personal development. They must be willing to confront themselves first - their core negative beliefs, the destructive self talk and behaviours that keep them from moving towards relationships that are mutually enriching.

Your relationships are not the source of your problems. Moreover, there are missing pieces in your personal foundation from unmet childhood needs and lack of instruction. There is distortion regarding reality and societies which keep denial in place. Co-addictive relationships are merely 'process addictions' which distract you from the intolerable reality of pain, anxiety and emptiness.

So if you did skim the earlier chapters and you are serious about wanting a happy, fulfilling relationship, please go back and read carefully the preceding information. 'First things first!'

WHAT IS LOVE?

Before I define the pattern of co-addictive relationships I'd like to give you my understanding of what love is. Love is about unconditional positive regard. When you love someone, you are able to honour and respect them as they go through their process in life. Your happiness and fulfilment do not depend on the mood that they're in. As long as they are not abusing or offending you, you can allow them to be angry, happy, sad or afraid. Love does not demand that you take away another's feelings ('Don't cry, it'll be all right' etc) or fix their problems.

Think of love as an energy of balance and definition. Love is the energy which holds things in place. It is the grand definer of separateness and the grand binder of closeness. In the context of relationship, love defines how close or how far apart we wish to be with others. When we can define our relationships clearly and without judgement, we will experience balance and harmony in them. For example, when I have a relationship with a client, I do not have the same expectations of them as I would have of a close friend or a lover. Similarly, I would not expect my lover to take care of me in a paternal way.

One of the most beautiful and clear expressions of love I have ever read was written by Kahil Gibran in *The Prophet*. The following extract represents, for me, the ideal way to relate lovingly in relationships.

"Love one another, but make not a bond of love:

Let it rather be a moving sea between the shores of your souls.

Fill each other's cup but drink not from one cup.

Give one another of your bread but eat not from the same loaf.

Sing and dance together and be joyous, but let each one of you be alone,

Even as the string of a lute are alone though they quiver

with the same music.

Give your hearts, but not into each other's keeping.

For only the hand of Life can contain your hearts.

And stand together, yet not too near together:

For the pillars of the temple stand apart,

And the oak tree and the cypress grow not in each other's shadow".

So why is there so much confusion about love today? And why don't we know how to love? The answer is... we were never taught how. We learn by observation. From the cradle to the grave, we observe love as pain, guilt, martyrdom, self-denial, sacrificing, suffering, being used and sometimes even denying our own existence. Let's look at our role models for love relationships.

The movies often promise us a 'magical' kind of love; our churches tell us how we 'should' love others and often, behind closed doors, we experience horrendous examples of 'love' within our families. No wonder we're confused.

Think of the lyrics of the popular songs we grow up hearing and singing. Nearly all of them are about love and the great majority have negative, dysfunctional messages (especially country and western songs) about the nature of love.

"Nothing you can say can tear me away from my guy; nothing you can do cause I'm stuck like glue to my guy"

"I don't want to be alone. Help me make it through the night"

"If you leave me now, you'll take away the very heart of me"

"I can't live, if living is without you"

"Give me just one more night"

And even... "If you leave me now, can I come too?"

YOU MIGHT AS WELL FACE IT YOU'RE ADDICTED TO LOVE

This is a common yet painful refrain in our society today. Like any addiction, co-addictive relationships can reach chronic or fatal proportions if left untreated. Critics and public alike regarded the movie *Fatal Attraction* as an extreme case, concocted by scriptwriters to achieve celluloid sensationalism. I will stick my neck out here and say that I believe that the love-addicted and pathologically violent behaviour of Glenn Close's character is not as rare as we would like to believe. In recent years in NSW, for example, 48% of all women homicide victims were killed by a spouse or defacto partner.

Pia Mellody defines a love addict as "someone assigning too much time, attention and value above themself to any person they're in a relationship with. This is coupled with *unrealistic expectations* for unconditional, positive regard".

Co-addictive relationships are set up by issues of neglect and abandonment. The addict has an inordinate need to be loved and parented and tends to marry a person who has their own parents' worst traits. Against all rational thought, they are attracted to partners who will abandon them. Through their relationship with these partners, they will react to or re-enact their unresolved childhood issues of neglect and abandonment. Co-addicts see a potential partner through their own distorted reality; they make up a fantasy about the other person (have unrealistic expectations) and then they get angry and/or disappointed when the fantasy (romance) wears off.

The greatest fears of the co-addicted are that of abandonment, engulfment, intimacy or being controlled. Addictive relationships take the place of true intimacy. They are loaded with lots of drama, game-playing and high intensity. The intensity of a co-addicted relationship is directly related to the degree that one's needs were unmet in childhood. Addictive lovers yearn to feel closeness, so they often connect through the intensity of anger and sex (fighting and making up). This pseudo-intimacy that co-addicts use is actually a wall of protection (isolation) against the possibility of experiencing hurt and disappointment. When you have true intimacy, you are vulnerable and open - to pain and disappointment, as well as to positive, euphoric feelings.

In the previous chapter, I gave you a generic definition for addictions, stating that addictions are 'any process which takes away intolerable reality'. Because of that, such a process becomes the highest priority in a person's life, taking away time and attention from other areas of their lives.

As a co-addict, if I am feeling worthless, not good enough, incomplete, empty, lonely, needy or afraid to be alone (because of my own childhood issues of abandonment), I'd call that a pretty intolerable reality. In this instance, I would strive to distract myself by focusing on another, rather than face my own pain. I would want to meet their needs in order to become valuable to them, so that they wouldn't leave me and I wouldn't have to be alone (to face my emptiness).

This method of distraction is not used continually, even by a chronic love addict, so many people reading this may remain in denial by reassuring themselves on this basis. However, the following check-list of attitudes and beliefs will help you to identify if you are co-addicted:

1. My good feelings about who I am stem from being liked by you.

2. My good feelings about who I am stem from receiving approval from you.

3. Your struggle affects my serenity, my mental attention focuses on solving your problems or relieving your pain.

4. My mental attention is focused on pleasing you.

5. My mental attention is focused on protecting you.

6. My mental attention is focused on manipulating you. In other words: 'Do it my way'.

7. My self-esteem is bolstered by solving your problems.

8. My self-esteem is bolstered by relieving your pain.

9. My own hobbies and interests are put aside, my time is spent sharing your interests and hobbies.

10. Your clothing and personal appearance are dictated by my desires, as I feel you are a reflection of me.

11. Your behaviour is dictated by my desires, as I feel you are a reflection of me.

12. I am not aware of how I feel, I'm aware of how you feel.

13. I am not aware of what I want, I ask what you want. I'm not aware, I assume.

14. The dreams I have for my future are linked to you.

15. My fear of rejection determines what I say or do.

16. My fear of your anger determines what I say or do.

17. I use giving as a way of feeling safe in our relationship.

18. My social circle diminishes as I involve myself with you.

19. I value your opinion and way of doing things more than my own.

20. The quality of my life is in relation to the quality of yours.

THE ADDICTIVE LOVE DANCE

As I've already stated, co-addictive relationships are set up from issues of neglect, abandonment, abuse, engulfment and unmet needs in childhood.

Like life, these types of relationships also contain a powerful paradox that people often dance between, going back and forth... just like a tango! Although confusing, this paradox promotes high levels of intensity, and is often mistaken for intimacy or 'true love.' I call this phenomenon 'The Addictive Love Dance.'

When people keep dancing this dance, it creates an addictive cycle which is like a marathon dance contest, where people start dropping one by one. As you may already know, in this 'contest' the winners are really the losers! They go round and round, bouncing back and forth between the fear of abandonment and the fear of being engulfed or controlled - and they both fear intimacy.

There are basically two types of dance partners. On the surface, one appears to be the leader and the other the follower, so I have chosen those names to identify the two types.

The apparent *'leader'* is one who has a surface fear of being controlled or engulfed. Really, there is a deep underlying fear of abandonment that the surface fear is covering up. The leader can be a 'commitment phobic', appearing strong, needless and in control. They often appear either passionate or aloof and are placed upon pedestals by their partners.

The apparent *'follower'* is one who has a surface fear of abandonment and rejection. Really, there is a deep underlying fear of intimacy that the surface fear is covering up. The follower can be quite a caretaker (need to be needed) sometimes appearing weak and needy. Because they place their partners on a pedestal they have unrealistic expectations and often get disappointed and/or angry. They are forever waiting for their partners to change, living with false hope to medicate their abandonment pain.

In reality, neither of these dance partners is a leader or a follower. They are caught in an addictive cycle that is an intense replacement for true intimacy, filling up the emptiness and loneliness in their relationship. Once the intensity is minimised, the partners often fear there is 'nothing between them'.

The emptiness triggers fear, loneliness and abandonment pain, causing the partners to unconsciously find ways to reconnect through intensity. This is often played out through sex, fighting or 'deep-and-meaningfuls'. Because these partners don't have a clue about how to create real happiness, fun and intimacy in their most important relationships, they stay forever stuck, dancing the same dance - feeling exhausted and disillusioned.

The addictive love dance is not only reserved for romantic lovers. Many mothers and daughters; mothers and sons; fathers and daughters; fathers and sons - or in fact, any two people (friends, employees, employers etc.) can dance this dance!

ENMESHMENT

Co-addicts have two choices in the way they relate to others - one is isolation and the other is intense, painful involvement (enmeshment). Generally, they vacillate between the two patterns.

Enmeshment is often mistaken for intimacy, when in fact it actually prevents it. When two people are enmeshed, they have no boundaries. They don't know where one ends and the other begins. This may be Hollywood's formula for true love and happiness, but in real life it produces a state of chaos and engulfment. When we are fused with another, we become con-fused!

ESCAPES FROM INTIMACY

I use 'co-addictive relationships' as a general term to cover many types of addictive relationships. You can be co-addicted to any person - not only to romantic partners. It can be with your children, parents, friends, counsellor, boss, sports coach, sponsor (in Twelve Step programs), minister, priest, rabbi, movie and pop stars, famous people (think of the international charisma of the late John F. Kennedy) or any authority figure.

However, in this section I intend to focus on romantic, sexual, spousal types of co-addicted relationships. The following information is a précis of the work presented in Anne Wilson Schaef's book *Escape From Intimacy*. Schaef breaks love addiction into three categories - romance addiction, sex addiction and relationship addiction. She claims that although these types of relationships appear to create intimacy, they are actually escapes from intimacy.

When I first read this material, it made a great impact on me because of its relevance to attaining personal freedom. Years ago, most of my relationships were addictive entanglements and the pain of these led me into recovery where I began the process of detaching and letting go. I discovered more about myself, what my personal needs and wants were and how to go about fulfilling them for myself. I began to feel free to do as I wished for the first time in my life. This was a liberating experience, learning how to be alone with myself - and enjoying it. But after a while, there were times when I felt incredible loneliness. I was moving into a new phase of my recovery where I realised there was a difference between being alone and being lonely. I also realised that my next phase of growth involved learning how to have freedom *and* intimacy in relationships, especially in my romantic relationships. I'm still learning how to do this and although I have a way to go yet, there is no comparison between the quality of my current relationship and those I had before I went into recovery.

ROMANCE ADDICTION

Romance addicts are addicted to their own fantasies and illusions about romance. It is the scene, the setting, the perfect picture that matters to them and gives them the high they are after. The sad thing about romance addicts is that in their quest to look good to the outside world, they miss the actual experience - the authentic exchange of feelings and intimacy. They love to pose. For them, the superficial appearance is the basis of the relationship. They're into telling others about it. It's very important that others know that they're loved and admired. 'He sent me flowers and he's taking me to a romantic restaurant' or 'she's so hot. All my mates were green with envy.'

Schaef says romance addicts are 'experts at instant intimacy'. They'll tell you about this close, intimate relationship, they've found in which they talk about everything, staying up until the wee hours. They insist they've found their soul mate, etc, etc. When you ask them how long they've been together, their reply is in the vicinity of: 'six weeks'. Real intimacy takes years to build. This 'romance escape' is really an enmeshed relationship with no boundaries, which merely gives the illusion of connection.

Romance addicts are also addicted to the cause. They're the crusaders, out leading the peace movement and saving the world. Romance addiction is often prevalent in religion, politics and war.

When you're engaging in any addictive process, it gives you an immediate and false high which wears off in due course. Meanwhile, it cuts you off from having the totally satisfying experience of what you truly desire. Sometimes you can be so out of touch with yourself that you can't even identify your deepest desires. And as long as you continue to fuel your romance addictions, you'll never find out what they are.

I am a recovering romance addict and here is an example of an incident from my life which, although it doesn't involve another person, effectively cut me off from having the experience I desired.

Several years ago I desired to embrace some of my fears and to feel a new level of trust and connection with my higher power. A spiritual adviser suggested that I should go and be alone with nature for at least seven days. For someone whose idea of a relaxing holiday was room service at a five star hotel, this presented quite a challenge. The picture of me alone communing with nature immediately brought up some fears, but also a stirring of excitement and anticipation.

When I began telling all my friends of my daring plans, they oohed and aahed with envy. My mother flew into a panic, which made the adventure more appealing. Off I went with all my camping gear (no books, radio, tapes or junk food to distract me) and set up camp in a near-empty national park. My unconscious expectation was to have a grand, spiritual experience. Each morning I rose and planned out my day with great ceremony. As I set out along one of the isolated hiking trails, I fantasised about what adventure might happen to me and how, on my return to the city, I would relay this to my friends at dinner parties. By the end of the third day, I felt tight, dry, unable to relax and meditate. I felt cut off from my conscious contact with my higher power. I was afraid I was going to miss the experience I'd craved. So I prayed and asked my higher power to help me.

Shortly after this, as I sat quietly, it dawned on me that I was operating in the same manner I did in the city. I was organised, with my list of chores. I constantly tidied my campsite, washed the dishes and imagined in advance each activity I was about to undertake. I didn't allow myself to just 'be' in the moment. I realised that nobody cared about what I was doing in the wilderness; they were too consumed with their own lives. If upon my return, they asked about my adventures, I saw that they would be doing this mostly out of courtesy. I was more intent on setting up the 'perfect' experience and 'looking good' to others than actually allowing the natural experience I desired to happen to me. I then sat down, took a deep breath and realised that I didn't have to do anything in particular. I was free to do whatever I wanted. I looked around and noticed what a beautiful, sunny, October day it was and decided that what I really wanted to do was just lie in the sun. So I did - and that's when I had the spiritual experience I'd been looking for.

What all of this taught me was that such precious experiences are internal and private and when I try to share them with others (the hallmark of a romance addict), they are somehow diminished.

I'm not suggesting that we should eliminate romance from our lives. It can be fun; it's a great form of adult play. However, the important thing is to acknowledge it for what it is, rather than assigning unrealistic meaning to it. Romantic interludes are delightful, but they are not life's ultimate experience.

SEX ADDICTION

This is the most 'personal' and hidden addiction in our society. Our sense of self starts with gender identification. Sex is a central part of one's self-image and we all have deep emotions about it.

Considering the negative attitudes, cultural myths, mixed messages (advertisers blatantly sell 'sex', not mouthwash, jeans and flash cars), lack of proper education and the highly charged emotions associated with sex, it is no surprise that much sexual behaviour is hidden and furtive.

Sexual addiction is so integrated into our social structures, it has come to be regarded as normal. Most sexual addiction is set up by sexual abuse in childhood and carries a large component of shame. Children with sexually repressed parents are often carrying and acting out the parents' repressed lust.

Sexual addiction is an obsession and preoccupation with sex in which most things are defined sexually or by their sexuality; and most perceptions and relationships are sexualised.

Having sex is a mood-altering experience which can be highly pleasurable, and this is fine. However, a sex addict will sexually act out or mentally obsess and fantasise about sex in order to avoid dealing with their uncomfortable feelings or their life in general.

Dr Patrick Carnes, in his breakthrough work on sexual addiction, *Out of The Shadows*, defines sexual addiction in three categories. According to Carnes, "*Level One* behaviours have in common general cultural acceptance... but each can be devastating when done compulsively." Such behaviours include masturbating, looking at pornography, patronising prostitutes, going to strip shows. In a sexual relationship with a Level One sex addict, "one partner sacrifices important parts of the total relationship in the service of sexual needs."

Level Two sexual addictive behaviours are intrusive enough to warrant stiff legal actions. They include voyeurism, exhibitionism, making indecent telephone calls, making inappropriate sexual advances.

Level Three behaviours are generally more severe and more overtly illegal. They include rape, incest, child molesting, sadomasochism and sexual torture. (There are a number of religious cults which incorporate sexual torture into their ceremonies).

Sexual anorexia is also a form of sexual addiction. The sexual anorexic is a person who is obsessed with sex... but they're obsessed with avoiding it. A new client once told me that she had dealt with her sex addiction/promiscuity about five years previously because it was causing her so much pain. This client was a recovering alcoholic and I was quite interested to hear how she had dealt with her sex addiction. She told me she had been celibate for the previous five years. This woman was also in my office because she longed for a fulfilling, loving relationship with a man. She was in her mid-30s and desperately wanted to have children. I explained to her that her sexual anorexia was not the solution to her problem. Her decision to be celibate was not a choice, but rather was based on her fear of trusting herself with her sexually addictive behaviour.

A person may be sexually anorexic because during their upbringing they received a lot of shaming messages about their bodies and sex.

Many religiously-addicted parents convey to their children shaming messages about the harmful consequences of sex. (Whatever you repress, you will become obsessed with.)

Another form of sexual addiction is the addiction to sexual fantasy. This does not take the form of sexually acting out, rather these addicts sexually 'act in' - in their minds. These types avoid dealing with their pain and emotions by losing themselves in constant sexual fantasies and 'affairs of the heart'. This can also be done when parents sexualise their relationships with their children at the emotional and intellectual levels, although not actually having sex with them. A graphic example of this was related to me by one of my former clients. She told me how when she was a teenager her father approached her before Christmas, asking her to choose between a diamond ring and a sewing machine. He told her that she had first choice and he would give the remaining gift to her mother. This made her feel terribly guilty and ashamed.

There is a widely held misconception that sex addicts are perverted people. Often, sex addicts are married or in committed relationships and they use these partnerships to get their sexual fixes. Sex is the basis of their relationships and they are afraid to leave because they don't know where they would get their consistent supply. With the rising concern of AIDS, Hepatitis and other sexually transmitted dis-eases and all the talk about the need for safe sex, remaining in a 'safe', sexually addictive relationship becomes paramount for them.

Despite the dangers of illicit affairs, some sex addicts are still rampantly promiscuous. The line of reasoning frequently used to blame a wife for her husband's affairs is that if she had been more sexually available to him, he would not have had to resort to having affairs. There is little understanding that the husband's promiscuous behaviour is often caused by an addiction, not by his wife. Just as alcoholics drown their emotional pain by drinking to excess, sex addicts medicate their emotional pain with the escape and relief they get through sexual affairs.

When a romance addict and a sex addict pair up, their relationship will often escalate into violence. This is the source of the 'Fatal Attraction' syndrome.

RELATIONSHIP ADDICTION

Schaef nominates three types of relationship addiction:

1. Being addicted to having a relationship.

The requirement here is to always be a couple, always be connected to someone. This relationship addict fears being alone and can only feel safe, secure and worthy when they are in a relationship. Their addiction is to the concept of a relationship. Their partner's values, personality and aspirations are not considered. This addict just wants someone to be in a relationship with them.

This type of person has overlapping relationships. Usually, they won't relinquish their current relationship until they are sure they have someone else waiting in the wings.

2. Being addicted while in a relationship.

This person can be out of a relationship for long periods of time and feel quite comfortable about this. Yet when they enter into a new relationship, they immediately get hooked. They become needy and whining and start to slip in areas in their lives where previously they were taking care of themselves quite well. This syndrome is common among women in high-powered jobs. Such women are successful and independent and these qualities make them very appealing to men. Yet within 90 days in relationship with a man, they become love-sick lap dogs.

3. Cling-clung addiction.

This type of relationship addict practises their relationship addiction on everyone they meet. Most of us have been around this type of person. These addicts have no boundaries, act intrusively and appear to be very needy, victim types. Usually they are adept at manipulating others to feel sorry for them.

Relationship addicts move from one relationship to another and they also have selective amnesia. In other words, they very quickly and conveniently forget the pain of their past relationships in order to maintain their relationship addiction. They are very controlling people who believe they can make relationships happen by sheer force of their own will. Relationship addicts do not have relationships - THEY HAVE HOSTAGES!

ARE YOU IN RITUAL OR ARE YOU IN RELATIONSHIP?

Schaef presents an excellent adaptation, in relationship terms, of Dr Patrick Carnes' 'cycle of addiction'.

Stage One: Preoccupation

This is the obsession stage of the relationship. It has a trance-like, mood-altering facet to it. The person is totally absorbed in the relationship. The woman may talk about it incessantly to her friends. The man may be unable to concentrate on the job because he's fantasising about his date with her that evening.

Stage Two: Ritualisation

This is the behavioural process undertaken when establishing a relationship. For women it may take the form of dieting, exercising, having beauty treatments, a new hairstyle; for men, courtship may be ritualised. *should* give her flowers and buy her dinner. It will make her warm to me enough to have her invite me in for a nightcap and then...'

Stage Three: Compulsive Relationship Behaviour

This involves establishing as early as possible the status of the relationship, or as Schaef says: "Nailing down the relationship and holding on to it for dear life". 'Are we committed?' 'Are we going to date others?' 'Are we monogamous?' Discussing marriage or getting married when the relationship is still in the 'romantic' stage.

Stage Four: Despair

This is when the addict realises that the relationship isn't going to 'fix' them and they sink into the feeling of hopelessness and despair. In other words, 'the honeymoon is over'. At this point, they will either move on to another relationship or fixate on some problematic aspect of their current relationship in order to become preoccupied. And so the cycle starts over again.

The three primary forms of co-addicted relationships are well summed up by Schaef:

Romance addicts MOVE ON.

Sex addicts COME ON

Relationship addicts HANG ON.

Identifying Dependent Relationships

Outwardly, there is usually one who appears strong, together, in control (anti-dependent) and one who appears weak, emotionally falling apart, and somewhat out of control (overly dependent). Unfortunately society judges the overly dependent one to be the one with the problem.

The dictionary defines a dependent person as: "Relying on or requiring the aid of another for support." There is healthy dependency and there is unhealthy dependency. An overly dependent person relies on others to meet their needs and take care of them because they feel incapable of fully taking care of themselves. These people can't tell the difference between their needs, wants and desires and haven't got a clue about how to get their adult dependency needs met. Outwardly, they are insecure and get lost in others and will fight to the death for anyone but themselves. They feel inadequate, seek approval and are caretakers because they desperately need to be needed. They lack boundaries and allow others to invade their space constantly.

Another form of unhealthy dependency is the exact opposite of the above behaviour. Such people are known as counter-dependents. A counter-dependent is a person who appears secure and independent, but inside they are fearful. This type of person requires a lot of support, praise and admiration from others, yet cannot tolerate others depending on them. They have difficulty acknowledging any weaknesses within them and they over-identify with strength and power. Counter-dependents are intrusive and invade others' boundaries without permission because they feel entitled to do so.

The characteristics of healthy and unhealthy dependency are listed below:

Unhealthy Dependency		Healthy Dependency
Overly Dependent	Counter-Dependent	
1. Insecurity	1. Grandiosity	1. Secure
2. Dependent	2. Anti-dependent	2. Inter-dependent
3. Other-centred	3. Self-centred	3. Socially interested
4. Overly-receptive	4. Intrusive	4. Responsive

When we are secure in a relationship, our self-esteem allows us to acknowledge our strengths and weaknesses without feeling guilt or shame. To be *inter-dependent* in a relationship means you are able to give and receive support. When we have a good sense of self and can see others clearly without the illusion of fantasy, we can then become socially interested. When we have mastered self-protection to the point that we can allow a trustworthy person to touch our souls or we can keep an untrustworthy person at arm's length, then we are in a healthy, *responsive* state.

EXAMPLES OF UNHEALTHY, DEPENDENT ATTITUDES AND BEHAVIOUR

1. Feeling unable to leave the nest, or leaving it with uncomfortable feelings.
Many adults have this problem. Although they may have left home physically years ago, they have not left home emotionally and mentally. A healthy, inter-dependent person is able to move away from their family of origin without feeling guilty or to move closer to them without feeling absorbed or enmeshed.

2. Feeling obligated to visit, telephone, entertain or chauffeur others around.
These activities can be enjoyable if done of your own volition, but they are not enjoyable when there is a 'should' attached to them. For example, many people spend Christmas with their parents when they would rather be socialising with their close friends.

3. Asking permission of a partner for anything - including spending money, authority to speak, use of the car, etc.
This doesn't mean you shouldn't have agreements with each other about finances and the like, providing these agreements are reached in an adult manner together.

4. Invasions of privacy, such as looking through doors and the wallets and private records of children or others.
This behaviour is a violation of another's boundaries and is usually done because the person snooping is feeling insecure and fearful.

5. Sentences like: 'I could never tell him how I feel' or 'She wouldn't like it'.
Dependent people will often tell their secrets to strangers or people they don't know well, or gossip about their close relationships. Instead, they should be communicating this information to their partner or other loved ones.

6. Feeling committed to a particular job and unable to try anything else.
'I've worked in the family business all my life and they expect that of me'. Or 'I've gone to school for over eight years to be a doctor and although I'm really miserable and don't want to do it anymore, I can't afford to do anything else.' Dependent people are too afraid to open themselves up to other possibilities and take a risk to do something else. They are always looking for a guarantee.

7. Having expectations of how a spouse, parent or child ought to be or act, etc or being embarrassed by their appearance or behaviour.
Because dependent people feel their family members are a reflection of themselves, they place too many expectations on them and then use controlling and manipulative tactics to have these fulfiled. How many parents feel uncomfortable being seen with their teenage children, especially if those children have purple hair or a dozen piercings? Or how does the pin-striped executive feel about taking his frumpy wife to the office party?

8. Being hurt by what others say, think, feel or do?
'What do you mean, you don't want to come over and be with me? That really hurt my feelings'. It's one thing to be disappointed when things don't go the way you'd like, but it's something else to lay guilt trips on people in order to get your own way. What's really happening in a situation like this is that the dependent person doesn't know how to get their needs met and they're afraid that if someone else doesn't do it for them, they won't feel fulfilled.

9. Feeling happy and successful only if your partner is feeling that way.
Maybe your partner is sad, angry or having a bad day. If you are a healthy person, you can still enjoy the flowers and trees on your afternoon picnic, rather than allowing his or her experience to spoil your day.

10. Allowing someone else to make decisions for you or frequently asking for advice before you make a decision.
As a young adult, I had this problem because I had been *told* what to do my whole life. This is why we often feel uncertain and afraid to make the 'right' decisions as adults. Many of my adult clients have said to me: 'I don't know why I feel stupid. My parents never put me down.' No, perhaps they didn't do this verbally. But when a child is constantly told what to do and how to be, the unconscious message they pick up from this is: 'I don't know anything. I'm stupid'. 103

11. Being obligated to others because you depend on them.
Some years ago, a business associate who was setting up seminars for me in another city, called to invite me to dine with him when he visited my city. Although my schedule was chock-a-block, I felt obligated to make time to see him because I was depending on the income he was generating for me. I cancelled and rescheduled a number of appointments in order to attend the dinner. But it transpired that we had no opportunity to discuss business during the meal because he had invited other mates to join us and the evening turned into a party. I sat through it feeling resentful, but learned a valuable lesson.

12. Not doing or saying something in front of a parent or dominant person for fear of their disapproval
For example, not smoking, drinking, swearing, eating sweets or being frank because you have a submissive role in that relationship.

13. Using careful language, lying about your behaviour or distorting the truth around a dominant person so they won't be upset with you.
Walking on eggshells around people who matter to you is a complete energy drain. To be on guard to this degree is to try to control everyone and everything in your environment. There is a huge amount of stress involved in constantly *presenting* yourself in the way you think will win others' approval.

PIN-POINTING YOUR 'PAYOFFS'

If you've read the above check-list and identified with some of the behaviours and attitudes, you may wonder why, since they cause so much stress, you can't simply give them up. The answer is that these produce unhealthy rewards which have become an essential part of our modus operandi. These rewards are also known as 'hidden agendas' or 'payoffs'. To pin-point your particular payoff, when you notice yourself in one of the above dependency patterns, stop and ask yourself what it is doing for you personally.

The following are some common payoffs born out of dependency patterns:

1. Being dependent can keep you in the 'safe', protective custody of others and give you the 'little child' benefits of not being responsible for your own behaviour. If you're dependent on

someone in this way, then when you make mistakes, you can claim it's not your fault. That way you don't have to face criticism or being put down. You give another all the power and then when anything goes wrong, the other person has to take care of it.

This dependent behaviour taught me an expensive lesson after my husband and I completed our therapy at the treatment centre. Prior to this, I had been shouldering the majority of family responsibilities, including the managing of our income and the payment of our bills. I felt burned out from the pressure of so much responsibility and told my husband it was time for him to manage our finances. I then took on the childish role in our relationship, ran up our credit cards and depended on him to arrest the situation. He didn't, of course, and we incurred a great debt. My unconscious payoff in this situation was to feel relieved of over-responsibility and to be able to blame him for this mess. After all, I constantly reminded him, we'd never gotten into debt when *I'd* handled the finances.

2. By staying dependent, you can blame your shortcomings on others. Another way to say this is that we can keep our character defects. Character defects really are self-defence mechanisms. We've used some of our undesirable, negative behaviour to protect ourselves because we have not learned a functional way to protect ourselves. If I stay dependent on you, I can abnegate my own personal power and remain jealous, judgemental, afraid, defensive, indecisive and critical.

3. If you are dependent on others, you don't have to undertake the hard work and risk of change. You are secure in your reliance on other persons who will take responsibility for you. The payoff here is that while others control you, you don't have to experience the discomfort of learning the balance between letting go and being responsible.

4. While you are pleasing others, you get to feel good about yourself. As children, we learned that the way to be good was to please mummy and daddy and now many symbolic mummies and daddies manipulate us. This is the one which 'runs' the caretakers and 'people pleasers' of the world. Their direct value is derived from what others think about them

and from what they can do for others. Above all, they need to be needed and this people-pleasing behaviour gives them that payoff.

5. To avoid the guilt you sometimes feel when you act assertively, it is easier to 'behave' than to learn how to eliminate unhealthy guilt. If you feel guilty when you assert yourself it is because you don't know that you have rights. The payoff is you don't have to face the shame you feel about not having certain rights.

6. By modelling yourself on the parent, spouse or individual on whom you depend, you needn't make choices for yourself. The payoffs here are that as long as you think what they think, or feel what they feel, there's no need for the hard work of determining what *you* think and feel and you don't feel responsible for any mistakes you make.

7. Dependents would rather be followers than leaders because they are usually looking for the easier, softer way out. As a follower, you can do what you're told and avoid trouble. It's simpler than taking all those risks that go with being your own person and facing the fear of failure. How many people resent Tall Poppies because they've dared to get out there and take a few risks in order to succeed?

The common thread in the above payoffs is the avoidance of personal responsibility. Think of responsibility as… responding to your own ability. People avoid responsibility because, sadly, they don't really believe they have what it takes to be responsible. And the reason for this is that most of them have had a heavy dose of shame.

Dependency is distasteful because it reduces you to less than a whole, independently functioning person. It may indeed be the easier, softer option in life, but it is by far the poorer one. Dependents miss out on the rich rewards of creating their lives the way they really desire them to be.

The following story from a former client of mine is great example of how a very capable and beautiful young woman almost ruined her life by remaining needy, confused about her capabilities and dependent on men.

KAREN'S STORY
A CLIENT'S PERSONAL VOYAGE

Being raised in a wealthy family with an Asian mother and a Western father created a childhood of pressure for me. Each one was going to raise their daughter to reflect the contrasting values they defended. These contrasts were to be the weapons of a tempestuous and unhappy marriage. As first born I held the honour and carried the burden of having to reflect their values, to be the best at whatever I did, to be top of the class, and bring honour to please each one as a reflection of the cultural refinement of their race. My mother insisted I have impeccable manners, excel academically and although I didn't know it at the time, she was skilful at showing me the art of manipulating men. My father wanted me to be his perfect little girl who never questioned authority. I was his little princess and our relationship refined what my mother had taught me.

Because my mother was jealous of my relationship with my father, and when I didn't live up to her expectations, I was beaten and told how much I had brought shame to her. She relentlessly lived and punished in the pursuit of excellence. I remember a time that seems so indicative of my formative years. I was in the third grade and had raced home excitedly wanting to show Mum I had done so well, how I had learned to do long division. She sat with me as I went through the homework questions. What I showed her though wasn't enough. She began to challenge me giving harder and harder examples. As I stumbled she would hit me across the head, whipping me with her hand and calling me stupid. I became so petrified of making the mistakes; in the end I just couldn't do them any more. In fact, I never did long division again without that fear. I vacillated from being extremely excited about doing something well, to completely losing every bit of confidence I had. This in many ways has been the story of so much of my life.

I often get excited about trying something new, like a new project. Trouble is, I then feel as though I have to know it perfectly from the beginning. When I don't, something inside of me gives up. I either check out, or go blank. This sabotaging behaviour caused me to abort most of my projects.

I was accepted into University and then dropped out so many times that they ended up kicking me out. By the time I was in my mid 20's I couldn't even hold down a job. My hyper vigilance and quick mind would dazzle people in interviews; I'd start really well, impress the pants off the company, come across as being so confident and capable, and then within weeks I would completely crumble. I became frightened, needy, dependant on my boss, and couldn't make a decision alone. Needless to say within 6 to 12 months I was either fired or asked to leave, because "although I was a good performer, I was too disruptive to the company and the team, and needed too much hand-holding".

In addition to not being able to hold down a job, or studies, I also couldn't get by without a man by my side. Alone, I felt I couldn't make it. Daddy had taught me a long time ago that if I wanted attention all I needed to do was be cute and seductive and a man would take care of me.

Being cute and seductive gave me the attention I so desperately craved from Daddy and with my need to be a high achiever, driven from my mother's influence, I stumbled upon the perfect vocation which would fulfil both of my parents unspoken expectations - I became a sex worker. What I initially saw was how badly managed so many of the massage parlours were, so I opened my own and made a lot of money at it. Finally, I was successful at business.

Erotic massage allowed me to use the clever behaviour I had learnt surviving two highly strung, love-addicted parents. I knew how to get my way through being cute, quick-minded and seductive I felt like I was in control (at least I thought I was in control). Although I made a great deal of money, it seemed to slip through my fingers. Making money was easy, but I didn't know the first thing about managing it.

For a while, I felt proud of my success and powerful that I had so many men under my control. It was as if I got all of Daddy's attention (each man represented Daddy for me) using many of Mummy's tricks - and I did it better than she did! Then things started to turn.

As the years went by, I had to keep upping the ante, doing 'extras' and even giving 'full service' at times. I watched the young girls I hired turn hard and cynical - like me. The business was soul destroying and the only way I could perform day in and day out was to completely cut off from what I was doing, numb out and run away from my self-hatred. A fog of blackness took over and I became lost and depressed. I had attempted suicide once and had thought about it again - after all that was the way my mother finally checked out (altogether). I felt I was sure to follow.

It was during a very black and desperate time that I was pointed in the direction of Shirley. Although frightening and difficult at times, for me the journey has been extraordinarily rewarding and I know I would not be here today if I hadn't faced the pain and realities of my adult life and childhood.

During my recovery journey, I had to go back into the memories of my childhood and unearthed the craziness that surrounded me. I was able to use my memories to gain insight into why things occurred in my adult life as they did. I understood how abusive it was of my parents to impose their racial and cultural expectations upon me. Now I can see how I was a pawn as they desperately 'dealt with their demons', and how I was 'set up' to project perfection. It is helpful for me to see that I have spent my life 'whipping the exhausted horse', trying to reach something I could never live up to. I have lived with the illusion of being a failure. This illusion more than anything else had perpetuated the problems and pain.

I found the courage to let go of my business and my boyfriend at the same time. This was the most frightening time in my life, because I didn't know how I was going to survive without a man and although I had saved some money, I didn't have a job or a vocation for that matter.

I joined a Twelve Step group that could support me with the love-addictive behaviour I relied on with men and participated in family-of-origin programs with Shirley's organisation. Gradually I learned to gain self-esteem through means other than the attention of men and my need to control them. I found the inner strength I needed to deal with different situations, and I made a whole lot of new friends who would give me 109 *honest and supportive feedback, which helped me tremendously in forming a clear perspective on matters.*

Through the various groups and programs I learned to live a day at a time accepting that everything is perfect in its own imperfect way. Today I'm in a new career and I participate with the intention of being a good employee, a day at a time and perform 'a good day's work for a good day's pay'. I manage my finances, budgets and savings and am well on the path to developing a strong and secure personal foundation.

I just left a job of nearly 3 years, which for me is a miracle. During that time I am proud to say that I was also able to negotiate a pay rise, and that I left happily and began my new job within 2 weeks of leaving the old job. In fact, the new job was created for me through my networking abilities.

I have now finished my degree, with distinctions along the way. One of the most important things I have learnt on my journey is that nothing is ever perfect the first time, and that as humans it's OK to make mistakes. I now know that out of these mistakes have come some of my greatest teachings. I have also learned how to have the faith in myself and love myself enough to rid myself of unhealthy and abusive friends. Today I surround myself with people who will help me both share and celebrate the wins.

My life is actually unfolding before me in such a way I could never have imagined.

Nelson Mandela's inaugural speech sits above my computer these days and what stands out for me are his words "it is our light not our darkness that scares us, and when we allow our light to shine we unconsciously give others permission to do the same". I never knew that letting my light shine was my biggest fear. It was because of my mother's jealously, her violence and threats of suicide, that I couldn't surpass her and let myself shine.

For the rest of my life, no matter how much fear comes my way, I have vowed to let my light shine and to surround myself with others who want to do the same. This is the reason I believe I have been led through the recovery journey, so I may live my life to the fullest with vivacity and passion! I certainly will not look back upon Mandela's words on my deathbed and mumble "If only I had given myself permission..."

THE ROOT OF DEPENDENCY

As I stated earlier, co-addictive relationships are set up from issues of childhood abandonment. The reason we have so much denial about this is that childhood abandonment exists in many forms beyond the average person's recognition and understanding.

Before defining some of the various forms of childhood abandonment, there is something important which must be understood first. This is that it takes many years for children to fully develop their intellect and their ability to reason. Their earliest way of thinking is through what John Bradshaw calls 'felt-thought'. Children gain understanding through their emotional reality. For children to grow, develop and mature, they have to be egocentric, putting a lot of focus on themselves. In their self-focused way of thinking, children take everything personally, including when they are neglected or abandoned. Until they are about seven or eight (the age of reason), they lack the ability to understand this logically. This element becomes very important in understanding issues of abandonment.

There are three forms of childhood abandonment – physical, emotional and abandonment through abuse.

PHYSICAL ABANDONMENT

This is commonly understood as occurring when there is parental death, desertion, divorce, adoption, or a serious parental illness. In addition, children are abandoned when their parents don't give them their time - for whatever reasons. Remembering that a child can't reason and will take things personally, no matter what the circumstances are, a child understands that what a parent gives their time to is what they love. If adequate time isn't being given to a child they will actually feel worth less than their parents' time. The parents could be workaholics or always on the go. Two-income families or single parent families are common these days, so parents are often pressed for time. Or in large families, with several children, the bottom line is that the parents cannot make enough time for each child.

Children, being egocentric, will always interpret these types of events as directly related to themselves. If mum or dad are not present for whatever reason, they'll think it's because of them.

ABANDONMENT THROUGH ABUSE

As I explained in Chapter 3, *Do You Know Who You Really Are?*: "As a child is being abused, no one is really there for them. They are all alone. Hence, abuse is abandonment."

Children have magical, non-logical thinking and because of their egocentricity, they make *themselves* responsible for the abuse they receive from their caregivers. Small children are *totally dependent* on their caregivers for survival. They are not able to reason that their parents may act crazily or be abusive. They think, 'something's wrong with me or my parents wouldn't treat me this way'. They can't afford to believe anything else because it threatens their survival. This idealistic thinking, therefore, guarantees their survival.

EMOTIONAL ABANDONMENT

Emotional abandonment occurs so extensively, I could write a whole book on it. In Chapter 3, I've already mentioned emotional abandonment in regards to narcissistic deprivation. There is another covert form of emotional abandonment which later creates devastating consequences in adult relationships. This abandonment occurs when a parent places the child into the 'emotional Surrogate Spouse' role. In dysfunctional marriages, it is very common for one or both parents to bond inappropriately with one of their children. An example of this might be if mum is mad at dad and is afraid to direct her anger at him, she may whinge, complain and express her disappointments to one of the children, or she may even ask a child for advice. By making the child her confidante, she is empowering him or her to feel a false sense of importance and mattering. This way of treating the child as an 'equal' (mummy or daddy's little man or little princess) constitutes extreme abandonment. The parents are getting their needs met at the expense of the child's needs.

THE FANTASY BOND

I believe the core issue of emotional abandonment is what Robert Firestone PhD calls the 'fantasy bond'. Let me explain: Children who are emotionally abandoned experience anxiety and a sense of emotional hunger. To deal with this, they imagine an illusion of connection to their mother. It is this imaginary fusion which Firestone calls the 'primary fantasy bond'. He contends that it is the core defence against reality. Without their reality available to them, children are abandoning themselves in the most profound way. Through this self-abandonment, the child in later life will be attracted to addictive relationships. Firestone has used the term 'bond' in the sense of bondage or limitation of freedom. It does not mean the same as 'bonding', which is a positive, nurturing process.

As a defence against emotional abandonment, the fantasy bond is a substitute for the love and care that is missing in the child's world. This allows the child to alleviate pain and anxiety and enables them to develop a feeling of pseudo-independence. Then, as adults, they say things like: "I don't need anyone. I can take care of myself". They try to become completely self-sufficient, needing nothing from the outer world. This is merely a more sophisticated defence against emotional abandonment.

According to Firestone, fantasy bonds also help to shield us from the realisation of our own immortality and from the awareness of our painful separateness. This is why people become dependent, clinging to family ties and fantasies of love - through these they can perpetuate the illusion of the connection they so inexorably seek. They sacrifice their freedom and any real intimacy in loving relationships in a desperate attempt to fuse with another person. This attempt to create a false sense of immortality through such fusions with others is obviously one that dependent people make on their lovers or spouses... but it doesn't stop there. They may also try to fuse with their children, religion or country!

Dependent people strive to maintain their fantasy bonds throughout their adults lives because to let them go, would mean they would have to experience real intimacy - and as Firestone notes, this: "would contradict [their] early conception of reality".

Bradshaw says: "Children idealise parents through the fantasy bond and therefore they will pass the rage, hurts, loneliness and shame of their own abandonment onto their own children. Instead of passing it back where it belongs, they pass it on."

GRIEF - THE KEY TO HEALING OUR ABANDONMENT

You will not be able to completely heal abandonment issues from your past without allowing yourself to grieve the relationships you once may have had, but lost. It is also important to grieve the relationships you misperceived as healthy and happy.

Grief is a normal and natural response to any loss. So why do people have so much trouble fully expressing their grief? The main reason is that the great majority of people are unaware (in denial) of all the losses, especially in relationships, that they've sustained throughout their lives. Another reason is that since expressing grief in our society is a big taboo, we are not taught how to grieve or how to deal with loss. Instead, we are constantly educated about how to acquire and hold on to things. As children, we also learn how to express ourselves by emulating the behaviour of our adult caregivers. Grieving generally involves moving through intense, emotional pain and this is usually kept hidden and private.

As we grew up, we learned how to suppress our grief. Because of this, most of us have massive, unresolved reserves of it inside of us. Intuitively, we fear that releasing our grief could be overwhelming. It is part of the human condition to fear emotionally letting go, yet this is exactly what we need to do if we are to heal our abandonment issues. When we allow ourselves to grieve one loss, often this will trigger the release of the cumulative grief we have stored - sometimes for decades. This happened to Sally, a client of mine. Sally socialised compulsively, yet she was emotionally isolated. Her friendships were superficial and she did not have a single, intimate relationship. When one of her acquaintances, Veronica, died suddenly of an aneurysm, the shock of her death pulled the plug on Sally's lifetime reservoir of stored grief. She fell apart, dramatically lost weight and had to take several weeks off work. Veronica's death had put her in touch with her stored grief and given her 'permission' to express it.

In order to heal our co-addictive relationships, we must allow ourselves to grieve over our childhood abandonment issues. Grieving will heal abandonment if we have:

- Enough time.

- Validation (by another).

- Non-shaming support.

As you can see, we cannot grieve alone! It is commonly accepted that we grow through being involved in relationships. Grieving is also a growth process, but seldom recognised as such. We can view our losses as an opportunity for personal healing and growth. Seen in this light, the pain of grief has many positive aspects and it is a finite process. However, staying in co-addictive relationships breeds a misery that is infinite.

In Chapter 10, I've provided more information on the importance of the grief process, not only for loss of relationships, but also as a necessary step before forgiveness can occur.

A QUICK RE-CAPITULATION

Most people in co-addictive relationships are willing to acknowledge that they have a problem and they're keen to learn skills and techniques to improve their current relationships. However, when I explain to them that taking the four steps is a graduated process, not just a nifty technique, many of them gloss over the first three steps and only tune in to the fourth.

Step 1.
Going into recovery from our co-addictive relationships takes us out of our misery and drops us into our pain, so we can finally heal. It enables us to be rigorously honest with ourselves and face the truth of our circumstances.

Step 2.
When we're in recovery, we begin to claim our dependent relationships (embracing our payoffs) instead of our dependent relationships claiming our happiness.

Step 3.
Recovery entails letting go and allowing ourselves to grieve the losses we've experienced in our relationships. Grieving naturally facilitates the process of forgiveness which is fundamental to our healing.

Step 4.
Once we've done the first three steps to the best of our ability, *then* we are ready to learn the skills and techniques necessary to build healthy relationships. (These will be explained in Chapter 9).

TAKE A DEEP BREATH AND...
FEAR FORWARD!

Now that you've read the first half of the book, you're probably feeling stirred up by the information given. It is a normal, healthy response to feel overwhelmed by your personal realisations at this stage. It means you have a great depth of honesty, open-mindedness and willingness.

You cannot begin to know and heal yourself until you break free from the thick wall of denial you have built up over your lifetime in order to survive.

It is unlikely that you will be able to digest and absorb all of the information presented in the previous chapters at first reading. But each time you re-read it in different stages of your healing process, you will probably have fresh realisations and new levels of awareness about your personal histories. Treat this rising awareness, too, as a positive sign that you are steadily coming out of denial, which is the first step to setting yourself free.

Often when people first recognise their co-dependency and addictive behaviour, they feel like I did that day in the treatment centre - i.e. a hopeless case! To stop at this point and wallow in self-pity will not get you anywhere. It's too late to go back into the 'Don't-tell-me-I'm-deluded, I'm-happy' phase. There is only one way to go - and that's forward. As I said in the first chapter, the only way out is the way through.

Now that you're somewhat out of denial, don't fall into the 'analysis paralysis' trap. It is time for you to metaphorically 'get up off the couch', as I did and take action. Action diminishes fear.

No one can take the steps for you, but you don't have to do it alone (as I will explain in Part Two). My first sponsor used to tell me gently after we'd spent hours taking inventory of my problems: "Well, Shirley, there's nothing left to do now but take a deep breath and... 'fear forward'."

At this point, I want to offer you the same choice. You can either stay stuck or you can fear forward and begin to set yourself free!

PART 2
'THE SOLUTION'

CHAPTER 6

KEYS TO KNOWING AND HEALING YOURSELF

In my professional experience, the hardest questions for the average person to answer are: 'Do you know who you really are?' and 'What do you really want?' In my workshops, I often tell the following parable to illustrate why we have so much trouble answering these questions.

FINDING YOUR TRUE COLOURS

Once upon a time there was a small, brown grasshopper called Henry. He lived in a meadow with many other grasshoppers. The meadow provided numerous adventures. It featured an abundance of trees, flowers, insects, lush, green grass and a variety of paths to take. Each grasshopper had his own path along which to hop, learning a great deal and enjoying different adventures on the way.

Henry was immature and hadn't worked out what he wanted to do with his life. He cruised along and went whichever way the breeze took him. One day while out strolling on his path, he came upon a rocky area covered with weeds. The weeds were growing so thickly that they were beginning to kill the grass. The rocks were numerous and some seemed so large it would take a bulldozer to move them. He really wanted his path to be pleasant and attractive, so he set about trimming the weeds and stacking a few of the smaller rocks to one side.

After a rainstorm a few days later, he noticed that the weeds had regrown and the rocks once again were strewn across his path. Every day he continued to trim the weeds and to shuffle the rocks around. He worked very hard, but he could not keep up to the job. Each night after he'd finished his chores, he was exhausted and afraid that he'd always be stuck in this weedy section and never have any new adventures.

One day he looked across the meadow and saw a cool, green grasshopper hopping along his path. His path looked a lot better than Henry's. There were no weeds or rocks on it. In fact, it was stunning. It was verdant, stylishly landscaped and covered with a profusion of gorgeous flowers.

Come to think of it, the cool, green grasshopper looked a lot better than Henry did, too. Henry was looking pretty shabby these days from working so hard on his path. Quite frankly, he wasn't having much success and he didn't know what to try next. On the other hand, the cool, green grasshopper seemed to be confident, energetic and to know just what to do to keep his path looking beautiful.

So rather than stay stuck with the mess on his path, Henry was irresistibly drawn towards the cool, green grasshopper's path. He quickly hopped on the stylish path and became a follower of the green grasshopper. At first this was lots of fun. His green friend taught him many new ways 'to be better' and he gave Henry plenty of tasks to keep him busy. Over time, he emulated his green mate in every way. So much so that after a while, Henry even started to turn green!

In due course, he became homesick for his own path. Even though it was overgrown with weeds and cluttered with rocks, it still held his dreams and desires. The green grasshopper's path may have been swish, but it was just not Henry's style. Besides, he found it was not easy being green. So finally he said goodbye to the cool, green grasshopper and returned to his own path.

When he got back there, he discovered that the weeds had grown very tall and now even the green grass was dead because it had not been cared for. He sat there, sadly looking at his shambling path. It appeared overwhelming. 'What am I to do?' he wondered.

Finally, it dawned on him that if he didn't get up and start moving, the weeds would completely take over his path. So this time, rather than trim the weeds off at the surface, he knew he had to dig down deep and pull them out at the roots. This he did with gusto - and was surprised to find he enjoyed it. Then he began to water his path regularly to revive the green grass. To the bare spots he applied fertiliser. As he was tending his path, he discovered he had lots of energy and for the first time in ages, he began to feel very good about himself. He didn't look shabby anymore because he found he had plenty of energy and time to spend on himself. In fact, he was soon the most beautiful shade of brown he had ever been.

As he remained focused on his path, he found, to his delight, that his creativity flourished. Many new ideas about things he wanted to do came to him. As he cultivated these ideas, he found that they formed the basis of a whole new set of desires. Soon his path was clear, beautiful and green, ablaze with a great variety of vivid blooms. It was apparent to him that by staying focused on his path and taking action, he could fulfil all of his desires.

Now and then when he encountered weeds or rocks on his way, he was sorely tempted to ignore them and go 'path-hopping' again. Then he remembered a wise adage imparted to him by the green grasshopper: "If the grass is always greener on the other side of the fence, water your own lawn."

Henry took this advice, stayed on his path and pursued his dreams.

NEEDS, WANTS AND DESIRES

Like Henry, many of us don't know who we really are or what we want. Doubting our own abilities, we often look for the easier, softer way to get through life. How many times have you been a path-hopper or a chameleon, changing yourself or your circumstances in the quest for others' approval? How many times have you denied your own desires because when things got tough, you didn't think you had what it took to fulfil them? Did you instead pursue someone else's path?

No wonder we get so confused and we don't know who we are and what we truly want or desire. The key to knowing and healing ourselves is to stay on our own individual path, focus on ourselves and water our own lawns (meet our own needs).

In differentiating between needs, wants and desires, you may look at it like this. You NEED food to survive; you may WANT food that tastes good and you may DESIRE gourmet food.

I mentioned earlier on that the most difficult question for people to answer is: 'What do you want?' I believe that what stops us from being able to answer this question is our inability to differentiate between needs, wants and desires. I've discovered three basic reasons for this.

1. To varying degrees our childhood needs and wants were not met. This makes us anxious, causing reactive behaviour, or leaves us needless and wantless.

2. Through the different stages of our upbringing, we were not taught how to fulfil our own needs, determine what we want or set desires (goals).

3. We have 'shame binds' related to many of our needs, wants and desires. Because we were either shamed or neglected by our major caregivers for having and expressing these, we become immobilised, feel that we don't have the right to have them or to ask others to help us fulfil them.

NEEDS

Our basic survival needs are for food, clothing, shelter, medical and dental care. The fulfilment of these needs gives us an experience of security.

Throughout our lives we will also need:

- instruction - learning 'how to' do things efficiently.

- stimulation - change, challenge, curiosity and fun. Without this, we become stagnant.

- self-actualisation - developing our own identity, individuality and creativity.

- self-acceptance - having self-worth and self-esteem.

- spiritualisation - having a sense of belonging and connection to all of life; to be spiritual is to be in touch with our very essence, to be open to new possibilities and the mystery in life.

The degree to which our childhood needs were not met will be reflected in the degree to which we feel fearful and insecure as adults. Because most of us were not taught how to meet our own needs, we continue to look to others to meet them. While we do this - and most of us do it a lot - we perpetuate the underlying fear of survival. The insatiable 'child' within feels he or she will never be satisfied, so we mask our fears with many false wants and goal setting.

One of the first personal development classes I took in my mid twenties, was on self-esteem and learning to ask for what you want. We were instructed to write lists of all the things we wanted, covering every area of our lives. Having finally been given permission to express this, I really got into this exercise. I wrote pages and pages of what I thought were all the things I wanted - from material possessions to the type of man I wanted, to the way I wanted my body to look. My needy 'inner child' had run rampant. Later I realised that it was fine to identify and allow myself to have what I wanted, but I didn't have a clue about what my *needs* were - or how to meet them.

As adults, needs can be as resources, people, feelings, situations or environments you MUST have to be your personal best. To have needs is to be human. Needs drive you and have an element of survival or urgency in them. This is why the idea of not having them met can make one anxious and ever fearful.

As previously stated, we basically need food to eat, a roof over our head, clothes on our body and medical care. Additionally, we have emotional, financial and sexual needs as well as a need for physical and emotional nurturing.

For many adults, emotional needs are the most neglected and where deep childhood wounds reside. Many feel ashamed if they even become aware of an emotional need. Yet, if we don't learn to recognise them and get them met, we become anxious, lose our confidence and we won't thrive. We also need to know how to create money and manage our finances in order to take care of ourselves, and if we do not fulfil our sexual needs our species would become extinct.

Because our needs are linked to survival, they are based in fear. This is not negative, but necessary. It's important to pay attention to our anxieties and learn to differentiate when we have an unmet need. Cutting off this natural warning sign can create much stress, confusion and even despair in our lives.

Our needs are formed from absolutes - from remembrances of the past. If our needs were not met in childhood, we lack a reference point and may have difficulty in discerning what our needs are. At the other end of the spectrum, if we stay 'needy', we can only look backwards. This causes us to look to our past for purposes of survival, rather than accepting that we're different today and we can open up to new possibilities and do things differently.

I believe that identifying and meeting our needs is the most important thing we can do - more important than goal setting! Our needs are part of our personal foundation. We need a strong foundation to weather life's storms and to survive earthquakes! If we put as much energy into getting our needs met as we do going after what we want, I think our results would be better, more fulfilling and happen sooner than we imagine.

Through many years of working intimately with people, I have learnt that most people don't have any idea of what their adult needs are and how to get them met appropriately. And, most people have shame attached to their needs, often because they were neglected in their formative years. People will either go without, having no idea why they feel stressed or somewhat unstable - or they become indulgent in other areas of their life to justify the hole in their foundation. This dynamic is a leading contributor to addictive behaviour. Addictive behaviour is mood altering, acting as a cover-up for the holes in our foundation.

When we don't identify and uncover our unmet needs, we often find ourselves falling short of the successes we want. We become anxious and left unattended, we will be prone to stress related diseases or creating stressful conditions in our life. Having said that, if we only meet our needs, the focus of our life will be about survival, effort and struggle, and we will remain a victim of life.

WANTS

Wants are more like objectives with a strong intention. They can be specific, yet not too precise. Fulfilling our wants gives us joy and provides gratification. Having a want show up or take form in one's life often involves an element of surprise which can be difficult for those who have control issues and trouble with trust.

The secret to getting more of what you want is to understand that wants do not have absolute pictures. Wants do not have the specific form that needs or desires have. They are somewhat formless and sometimes intangible. Letting go of control is vital to creating what you want. Let's take the example of food. You need food to survive, you want food that tastes good and you might desire gourmet food.

If you are going to eat something that you want, you may not care if it's as desirable as steak, prawns or a favourite food as long as it tastes good. If you need something to eat and you feel as though we're starving, a Vegemite sandwich may suffice. You may not be as precise and go to as much trouble to get a specific food or feel threatened if there is nothing in the house to eat. More often than not, if you let go of controlling the situation (either through fear or desire/indulgence) you will usually get something you want to eat easier and more quickly - and it will probably come about in a way that you didn't precisely plan.

WHAT'S STOPPING YOU?

I have found four circumstances that stand in the way of having what you want.

The first one is *shame*. Shame makes you feel worthless, stupid, and as though you don't have rights. If as a child, you were shamed or criticised for asking for what you wanted, or you were not encouraged to say what you wanted, you may have shame attached to your wants. As a result, one or two things will happen. Either your subconscious mind will not allow you to know what you want, or you may know what you want yet be unable to express it or pursue it.

The second obstacle to discovering what you want is *unrealistic expectations*. When you were a child and you wanted something, it was expected that someone else would give it to you. This pattern may have set you up to look to others to satisfy your wants, rather than allowing you to take steps which would lead you into discovering your own purpose and intention. Or, you may not tell others what you want and therefore you do not reach agreements to have your wants satisfied.

The third one is *dramatisation*. This is when we take a want and turn it into a need. For example you may say, 'I want a relationship, but if I have one more lover who leaves me I will die!' Although, we may be motivated to move by pain, fear or joy, we often distort emotional pain into a survival issue. Rather than motivating us to focus more clearly on what we want, we use drama to stay stuck, remaining a victim and wading in a cesspool of underground emotions.

The fourth circumstance is the *making of pictures of your wants*. What I mean in this instance is being exact and precise. This is what's advised in goal setting and prohibits fulfiling wants. When you begin to make pictures of what you want, it will either turn into a desire (goal), taking much longer to manifest, or it will become a need with that driving survival energy behind it. Placing pictures to your wants limits them and reduces the spontaneity and the adventure of discovery.

Wants are activities, preferences, or behaviours that we are naturally drawn to and gravitate towards. When our wants are fulfilled, they 125 bring us joy. However, determining what we want is a process. You have to stop and think about it. Check in with your feelings and values. Consider the responsibilities involved.

If you have no idea what you want, start by making a guess. Then go into discovery mode and as you go, notice if you continue to feel like moving forward... or not. This can be misleading if you have a specific, or preconceived idea of *how you should* get there or *what you must do*. For example: You want to work in sales, but you hate 'cold calling' and you've been told that if you work in sales, you *must* cold call. Therefore, you decide sales are not for you. Then, you meet someone that has a fabulous sales position that is only required to call on established accounts, to customers she has personally been introduced to. So, be careful not to let *how* or what you *must do* get in the way of what you want to do.

Wants just seem to show up when you least expect them. Usually because you are present and engaged in a process of discovery, enjoying each step along the way. If there is too much effort and struggle and you feel dissatisfied, then it probably isn't what you really wanted, so let it go.

DESIRES

Desires have more passion in them than needs or wants. They are linked to our dreams and goals, giving us a sense of purpose. Our desires determine the quality of our lives and the direction we will take. To find your desires, look for the things that do not bring you fear - for example, you may have a goal to be wealthy, yet, if that goal is driven from the fear of not having enough (and this may have been your experience in childhood), pursuit of financial wealth may backfire on you or cause other destructive ramifications in your life.

To help clarify your desires, you may ask yourself questions such as: 'Do I want a partner or do I want to be single?'; 'Do I want children? If, so how many?'; 'Where do I want to live? Do I want to live in another state or perhaps another country?'; 'What career path do I want to follow?' Whatever you ask yourself, if the answer is driven by fear, it will be a need masquerading as a desire.

Unlike wants, desires are precise goals that motivate with passion and enthusiasm. Sometimes desires can be confused with needs or vice versa because they also have absolute pictures. Formed from new ideas as well as remembrances of the past, desires require more steps and take more time to manifest. When the absolute picture of a desire is so important to you, you won't mind taking extra steps and spending more time acquiring it.

For instance, you may *need* a car. You *may* want a red convertible sports car with a great sound system. You may *desire* a new Jaguar convertible, which is fire-engine red, with white leather seats. More than likely it will take a longer time and require more steps to get the Jag, but you wouldn't find it a sacrifice. In fact, you'd probably enjoy every aspect of getting it - saving; exploring; researching; the anticipation and finally the achievement of the goal. There is a need and want part within each desire, yet being clear about their differences and the way you interact with each part can make the voyage a first-class experience where you feel in control.

Energetically, fear and passion can feel similar and often get confused. Need is the driving force of a desire. It is the starting point. As you form desires from your wants, don't limit yourself by giving loyalty to the need. Need is an absolute from the past that is linked to survival and is based in fear.

Secondly, determine the 'want' part of your desire. Ask yourself, 'what is my purpose and intention about this?' Then you can allow passion to ignite your vision and present you with the first part of an action plan towards your desires. *Staying focused on the purpose and intention in your desire* will take you away from your fears and move you towards things that give you joy. While in the process of forming your desires you are able to look forward to new possibilities, look backward to past knowledge and be in the here and now simultaneously.

What is it about desire that everybody wants? And why is desire so desirable? Because, if you have gourmet food all the time, you will always have food that tastes good to you. Or, at the very least you will always have food. Then you'll feel secure. When you won't settle for anything except your desire, it is almost a case of settling for second best. Your desire (precise goal) will only marginally fulfil your purpose and intention (the want part). There are an infinite number of other possibilities that will fulfil it better, but when you only have the absolute of your desire, you often won't recognise other alternatives. You may have difficulty with this because things learned in your lifetime set up filters that arbitrarily ignore better choices and limit the greatest possibilities. Using purpose and intention allows you to be flexible while you are taking steps, so you can reach a place of the greatest fulfilment.

Here's an example. My friend Steve often travels overseas for his work and we hadn't been able to get together in a long time. We always look forward to spending time together because we laugh a lot and have stimulating conversations. Last Friday night we decided to go to dinner. We were both very hungry and needed something to eat. I said to Steve, "I would love to have Mexican food - a Taco - my mouth is watering for a Taco". As we walked down the street, Steve saw the picture menu in the window of the local Thai restaurant. His mouth began salivating because Thai is his absolute favourite food. I wanted to go to the Mexican restaurant up the street and Steve wanted to eat Thai food.

We had a conflict. It appeared one of us had to lose and compromise. That is only because we were confusing our wants with our desires. I was really desiring a Taco and he desiring Thai food, because we had a picture of it and perhaps a memory of the taste. What we both really wanted when we made arrangements to get together was to share each others' company and have something to eat. I could go to the Mexican restaurant, Steve could go to the Thai restaurant and we could both have exactly what we desired to eat, but we wouldn't get what we wanted (which was sharing each others' company) and we would have to eat alone.

So we looked at the purpose and intention of our evening. It was to get together, have some good conversation, share a good meal and have a good time. We could both have our wants fulfilled if we stuck to our purpose and intention. We did this by having dinner at the great new Indian restaurant that had wonderful food and an atmosphere that enabled us to enjoy each other's company. This is a case of a want being much better and more fulfiling than a desire.

People often get hung up on their precise desires (goals), which limit and stop them from experiencing their heart's desire. This is the pitfall of 'creative visualisation' and goal setting. More often you will receive greater spontaneity, richer rewards and delightful surprises when you go for the wants. Desires aren't necessarily the 'be all and end all', unless of course, nothing else will do except that Jaguar!

SHAME BINDS

I've already explained that as we were abused as children, we carried the shame from our major caregivers. When we were shamed for having and expressing our needs, wants and desires, that shame became bound to them. As a result, one of two things will happen. Either our subconscious mind will not allow us to know what they are (remember, shame is about not wanting to be exposed. So our needs, wants and desires will stay buried and hidden) or if we try to express them, we will go into a 'shame attack', rendering us unable to ask for them. Knowing that we have the right to our needs, wants and desires always diminishes and moves the shame. First you have to find out specifically where your needs, wants and desires are shame-bound. Try saying aloud, for example: 'I have the right to eat' or 'I have the right to get my teeth fixed' or 'I have the right to ask for a hug'; 'I have the right to be sexual with another and to ask him/her for what I want'; 'I have the right to drive an expensive car'; 'I have the right to take a holiday', etc. You may have to get support for this.

SUMMING IT UP

When we are in *need*, there is more sacrifice involved.

When we are in *want*, there is less sacrifice involved.

When we are in *desire*, there is no sacrifice involved.

When we are in need, we are in a state of survival and can only look backward to the past as a reference. When we are in want, we are more in the moment, but we can also look backward as well. When we are in desire, we can look forward and backward and be in the moment, simultaneously.

In order to get in touch with our needs, wants and desires, first we must go within and learn how to tap into our internal information system. Then we can go out into the world and get help in learning how to take care of the needs we didn't learn how to address in childhood. We also have to learn how to negotiate our wants and desires and to ask for emotional support from others.

GOING WITHIN - RECOVERY STARTS WITH DISCOVERY

Through going within and discovering our authentic selves, we begin the process of self-knowledge and self-healing. In doing this, we start to understand that we can create the love, security and serenity that we have been seeking outside of ourselves.

The simplest way I have found to understand and communicate with our inner self is to put it in the context of a family. Through my own recovery process and the many clients and students with whom I have worked, I've developed a model called the 'Inner Family'. (This model is not to be confused with the one used by Transactional Analysis, which was developed by Eric Berne. Although my Inner Family model may have some similarities to the TA model, there are significant differences). I've found this to be a very effective and creative method of going within in order to re-connect with the authentic self and to tap into what we truly want.

There are many resources available today for healing your 'inner child'. However, I've discovered that the interaction of our inner family members is a much more powerful dynamic than anything that was or wasn't done to or for you in childhood. We will unconsciously re-enact family dynamics from our childhood and treat ourselves as we were treated in our family of origin. We also parent ourselves and interact with ourselves in ways familiar from our childhood.

Our inner family consists of a child, adolescent, adult, a pair of functional parents and a pair of dysfunctional parents. In the process of growing up we all have learned to model aspects of our parents, teachers, heroes and the many caregivers with whom we've interacted. It is through our stages of development, our perceptions and the major caregivers who have empowered or disempowered us, that we have formed our inner family members.

Using the inner family system is an innovative method of going within in a focused, balanced way. These parts of your character mostly operate on an unconscious level and are responsible for many of your choices, as well as knee jerk reactions. I believe we might as well use these different aspects consciously so that we may have more freedom of choice and appropriate expression.

Each inner family member has his or her unique attributes, abilities, talents and characteristics. Learning to identify your inner family members and the role each one is playing in your life today is extremely beneficial to identify your needs, wants and desires and to discover what is blocking you. This is also a highly successful method to integrate your best internal resources and discover the steps to take to be true to yourself, get the support you need and to live a happier, fulfilling life.

The child aspect of us is the precious, vulnerable and victim part of our character. The adolescent is the character who likes to learn, have adventures and express its individuality. The parent is the discoverer. As the child part of us generates a need, the adolescent goes out to explore and the parent is the one who actually makes the discoveries.

The adult is the aspect of us that is the master of methodology and gives us a sense of security by managing all the characters.

The happy, functional family we've longed for lives within us. By discovering our inner family and learning how they can cooperate, we CAN uncover our true selves and define our needs, wants and desires.

YOUR INNER FAMILY

Let's explore each Inner Family member in more depth.

THE CHILD

The child is that part of you which is creative, spiritual, expressive, precious, vulnerable and innocent. These beautiful, childlike attributes are extremely valuable in our adult life, especially when creating something new, thinking outside of the box or getting in touch with our true power. The child understands the importance of playing; is spontaneous; expressive and moves freely. When you feel stuck, it is the child in you that will help you to move. A child is perfectly imperfect, making mistakes in order to grow.

I believe there are three ways in which most people express the child part of themselves. They are...

child*less*

child*ish*

child*like*

When we are acting *childless* we are often overly responsible and too serious. We lack spontaneity, playfulness and feel blocked in our creativity. Those positive aspects of our Inner Child become invisible.

When we are acting *childish* we are often more reactive, feel victimised and let our responsibilities slide and our structure collapse. In recovery from addictive behaviour, we talk about 'self will run riot'. This is the *childish* part of our inner child, which can masquerade as innocent and cunning.

The more balanced aspect of our Inner Child is to be *childlike*. When we are childlike we are able to tap into our creativity. We move through our daily living in the spirit of play, which gives us the capacity for real joy. As we learn to embody and express the childlike aspect of ourselves it helps us to connect with our heart and the core of our authentic self.

Vulnerability leads to authenticity. Society shames and persecutes vulnerability. When we are being vulnerable as adults, we often get shamed (or we shame ourselves) and then feel like a victim. Not only do we feel like a victim in the adult situation, but this also triggers our childhood pain and emotional memories of being a victim. Is it any wonder that people hate feeling powerless?

To the degree that we keep this victim mentality and behaviour in our adult life, it will drive us to be childish or childless and block our childlike nature from manifesting. When we are being childlike as adults, we learn to embrace our vulnerability, which leads us to become more authentic and then lets us access our true power - perhaps for the first time in our life!

THE ADOLESCENT

In the past fifteen years, I've run several programs focusing on healing the wounds of adolescence, specifically focusing on issues of shame, sexuality and anger. I've witnessed deeper wounds and hurts coming from people's adolescence, than their early childhood. There is a tendency to think of the adolescent as awkward or negatively, yet our inner adolescent is curious, adventurous, enthusiastic, sexual and fun. Sometimes people who feel inadequate sexually have difficulty finding their adolescent because they were shamed as teenagers. The adolescent can be self-accepting, make his or her own choices; is inquisitive; takes risks; wants to learn and experience life.

Adolescence is a time when we are preparing to leave home and make our way in the big world. The adolescent part of our character is an explorer - the trailblazer of new frontiers, a pioneer who rallies in the excitement of breaking new ground. The enthusiastic adolescent is the part of us that will forever remain a student and loves the experience of learning and expansion. As we embark on a learning experience, it is the adolescent part of our character that often asks for advice from a teacher or authority figure. Although seeking advice or instruction is only *one* way we learn, it can still be a useful method to acquire new skills.

Negative judgement comes into the picture when we enter a new situation as the student and then expect ourselves to immediately act as if we already know what to do. We do this because in the physical sense we are adults, and often think we *should* know what to do and how to do it. Because the adolescent part of us has black and white thinking, it is constantly looking for the right or wrong way to do something and monitoring what is good and what is bad. The adolescent strives to discover how to do it perfectly. Criticising, berating and shaming ourselves if we're not perfect, causes us to become critical of others, and ourselves and stagnant in our growth. Instead, we need to recognise and validate the student part of ourselves that has the thirst for learning and embrace our delightful adventurer for the willingness to risk and learn by making mistakes. If we shame ourselves for learning through our mistakes we only drive the adolescent part of us to strive harder for perfection (becoming controlling and neurotic) or go into hiding.

Our adolescent carries a double-edged sword. One edge is densely coated with judgement, fear and shame, and the other edge cuts the way clear to freedom of choice. To stay clear of the dense edge as you're exploring new territories, it's important to determine if you are making your choices from judgement, fear or shame, or freedom of choice. When making a choice, consider your needs, wants and desires. Then, if you want to have more clarity about your choice, ask yourself, 'what do I want to allow and what will I not allow?'

Part of our adolescent character, which is left over from early childhood, is to copy and mimic rather than to choose or say what we really want. Many of us let our unconfident adolescent part go along with others to be part of the pack. It's easier to mimic rather than to break new ground. Why is it easier? When too many things happen at once, we lose our focus, making us confused. Too many good things at once may seem like nirvana, yet, it robs us from reaping the richness and greater satisfaction. When you narrow your focus, only a limited number of things can be created and experienced at one time. Doing this lets you savour your creations and allows you to observe them more realistically and clearly. But if your focus is too narrow you can become close-minded and have fewer choices.

To not focus at all leaves us wide open for anything to happen (positive and negative). For example, you didn't desire or 'choose' to have your house robbed, but perhaps you didn't choose *not* to allow it. (Maybe you have a victim consciousness and forgot to lock your window.) What prevents us from focusing? *Fear* - the fear that we will lose; the fear of failure; the fear of success; the fear of surpassing our parents... the list goes on. And so, we allow all things. Whether we realise it or not, we are always choosing. Therefore, by allowing all things and not choosing - *you are making a choice.*

To help our adolescent move from the explorer to the discoverer it is important to narrow the focus so that only a limited number of things may be experienced at one time. This is how your choices can become more **apparent**, allowing you to mature and become accountable for what you are choosing, or what you are *not* choosing.

During adolescence we are exploring who we are and begin forming our identity. As I said previously, we are getting ready to leave home. This is the time when we begin to separate from our major caregivers and discover more of the *Self.* Because many of us did not grow up in an environment that allowed us to discover our true self, as adults, the adolescent part of us continues the struggle to find its identity.

I've discovered three different types of behaviour that people express when they're coming from their adolescent self

Self*less*

Self*ish*

Self*ing*

When we are acting *selfless*, we allow too many things to happen at once and lose our focus. We can become too allowing and accommodating, causing us to be afraid to choose and therefore unable to commit.

When we are acting *selfish*, we have gone to the other extreme and made our focus too narrow, perhaps on only one desire. This causes us to exclude all other things and become more self-centred and close-minded.

When we are acting *selfing* we are able to say what we want and what we don't want. We are able to set healthy limits for ourselves and still remain open to new possibilities. When we focus on what we will allow and what we won't allow in a balanced way, then we are being selfing.

THE PARENT

The parent aspect of our character is the *discoverer*. This is the part that allows us to make new discoveries, expand and grow. Isn't that what healthy parents do? They provide a fertile environment so we can expand our minds, allow our bodies to grow and discover more appropriate behaviours.

When the adolescent goes out to explore, it is the parent aspect of ourselves that discovers the appropriate steps and actions to take. These steps become **AP-PARENT** as we explore and discover. When something is **apparent**, it is obvious - readily seen or understood -

because of our participation. The key to knowing your inner parent is to jump in and take action. Out of your involvement, your parent will discover more than one appropriate behaviour for any given situation.

Many people today are interested in the process of re-parenting themselves. I've found that often people have tremendous difficulty being their own loving parent. *If you didn't have a healthy model to learn from in the first place, how can you possibly re-parent yourself?* In my opinion, we can't re-parent ourselves, although we can give ourselves permission to expand and grow. When embarking upon new territory, most of us look for the right or exact thing to do. If we are willing to take different steps from the ones we've been taking, we will be lead to discoveries, which are more appropriate for us in any given situation. This process allows more expansion for the development of our identity. In other words:

**be
ap-parent!**

When we find ourselves repeating the same behaviour patterns, usually our focus is too narrow and it appears there is only one way to do what we're doing. The parent part of us comes into the picture when we begin to have an inkling that there is a better or different way to do it. Whereas the adolescent likes to explore for the adventure of exploring, it also wants to be told what to do and how to do it - the right way. Through the parent part of us, we discover a number of ways to do something, because it is the expanding and growing part, rather than the mimicking and advice seeking part.

INNER DYSFUNCTIONAL PARENTS

The dysfunctional parents overly control you and others. They are the voices inside your head telling you when you 'should', 'must', 'ought to'. Dysfunctional parents are righteous, dominating, critical, neglectful and judgemental. They attack, give orders, demand perfectionism and invite the child and adolescent to fail. Dysfunctional parents think they have all the answers. They have no higher power and think they are God.

When I'd been in recovery for about a year, my sponsor said to me one day, "Shirley, I think you're getting a lot better" "Why", I asked? "Because you don't say '*I know*' all the time like you used to". I smiled and realised that by relinquishing the idea that I 'knew' so much, I'd actually cleared a space to discover more, to connect with the realm of spiritual wisdom. This wisdom is strongly evident in our inner functional parents.

Inner Functional Parents

Functional parents honour and respect you and others; they give instruction, are patient, protect, and they know how to nurture and give love. They seek guidance from a higher power and are open to receive and express wisdom. The functional parents are balanced in intellectual, feeling, physical and spiritual realities.

THE ADULT

The adult is mature and can facilitate the expression of the child, adolescent and parent qualities in a positive way. The adult is intellectual; secure; accountable; dependable; able to create structure; and knows how to meet dependency needs. This part is also a protector, but in a different way than the parent.

Sound boring? Too much responsibility? When do I get to play, you ask?

Of all the inner family members, the adult sometimes appears to be sitting on the sidelines, not getting a chance to play. That's because the adult is more like a coach. The one who instructs and manages the team. Being the master of methodology and routine, the adult holds the responsibility for the other team players and creates structure. Have you ever noticed the expression on the coach's face during a ballgame? It often looks intense and serious. Let's face it, adults don't seem to have as much fun as children, adolescents or even parents. No wonder most people seldom view the adult aspect of life as spontaneous and exciting. In fact, being an appropriate adult is boring! That's why it's called A-**DULL**-T.

Before you unload your responsibilities and become more childish or selfish, let's take a closer look. A dull person is one who is habitually predictable and boring. After all, when we're adults we *have* to be responsible even though at times we'd rather be childish and selfish. Although the adult aspect of our character seems a bit monotonous, since the majority of our life is spent in adulthood, we may want to learn how we can shift from the drudgery of a '*have to*' to the delight of a '*get to*' and perceive our adult more positively.

The adult part of us is the part that knows what to do and how to do it. Adults know how to 'bring home the bacon'. Because the adult always succeeds at the hunt, its hunting is often taken for granted rather than seen as an accomplishment. It becomes expected. It would truly be more amazing and get more attention if the adult only rarely succeeded at the hunt. Although the adult's success at routine tasks may be ignored, when the tasks are grouped together and produce an event, then there is usually recognition and appreciation given. For example, when the adult brings food home from the hunt, he or she may not get recognised. But later, when the full meal has been prepared and eaten, this is the time for the adult to receive compliments and appreciation. The adult part of us knows how to wait for delayed gratification.

Another rewarding feature of our adult part is the ability to create security. The adult provides security because it has the ability to select the most appropriate behaviour in familiar situations. This is a different way of protecting than the *ap-parent* way. Our predictable adult has the knowledge that no matter what it does it can easily succeed every time. People begin to ignore that it's just as much effort for the adult to go hunting as it is for the child, adolescent and parent to do something that is routine for them. The adult is ignored because it is using a different tactic. The tactic that the adult uses is the one that works best to combine many of his/her abilities and resources.

In a sports team, the various team players may take a tactic that allows each individual's abilities to shine. But it is the coach who knows how to utilise the talents of each team member and pull them together in a method that makes a winning play. The method doesn't have to become apparent to the coach because he already has an inner experience of success and knows how to pull out the best in each team member.

When we are feeling comfortable and assured we are coming from our adult. We are secure with what is going on and don't feel the need to change things. The desires of our child are picked up by the exploring adolescent, who pushes us to be the discovering parent who wants to expand. The adult integrates the new discoveries until it can become a teacher of them. That is when the curriculum becomes boring. Being an adult allows us to expand our creativity under the umbrella of self-knowledge and self-security. This keeps us from seeking approval from others and allowing them to rain on our parade.

SUMMARY

By developing a relationship with each one of your inner family members, you'll find the talents and strengths they have to offer. You'll also be able to pinpoint what your fear, anger, pain and shame are about and where you need to heal. It is important to learn to acknowledge and love *all* the aspects of yourself. Those parts you refuse to accept and embrace are the ones which will end up running you and prevent you from fulfilling your needs, wants and desires.

I'll give you an example of this from my own life. I used to be appalled by women who appeared needy and helpless. Because of my family history, one of my greatest fears was being controlled by someone (read 'man'). I was afraid that if I ever allowed my inner child to express neediness and helplessness, I would fall prey to someone more powerful. I wanted to feel strong, be independent and take care of myself. In order to do this, I believed I had to *disown* any parts of me that seemed needy. By disowning my inner child's neediness, I unconsciously acted so strongly, I became a counter-dependent. I lost touch with my softness and vulnerability, yet these gentle qualities felt natural and satisfying when I occasionally allowed myself to feel them. To be true to myself, I needed to allow them more expression in my life. Until I began to do this, I kept attracting and being attracted to the wrong types of men for me. They were wounded bird, addictive types or so boring to me because my needy inner part was looking for an adult.

There are two different dynamics in operation here. The first one is: while I projected an exaggerated air of strength and independence, I attracted, like a magnet, those men who were deficient in those qualities themselves and unconsciously sought them in me. The second dynamic is: Because I had disowned and refused to express my own neediness and vulnerability, I handed my power over to *someone who obviously knew better than me.*

One of the benefits I've found in acquainting myself with my inner family is that it helped me to release and develop my natural creativity in areas I'd not previously considered. As my creativity blossomed, *my addictions and compulsive behaviours began to fall away.*

As you allow your inner family members to express themselves co-operatively, make conscious choices and contribute to your life, you will start to feel fulfilment, increased joy and serenity. Your growing connection with your inner family members will foster self-love and approval.

The following inspiring story from a former client illustrates just how important our inner family can be to us.

PETER'S STORY
A CLIENT'S PERSONAL VOYAGE

It has been said, word of mouth is a great way to hear or learn about something. I have learnt much on the so-called grape vine. A good friend of mine first told me about Shirley Smith and gave me her book Set Yourself Free *when I was involved in Twelve Step programs. These programs opened a door to my life. Talking about my experience of being raised by an alcoholic father helped me understand the damage inflicted living in a household with a drinker. Worst of all, I discovered how I had become like my father, in many more ways than simply mimicking the drinking and the drugging.*

What my friend said rang true in my ears: "it's one thing to talk about our experiences, it's another to be expertly guided by someone who can help you become the person you were meant to be".

I rang Shirley in 1992 and two weeks later I found myself sitting in a room with nine other strangers one Friday afternoon. At the time I was working in the building industry with teams of tradesman working for me and while they were at work I was sitting in my first Family of Origin group. And although I didn't let it show - boy, was I feeling scared!

Sitting in those groups I began working through my past. I saw how I reacted so sharply to everyday issues and situations out of defences I had built in the past. I had learned to protect myself, blow by blow in my tough and savage world. The groups showed me how my father, my teachers and other caregivers had delivered to me this unforgiving world. Seen through many new eyes, the group reflected their concern for me as each of my stories, my almost forgotten childhood memories, revealed the tortured beliefs I had absorbed from the often callous behaviours dumped upon my young shoulders.

My father's constant criticism had me walking around believing that I was not a smart person. In his eyes, I was never good enough. He would swing between punishing drunken outbursts and brutal silences. I lived in a world of rules and 'toeing the line'. I was terrified of making a mistake, I knew only too well what would happen if I did.

My experience of school had not been a happy one. Throughout my childhood school report cards echoed loudly that I was not enough. I lived in fear of the nun's painful and punitive ways. I did find a place I excelled at and became obsessed with pleasing my sports coaches. I secretly wanted my father to be pleased but I never got him to a game, not even when I was selected at representative level. When he left my mother for another woman my yearning for praise and attention became a dull, background ache.

At 16 my world collapsed when my mother died. She had been the one warm heart in a bleak and barren world. With my sporting days, my adolescence and my innocence over, I left school and moved from a country town to the city. I fulfiled a promise, though disinterested, and took an apprenticeship. It wasn't long before I discovered that drugs could take the emptiness and pain away, at least for a while. I was 34 when I finally landed myself in Narcotics Anonymous. Alone, empty, hurt and angry.

In 1994, after I had been working with Shirley for some time, I decided to attend one of her programs on creativity. I didn't believe I had a creative bone in my body as I had been slogging it out brick laying for many years. It seemed like the exact opposite of who I had become, but something in me wanted to give her workshop a go. On that weekend magic happened as a part of me was set free. What came to life was the kid in me I had forgotten. A long, long time ago there was a kid, a little kid who had a sand pit. This boy loved to play and build and imagine all sorts of wild and crazy things. During the *program a part of me came alive again. I remembered how much I loved to play in that sandpit and how when building my palaces and castles I was always making up stories to go with them. I was a kid who could entertain himself and his buddies for hours. No one criticised my sandcastles or said they were poorly built. If they fell over, I just built another one for another adventure. I finally understood the magic of my sandpit - there had been no rigid structure or rules. That particular program on creativity was the beginning of a new life for me.*

My sandpit story-making awakened an extraordinary creative urge. I wanted to make up more stories. I realised to the core of my being that the creative self doesn't need rigid structure and rules and when being creative, you can never make a mistake. I also discovered I had a vivid and electric imagination. Something about this idea set me on fire. I began to yearn to let the little boy in me or the creative self play. Up until that moment every thing I had been doing in my life seemed in some way to be for someone else. For the first time in my life, I found something I loved that was totally for me and my pleasure - telling stories.

I took my newly discovered imagination to Shirley's Empowering Communications Program and was truly inspired by the result. Excited, I decided I wanted to write my stories down. To do this I not only had to teach myself to type, I had to learn how to sit down (and stay still) at the computer as well, a bit tricky with the gnarly old hands of a builder. I even had to pick up where I had left off at school and teach myself how to write again; pouring over book after book to learn the structure of storytelling.

As I write this short piece about my journey for the anniversary edition of **Set Yourself Free***, I am proud to say that I have finished my first novel and am now deeply into my second, its sequel. When I stop and think about how far I've come, I am filled with gratitude... and I am so glad I was able to pick that juicy fruit from the grape vine, all those years ago.*

HOW TO FIND YOUR INNER FAMILY

There are different ways in which you can access and communicate with your inner family members. One powerful method is a closed eye process using the imagining power of your mind. Locate a quiet, private place, close your eyes, take some deep breaths and call forth each one of them. Allow yourself to get an energetic sense of them. Carefully visualise each one, noting their age, the colour of their hair, the style of their clothes, their surroundings etc. Then begin a dialogue with each one. Ask them what they're thinking and get a sense of what they're feeling. Ask if there's anything they want to tell you. Do they have any secrets they want to share? Let them know that you want to get to know them and have each one of them contribute to your life.

In my workshops, after people go through this process, I ask them to draw their inner family members, taking into account the predominance each one seems to have in their lives. Another method to make contact with the inner family is through journal writing. Sometimes you can write a question (to a specific inner family member) and then obtain the answer by writing it with your non-dominant hand.

You may see your child as big and obvious, in a self-will run riot mode. You may hear crying or perhaps find yourself crying. Sometimes your child is hiding and not present. There is usually a good reason for this and you are the only one who can find out. You may feel a daring adolescent or you may see a very feint, shrinking violet. Your child or adolescent might use swear words to test your trustworthiness or maybe they are angry.

Your adult may appear rigid and excessively responsible with little capacity for spontaneity; Perhaps you'll find a confident adult who loves a challenge. Or your adult might say: 'I can't take it anymore. I want to stay in bed and pull up the covers'.

Sometimes the dysfunctional parents appear in the form of words. These are usually shaming and judgemental criticisms. You might see a large, angry face or pointing finger; or you may sense that you are totally alone and no one is there for you. The functional parents tend to appear in a more symbolic context, as flowers or animals or looking saintly. When you are in touch with your functional parents, you might 'hear' the answer to a question or problem or sense the presence of a 'guardian angel'.

When you first begin, one or two of your inner family members may be completely missing. This commonly occurs, but if you just persist, it will pay off. It doesn't matter how your inner family members manifest for you. The important thing is to trust in your own process and to go with it. As you regularly begin to visualise, draw, write to or dialogue with the inner family, they will become more and more obvious and present. Treat them like friends and the things they will reveal to you will sometimes astound you and always benefit you.

All of the above examples are normal - in fact, whatever you find is normal and necessary for your healing and inner security. FEAR FORWARD!

If you find it difficult to do this process, you might need some assistance from a counsellor or someone who has expertise in facilitating these types of exercises. Or you may prefer to use a guided visualisation tape/CD. Go to **www.theradiantgroup.com.au/products.html** or send an e-mail to **products@theradiantgroup.com.au**

REGULAR FAMILY MEETINGS

It is important to have regular family meetings as this assists you to better know yourself and to identify your needs, wants and desires. There are various ways to have regular family meetings, but the important thing is to use your creativity and imagination. This process doesn't have to be a major production. If you don't have the time or the place to do a closed-eye process, you can dialogue with your inner family members in the shower or while driving. Or you can talk to them silently while working or riding on public transport. What we're after here is that inner communication with the self. Just ask and then allow the answers to come. Try not to censor and analyse the answers you receive. The first things that come to mind are usually the right answers for you.

A former client of mine who is a solicitor told me about an effective way she found to hold inner family meetings at work. In the early stages of her recovery, she would sometimes become distracted from her work by thinking obsessively about problems she had in her private life. At these times, she would close her office door, sit down with pen and paper and list each inner family member. She would then close her eyes and ask each one of them what was bothering them and what it was they wanted. As the answers came to her and she observed 'the big picture' on the page, she became clear about the real problem and what course of action to take next. This whole process took a maximum of five minutes. After this 'meeting' she was able to return to work with full concentration and without feeling that she was compromising or sacrificing some of her personal needs.

DEVELOPING COOPERATION AND BALANCE

The next step is learning how to have the inner family members cooperate. Each one expresses individually and has different needs, wants and desires - and these have to be satisfactorily reconciled.

If you neglect their needs, wants and desires, they will usually find a way to get your outer attention in an inappropriate or even harmful way. For example, if I'm working too hard or too long and I haven't given my adolescent or child any attention or outlet for expression, they will react. My child might indulge with food or drink that is unhealthy or fattening or my adolescent may rebel by getting a speeding ticket.

It is possible to reconcile these apparently conflicting needs. What you can do is have your adult talk to your child and adolescent. 'If you can just hang in there for two more weeks until I finish this project, I'll make enough money to take you on a special fun holiday and buy you some new clothes.' Another way to handle this is to let each family member have some regular expression. The child gets to go cycling in the park or playing on the beach, the teenager gets to go to the shopping mall and the movies and the adult gets to attend the theatre or dinner with friends. The functional parents get opportunities to give love and guidance and to make a contribution.

It is important to find out the needs, wants and desires of each inner family member and allow them to be expressed in a healthy balanced way. Equally important is learning how to maintain the correct balance of power among your inner family members. This balance changes according to your age, status and activities at any given time. If you are 18 and single, your expression of your adult will be different from someone who is 35. If you are enjoying a day at Disneyland, you would want to allow more of your inner child to emerge, whereas if you are attending a job interview, you will want to have more of your adult present.

In recovery, the goal is to have more of your balanced, functional adult and parents on board and less of the child and adolescent. The attributes of the latter two, however, still need to be available and expressed through the adult. In short, maintaining this balance is the key to having your inner family members cooperate.

During the first few years of your recovery, having a relationship with each inner family member is fundamental to your healing process. 'They' will help you to rediscover your authentic self, to determine and fulfil your needs, wants and desires and they will progressively heal your distorted reality. As you heal, your inner family members will become more integrated. For instance, you may not be frequently communicating with your inner child, but the characteristics of vulnerability, creativity, spontaneity and preciousness may be evident and utilised in your daily living. Or you may find you've sharpened your parenting skills to the point where you nurture and take care of yourself very wisely.

THE MAGIC OF PURPOSE

As a result of losing contact with our authentic self and our true needs, wants and desires, many of us have given up our own dreams and adopted someone else's. When we do this, we go through life without a sense of purpose. In many instances we get side-tracked, forgetting what our intention was in the first place. Then we are 'off-purpose',

A purpose is a general statement of your intention; it's a result you would like to achieve. I'm not necessarily talking about a life purpose here. Although we have purposes for some of our most important desires, we also can have purposes for our wants and our needs. When I began to write this book, the first thing I did was to define my purpose in writing it. Whenever I conduct a workshop I do the same thing. I've also done it when changing jobs, moving house, entering a new relationship or having a business meeting. Without clearly defined purposes, we become scattered and have to strive harder.

Setting a purpose is a focusing tool that takes a lot of the stress and struggle out of achieving the desired results. In order to fulfil our needs, wants and desires, it is essential to stay focused. In fact, it has been said that "genius is the ability to focus". When you are focused, you stay on track and don't allow distractions.

A way that we set ourselves up to fail is to have our purpose be larger than the focus we can hold now. If you are in debt and on the dole, it would be pointless for you to set a purpose to have complete financial freedom within 12 months because this is a purpose of such relatively staggering dimension that you could not possibly hold it in your current focus. To set yourself up to succeed, you would start with a smaller purpose. To help define this smaller purpose, you need to keep your focus in the present, asking yourself what it is that you need, want and desire *now*.

- An appropriate purpose might be:

  To be self-supporting and experiencing ever-expanding levels of freedom.

- Your intended results might be:

1. To find, as quickly as possible, a job which affords you the freedom to incorporate the other activities which will allow you to expand - e.g. taking classes to develop a new skill, exercising, meditating.

2. To quit the welfare system and begin to reduce your debt by making steady repayments that you can afford.

To determine your purpose, ask yourself:

1. What are my motivations and my intention?

2. Why do I want this?

3. What are the results I want to experience?

These results are not necessarily tangible. They may be things such as experiencing more trust, receiving support from others, having more fun, feeling safe in relationships or creating cooperation in your relationships.

In the process of achieving a desired result, often the form may change. However, if you have a clear purpose, you can be flexible when the form does change and still attain your desired result. About three years ago, I wrote out a purpose for a new career path. This included writing a book. My purpose in writing it was to help people to give themselves permission to do what they really wanted to do and to know that they're never alone.

Three months later I was working with a career consultant and a tremendous idea for a book emerged. So I began working on it. A year later, just as I was about to emigrate, I met an American publisher who was interested in publishing it. He introduced me to my Australian publisher. She was keen to publish my book, but saw it as a sequel to another, introductory book - which turned out to be this one. So I put my original notes on the back burner and started work on *Set Yourself Free*.

The point here is that this book, although very different from the one I'd commenced several years ago, still allowed me to fulfil every aspect of my original purpose.

If you try to be too absolute and detailed when you're writing a purpose, you will usually limit yourself. When I originally wrote my purpose for a book, I didn't say it had to be called *Set Yourself Free* or that it had to be published by a certain company in a certain country. But I did focus on and write out some intended results that I wanted my readers and myself to experience.

One of the attitudinal pitfalls in our 'quick fix' society is: 'I have to have it all - RIGHT NOW.' Patience is a quality that we need to cultivate and it is formed through having purpose and focus. Patience is not only, as we are so often told, a virtue, it also has a practical side. Believe it or not, patience can be regarded as something to be desired rather than something to dread. Try thinking of it in this context: time is a bookmark to prevent everything from happening at once. Time segments things into events so we may see, feel and perceive them and be able to savour them to the fullest. If we received several of our wants and desires all at once, we would be overloaded and unable to relish them fully.

Imagine that within one week you bought the new red Jaguar sports car you'd been desiring, you got the big job promotion you'd waited for five years and your firm immediately wanted to send you on an overseas business trip, your fiancé finally wanted to set the wedding date and your real estate agent phoned you with the news that the sale of your apartment came through. This all sounds great in principle and undoubtedly you'd be extremely excited, but you would not be able to fully cherish and appreciate the fulfilment of your desires if they manifested all at once.

I know you all have dreams, goals and things you want to manifest in your lives. Everyone is valuable, precious, talented, creative and able to respond to their individual abilities. You *can* have a fulfilling career, a life-partner, friends, material possessions, harmonious relationships with others, serenity or whatever you desire. Happiness and fulfilment are an inside job. To create what you desire in your outer world, you have to go within - and your 'Inner Family' is waiting to help!

CHAPTER 7

YOU DON'T HAVE TO
BE A JUGGLER TO
BALANCE YOUR LIFE

As I said in Chapter 1, I believe that the fundamental key to personal freedom lies in attaining and maintaining balance in our lives. En route to this coveted state are many exciting adventures, personal discoveries and a life that finally feels like yours. Yet when people first begin their recovery journey, there is often apprehension. It's amazing to me to watch the '*coincidental*' disruptions that arise, getting in the way of their recovery program... They say things like: 'It's all too hard and complicated'. 'I don't have the time to spend on this'. Or the old standard, 'I don't really have a problem, it's my partner who is the problem'. Or better still, 'I'm only doing this because my partner is insisting - things are not that bad'.

Two fundamental fears are underlying these excuses. One, the fear that life is now going to be boring. Two, feeling overwhelmed at the realisation of the imbalance of their reality (intellectual, emotional, physical and spiritual states), which makes them feel out of control. The fear of being out of control, deeply threatens our survival.

I can assure you right now that if you are sincere and are actively participating in your own recovery, you will never be bored again! And, although you may have a few times when it's a challenge to get out of bed and front up, your life won't fall apart. It's just that your old life will die and slowly fall away, making way for the life you've been dying to have.

I can't promise that the road ahead will always be easy, but the process of recovery is *simple*. And it works! In fact, if you are co-dependent, an addict of some type, or were raised in a family with alcoholism, other addictive dysfunctions, or where the adults behaviours were extreme, most counselling and personal development programs will only scratch the surface. Treating the addictive personality and those raised in an addictive, dysfunctional environment requires fundamental, foundational, lifestyle change. The approach is different. The healing has to take place at the core or you will go back to your survival patterns, no matter how dysfunctional they are or how much you don't want to. Your biggest illusion is that you were in control in the first place - and somewhere deep inside of you, you know that and fear you won't make it if you let go of your behaviours that have allowed you to survive.

When I first wrote this book, the mind body connection was just being introduced to the masses. Today, this holistic approach to health and well-being is generally recognised as essential - and *balance is the key.* But exactly what is balance and how does one attain it?

Balance is a state of equilibrium, derived from our intellectual, emotional, physical and spiritual realities being integrated. When we are balanced, we feel centred, focused, stable, harmonious, and more importantly, clear about our choices.

When we are out of balance we operate in a state of instability, disharmony, confusion and insecurity. We feel scattered, stressed, distracted and are unclear about our choices.

Co-dependents and addictive types experience imbalance by operating in extremes. They juggle life and every once in a while - it all seems to come crashing down. Or they come so close to reaching that goal and having all their ducks in a row, just before it all falls apart. So, why are we so unsuccessful in our efforts to create and sustain balance? Because we go about it back to front. The way to achieve a high degree of balance is from the inside out - not the outside in!

I'd like to draw an analogy to explain this: picture the jugglers at the circus. We are fascinated with the way they can juggle different objects in their hands, walk on tightropes and keep numerous plates busily spinning on the end of thin sticks. In keeping everything going, the juggler appears to have incredible balance. We watch in anticipation, feeling the adrenalin pump. As long as he keeps moving fast, he can keep those plates spinning! The jugglers' act usually lasts only a matter of minutes and when they conclude their performance by gathering up their plates and taking a bow, the audience applauds out of relief as much as admiration.

Sometimes, in our efforts to have a full and balanced life, we are very much like jugglers. But unlike the circus entertainers, we often keep our juggling acts going for years and we can wear ourselves (and everyone else) out in the process. Then why do we do it? Because we think that by keeping ourselves very busy, juggling loads of activities and people, we will impress others and add a perceived significance to our lives. We also do it because we are running the biggest addiction going - we are addicted to our own adrenalin.

Adrenalin is a gift from God, helping us to survive and act wisely in emergencies. When you hear stories of a small woman lifting the front of a car to free a child pinned underneath, it's the adrenalin that gives this incredible strength. In emergencies or times when we have to kick in and go the extra mile, adrenalin is great. However, we were never meant to live in this 'fight or flight' state for a good portion of our life.

Operating in extremes keeps the adrenalin flowing through our veins just like a drug. We become addicted to it because adrenalin cuts off feelings and gives us the illusion of being *alive* and in control. We do not do this consciously. In fact, many of us feel that running on adrenalin is normal. When we consider our history and the environment in which our behaviour patterns were learned, it makes sense.

One of the definitions that Webster's gives for a 'juggler' is a 'deceiver'. Underneath that frantic juggling syndrome, we feel that we are not enough. One of my teachers once said to me: "If you think you're not enough... already you're *too* much!" People who have an underlying feeling and belief that they are not enough believe that only by constantly adding to themselves can they be enough. By doing this, they become over-the-top, *too* much. When they are not busy, alone or when it's quiet, they become disturbed or frightened. In the stillness, they think things such as: 'People don't like me. What are they thinking about me? I'm not good enough. I don't have what it takes. They will find out that I am a fraud - that I don't know what I'm doing. I don't know what to *do* .. I'd better add another plate!'

'Jugglers' usually look as if they have a full life. They are hooked on filling up every moment so that they don't have to be alone to face their distorted and painful reality. When we hide who we really are in this manner, we create a stressful imbalance. Yet we mistakenly keep trying to juggle those plates and even add some more in the illusory pursuit of balance. Instead we need to stop 'adding plates' and examine our thoughts; experience our feelings; take an honest look at our behaviours and connect to our true self. If we don't, the stress of struggling for balance progresses until we're in a state of 'burnout' or we have a 'breakdown' or hit 'mid-life crisis'. At this point, we're usually almost worn out in our physical addictions, emotionally depressed or distraught, have over-reactive behaviour or we are intellectually negative and defensive.

When this happens, we go looking for a 'fix'. And so we begin the search for meaning in our lives. We want to fill up the hole inside of us and feel whole. If we've had a religious upbringing, we may revert to that in our quest for meaning. Or we may explore other spiritual avenues. This search for meaning is pointless unless you have 'emptied your bucket' (acknowledged and begun to heal your distorted reality). Without having done this, such spiritual searching is reduced to a mere diversionary tactic that I call the 'God Fix'. Spiritual searching is not the panacea, although many use this to avoid doing their emotional work. We will only discover who we are, what we want and how to create it when we examine all four realities - intellectual, feeling, physical and spiritual - and learn how to balance them. A great teacher once told us that we need to *"live in this world, but not of it"*.

CREATING BALANCE

As children, we learned to contain and suppress our realities and along the way most of us lost track of them. If you grew up in an environment where your reality was not allowed to emerge or if it went unsupported, then as an adult you have to learn to balance your four realities. This is fundamental to building a solid personal foundation and involves 'Emptying Your Bucket'

But, there is a catch to emptying your bucket. It's called *denial*. Most of us don't know we need to empty our bucket, and the ones who do know they need to - don't know how to.

One way of emptying your bucket is to have a trauma or crisis in your life. Some people wait and have a mid-life crisis, which is a warning that your bucket is long overdue to be emptied. *There is another way.* You can do it by choice. And balancing your four realities will allow you to make better choices.

In attaining balance, you will need to take actions that will prompt you to:

- Become aware of your own individual thinking, beliefs and the meaning you assign to things.

- Tune in to your own individual feelings (including 'emptying your bucket' of the fear and shame that keep you from doing and having what you want). Rather than suppress them, learn how to manage your feelings in an adult manner.

- Honestly confront your behaviours and observe your physical reality. Then learn how to take action with balance. If you have an addiction - seek treatment.

- Develop your creativity, imagination, intuition and a relationship with a higher power. Connect with your true essence.

It is extremely important to take these actions if you want to have a sense of self, discover what your needs, wants and desires are and learn to attain balance - from the inside out.

THOUGHT IS CREATIVE

To begin the process of attaining balance, you need to examine your negative thoughts, beliefs and attitudes and where you got them. Beliefs, thoughts and attitudes shape your intellectual reality (thought creates form).

From our thoughts, beliefs and attitudes flow experiences, which reinforce them. Because so many of us have distorted thinking, we sometimes have difficulty in knowing what these are. If this is the case, simply look at your current situation and ask yourself: 'What would my thought/belief/attitude be, given the circumstances I'm in?' Once you've identified what your negative thoughts, beliefs and attitudes are, state them honestly to yourself and then write them down. Now you are ready to create affirmations to counteract them.

Affirmations are a statement or declaration of one's desires, wants, needs or beliefs. They must be written in the same sentence structure as the stated negative beliefs.

There is much information available today about affirmations. There are people who malign their effectiveness, claiming they don't work. This is because they don't understand the principles behind them. Affirmations won't work for you if you're writing them from the perspective of your distorted reality. In other words, you don't know what to affirm. You select a few phrases that sound good and away you go. Doing this is what I call 'frosting a rotten cake', putting the trimmings on and trying to make things look good from the outside in.

Affirmations need to be tailor-made for the individual. Affirmations do two things:

1. They act as a catalyst in bringing up the 'mud' from the bottom of your 'bucket'. In this sense, the affirmations represent the clear water (the truth about you). As you affirm, it's like pouring water into your bucket. As you do so, they will cause the mud (which is the opposite of them) to surface. This is the first step on the road to healing. (In the next section, I will outline a process to use to help you to empty your bucket and embrace your fears.)

2. Correctly written, in the same syntax as the negative statement, they reprogram and help to eliminate your negative beliefs, thoughts and attitudes. I will illustrate this below.

Here are some common negative thoughts and beliefs:

- I am stupid.
- I never have enough money.
- I am a failure.
- My body is ugly.
- I can't have what I want.
- Men are emotionally unavailable for me.
- I don't understand women.
- Love hurts.
- I'm not good enough.
- People will reject me if I tell them what I want.

Rewritten as affirmations, they would read:

- I am smart.
- I always have enough money.
- I am a success.

- My body is beautiful.

- I can have what I want.

- Men are emotionally available for me.

- I do understand women.

- Love heals.

- I am good enough.

- People will accept me if I tell them what I want.

When you're reprogramming your thoughts by using your specific positive affirmations, it is important that you see them by writing them, *hear them by speaking them* aloud and get a *sense* of them by repeating them over and over until they feel real. Repetition is essential for reprogramming, so the more you do them, the closer you come to balancing your intellectual reality.

When writing and saying your affirmations, do them in the first, second and third person with a response column. In the response column, write the first response that comes to mind, even if it doesn't make sense to you.

The response column will increase your awareness of your negative and distorted thoughts. Don't judge yourself for having these. Instead, use them as raw material from which to create the opposite meaning in the form of new, life-enhancing affirmations.

Affirmation *(1st person)*	**Response**
I, Shirley, am good enough.	No I'm not!
I, Shirley am good enough.	What about all the mistakes I've made?
I, Shirley, am good enough.	Maybe... After all, nobody's perfect.
(2nd person)	
You, Shirley, are good enough.	Who said that?
You, Shirley, are good enough.	I hope no one finds out I'm stupid.
You, Shirley, are good enough.	I wish I could believe that.
(3rd person)	
Shirley is good enough.	I've certainly tried hard.

Shirley is good enough.   Do you think so?

Shirley is good enough.   Thank you, yes I know!

There is no limit to the healing and creative power of your mind. It will always bring you, sometimes with startling precision, the full measure of your thoughts, attitudes and beliefs. When you fully acknowledge that your mind has the power to change everything about you for the better, you will feel free to calmly set about changing your state of mind and using your imagination to establish a new set of ideas.

VISION - A BRIDGE TO OUR BRIGHT FUTURE

Once we discover the power of a positive mental attitude, we get excited because we realise we can harness it in the form of creating a vision. A vision is a mental image produced by imagination that always refers to a future state and a condition that does not presently exist. With our imagination, we lay hold of ideas and give them substance. A vision provides the all-important bridge from our present to our future.

Vision is inspired by our needs, wants and desires, formed by our imagination and purposes and attained by our willingness, commitment, persistence and ability to focus.

As we begin the process of creating vision, we need to consider embracing our past as well as our future. To embrace is to have eager acceptance, to encircle or surround something as a display of affection. We embrace things in two ways - as a lover or a wrestler. When we're healing our distorted reality, the thing to ask ourselves is: Are we wrestling or struggling with the mistakes that we've made or are we eagerly accepting them and encircling them with love? Are we feeling grateful for what we learned from them? And how has that inspired us to create something new?

When we have not embraced our past, we have not allowed ourselves the feeling of completion with it. Completing the past swings the door wide open to new beginnings so that we may embrace future desires.

WRITE IT DOWN

Once you know what you want, you need to **write it down.** If you don't do this, you'll get caught up in detailed thoughts and plans such as: 'What should I do?', 'How will this happen?', 'How can I make it work?', 'Maybe if I try such and such...' In other words, you'll become obsessed with *how* this will happen. Far from helping you to fulfil your vision, this kind of thinking will keep you stuck. This is why you need to extract the vision from your mind and write it down.

YOU CAN IF YOU WILL

Once you've written out your intention, the next important element is to **be willing** for your vision to manifest. Willingness is a frame of mind open to every possibility without judgment, reservation or refusal. Willingness does not require physical action, but it does require a shift in attitude. There is no process involved in achieving willingness. You get it by having it.

WHEN IT'S TIME TO COMMIT

Once you know you're willing, you need to **commit** to your vision. Commitment is not an obligation, duty or something to entrap you. It is an attitude that calls forth your abilities and all the other ingredients needed to realise your vision. Commitment will give you certainty, freedom and the excitement of living. If your passion starts to die, commitment brings it alive. It generates a feeling of confidence and is a firm belief that what you want is so desirable that it is worth going the extra mile to achieve it.

PERSISTENCE PAYS OFF

An element that seems to be necessary in the fulfilment of a vision is discipline. Most of us fall short of our desires and expectations regarding discipline. Discipline has a joyless quality to it because as children most of our discipline was really abuse. In attaining your vision, there is something better to use than discipline and easily achievable - and that's **persistence**. Persistence is possible, even when discipline is lacking. To be persistent is to continue steadily, especially in spite of opposition; to hold firmly and steadfastly to a vision, despite obstacles. It goes beyond faith and hope. Persistence is simply doing it anyway. At times when I've felt bogged down or despondent, I've often been cheered and inspired by the words of former US President Calvin Coolidge who said: "Nothing in the world can take the place of persistence. Talent will not: nothing is more common than successful men without talent. Genius will not: unrewarded genius is almost a proverb. Education will not: the world is full of educated derelicts. Persistence and determination alone are omnipotent. The slogan 'press on' has solved and always will solve the problems of the human race".

WHAT ARE YOU WAITING FOR?

So why do we avoid setting a vision? There are a number of reasons for this.

1. We fear failure. Remember, vision is something we desire for the future. Through our limitations of the past, we can't see how it will happen, so we are afraid to try at all.

2. We fear success. If everything was working in our lives, what would we talk about to our friends? Or perhaps we fear it will be boring or lonely at the top or that we'll lose our friends if we're too successful.

3. We fear being locked in to the vision and that we'll have no freedom to change.

THE LITMUS TEST FOR YOUR TRUE VISION

How can you tell if a vision is really your own or if it is one that you've subconsciously taken on from one of your caregivers? Did you really want to be a doctor or go for that safe, secure job you're in - or was that your parents' vision for you? If your vision has the following qualities, it is almost certainly your own.

1. It's simple (although attaining it may not be easy every step of the way).

2. It's easily understood. (Vision also has the quality of re-vision, meaning it's constantly reviewed as the form changes).

3. It's clearly desirable. (You are excited about it).

4. It's energising. (Even if it is challenging at times, you still want to apply your energy to attaining it.)

IGNITE YOUR VISION

Having vision is a wondrous quality in human beings, but bringing your vision into realisation is even more so. If you can't find the ignition switch to your vision, it will never spark into manifestation. So what is it that ignites and fuels your vision? It's PASSION. Passion is the energy which produces intense feeling and desire in us. This energy is love-directed.

In our society, passion is often thought of as being synonymous or interchangeable with sex. Passion is distinct from but related to sexual energy of creation - a driving force in our creativity. When we are passionate about our vision, all of our senses are awake and aware. In this state, it is easier to stay focused on our vision. Passion occurs when you live from and trust your feelings and intuition. When you're passionate about your vision, you have the sense of being totally alive in every cell of your body. It's a great feeling!

THE GIFTS OF FEELINGS

If you don't completely understand why the feeling reality is the most damaged for the co-dependent, please re-read the section on *Feeling Reality* in Chapter 4. Without having our feeling reality fully available to us, we cannot be balanced.

During my workshops when I list the raw feelings (joy, pain, loneliness, fear, anger, guilt, lust and shame), I ask people to nominate the ones they consider positive. The majority of the group say there's only one - joy. I then tell them that all of our feelings have a positive purpose and they also have special gifts to offer us. We need to learn to make friends with our feelings in order to receive their gifts and be a fully functioning, balanced person.

The gifts of joy are healing and hope. When we're joyous, there is a sense of well-being and optimism.

The gifts of pain are growth and healing. Pain is a great motivator: it motivates us to change and change is the only constant in life. If we're not changing and growing, we become stagnant and lifeless. To recognise the healing gift of pain, think of the 'good hurt' you feel when a masseur works on the sore points in your body. As they press on a knotted area, it 'hurts so good' that you don't want them to stop because it's a release. The same principle applies to our emotional pain.

Although our thoughts and ideas about pain and joy are quite different, the pure feeling of them is very much the same. Some people experience this as pain-filled joy or joy-filled pain.

The gift of loneliness is reaching out. To be engaged in any addictive process is very isolating and lonely. The feeling of loneliness is very close to the feeling of pain. However, loneliness is not the same as being alone. It is rooted in isolation. Fantasy is a way to defend against loneliness and will ease the pain of it. If you use the gift of loneliness and reach out, you can enjoy rich, rewarding relationships and you won't have to rely on fantasy to ease the pain.

The gifts of fear are wisdom and protection. Fear alerts us to danger in our environment. Many people aspire to eliminate all their fears, but this wouldn't be a wise thing to do. Without the feeling of fear at our disposal, we might take a course of action that could bring harm. We've all seen people get drunk, lose their inhibitions and fears and do foolhardy things - such as driving their cars or swimming at night in unsafe waters - with terrible consequences. We can learn a lot from our fears and although they may feel unpleasant, we can gain great wisdom by embracing them.

The gifts of anger are strength, honour and dignity. Anger is a very powerful, energising emotion. When we're in a state of procrastination, we sometimes get angry with ourselves. It's this healthy anger that helps to get us moving. If you are violated or offended in any way, the expression of your healthy anger will restore your dignity. Anger helps us to have self-respect. Sadly for them, most co-dependents would rather be nailed to the cross and die than express their anger. So they remain victimised people-pleasers. I've heard this syndrome referred to in Twelve Step meetings as: 'Get off the cross. We need the wood.'

Healthy guilt helps us to retain our values and integrity and prompts us to make amends when that is necessary. When we've acted outside of our value system, guilt gives us a gnawing feeling which alerts us to this transgression. Healthy guilt is like our conscience and it helps keep our integrity intact.

In the physical sense, the gift of lust is the preservation of our species. Yet lust is not only about our sexuality. Lust is the passionate, feeling energy contained in desire, it is an energy in motion that fuels our desires and helps us to realise them. In this sense, it also stimulates our natural creativity.

The gifts of shame are accountability, humility and spirituality. When we experience healthy shame, we are willing to note the impact of our actions on someone else. Healthy shame reminds us of our fallibility and imperfections and gives us permission to be human. It gives us humility, reminds us that we are not God, that we need help and that we can and will make mistakes.

One of the keys to personal freedom is learning how to identify and express our healthy feelings and how to embrace the overwhelming ones that dictate the direction of our lives.

MAKE FRIENDS WITH YOUR FEELINGS

Making friends with your feelings is integral to balancing your feeling reality and expanding your sense of personal freedom.

Here are some simple keys to assist you:

- When you're feeling pain, allow yourself to purge it - perhaps by crying or sharing with someone that you're hurting. Allow another to validate your experience. Look within your pain and see what actions you may take to change and grow.

- When you're feeling lonely, you must force yourself to take action by reaching out and finding some support. Allow yourself to be vulnerable and tell people close to you that you're lonely and would like their company. If you don't have an intimate support network, you might consider attending a Twelve Step meeting and sharing about your loneliness in the context of the meeting. Don't wait for people to come to you or you may be lonely for a long time.

- When you're feeling anger because someone has offended you or is not keeping their agreements with you, you need to directly confront *them*. Co-dependents typically tell everyone (except the person with whom they're angry) about their anger. If suppressed anger from childhood arises, throw a 'creative tantrum' - punch or scream into a pillow, lay on your bed and kick your feet and while you're doing this, acknowledge to yourself that you are purging this anger from the past.

- When you're feeling guilty, ask yourself if there's someone you've offended and if you owe them amends (including yourself). If you've done something outside the bounds of your own values, then take the appropriate action to get yourself back on track. But if you haven't, do not analyse *why* you feel guilty. It is more important to recognise *when* you feel guilty. Then begin to do something about it. It is that *unrecognising* of guilt that will perpetuate your co-dependency and drive you into addictions. The same principle also applies to shame.

- When you're feeling your healthy lust about a goal or a project that you have, use it as a powerful catalyst to take the actions necessary to create your intended result. Healthy lust also enables you to get in touch with your desires.

- When you are feeling shame, take the time to make an affirmation tape which disputes the shame statements you have about yourself. Listen to it daily until you feel your shame attacks diminishing. Because shame fears exposure, in order to heal it you need to share it with another. Make sure that you do this with a person or in a group where you can be validated and not judged. In a Twelve Step program, the fifth step reduces one's shame. Because toxic shame is so pervasive and immobilising, you may have to seek the help of a therapist skilled in shame reduction work.

- Although shame and fear have their healthy aspects, most of us are overloaded and thrown out of balance by our toxic shame and unhealthy fear. Shame and fear are the root causes of our inability and unwillingness to feel and express our other feelings. They also prevent us from doing and having what we really want in life.

Like shame, fear also immobilises and entraps us. In order to experience freedom, you must have a conscious understanding of your fear. If you have clarity in this regard, you will not allow your fear into your relationships, career or finances.

It is also important to distinguish your own fears from someone else's. Often, the fears that keep us from doing and having what we want are either carried fears (from others) or childhood fears, which weren't fully expressed. While they may feel very real and intense, neither of these types of fears has any basis in our adult reality. In actuality, they are *reactions* to childhood incidents that we unconsciously hold on to. If you don't recognise, face and embrace your fears, they will engulf you, limit you and slowly squeeze the life out of you.

When I started this journey, someone told me I should embrace my fears. I thought it sounded like a cool idea, but I didn't have a clue how to do it. It has taken me years to understand, learn and practise embracing my fear. The first thing I had to grasp was that embracing my fear meant learning to see the love in it. I describe love as the energy of definition and balance (refer to Chapter 5). Using the energy of love in this way has helped me to define things clearly and see them, without judgement, in a more balanced perspective. Once we embrace (accept, encompass, take up willingly) our fears, they can begin to bring us wisdom instead of controlling our lives. The following process is designed to help you to do this. I've spent years designing this model and have hundreds of my clients who have used it to identify and free themselves of core fears.

EMBRACING YOUR FEAR

The following exercise will help you eliminate over-reactive behaviour caused by fears you've carried into your adult life from childhood experiences. As adults, we re-enact our childhood fears even though we dress them up in a variety of different ways. This very powerful exercise will help you to break down your fear and relieve the pressure that causes you to react, giving you more balanced choices. You may use this exercise repeatedly to embrace fears in your adult life and more importantly to identify and embrace the original source of your fears, which come from childhood. These are called *core fears*. To receive optimum value, it is important to allow your feelings to connect with your thoughts and memories during this exercise. When you respond to the various questions in this process, make sure you note when the instructions change from writing with your **non-dominant hand to your dominant hand.** You will receive more value from this process when you alternate hands.

• This process can also be done as a closed eye guided visualisation.

The guided version of this process, facilitated by Shirley Smith, is available on CD or Tape from The Radiant Group. Contact them at PO Box 1605, Neutral Bay, NSW, Australia 2089, Australia - Phone: +61 2 9953 7000, e-mail: info@TheRadiantGroup.com.au

What you will need:
Coloured felt pens or pencils.
A quiet, comfortable and safe place where you won't be interrupted. 163

Allow about an hour
- In this exercise I have given some examples, write your own responses to each question beneath my examples.

Step One

To begin this exercise it is important for you to relax. This will help you to connect with your feelings. You can use any technique you know of that helps you to relax, or you may close your eyes and inhale to the mental count to eight - then hold your breath as you count to eight - and exhale slowly as you count backwards from eight to one.

Think of a current fear in your life, one that relates to a specific situation which has emotional intensity, causing you to over-react. Then close your eyes and allow yourself to call up that fear in as much detail as possible. Once you have done this respond to the following questions writing with your *dominant hand.*

1. My Fear Is:

I am afraid of Mr Sanders, my boss.

In order to lessen the intensity of the fear, you may now want to see what lesson you can derive from your fear. It is usually something which gives you value in some way and has a positive intent.

2. What does this fear do for me? What does this fear protect me from?

It allows me to keep a defensive wall up so I can keep a distance from him, which helps me to stay in control.

The behaviour generated from my fear protects me from feeling rejected.

3. What payoffs am I receiving when I react in this fearful way?

It keeps me on my toes.

I feel an adrenalin rush which gives an element of excitement to my boring job.

I feel a sense of power by staying in control.

4. Does this reactive behaviour give me a false sense of power? If so, how?

Yes. Even though he was my superior, I knew at times I could control his behaviour, which made me feel superior to him.

Step Two

As you know most of our unhealthy fears are re-enactments of childhood incidents. In order to examine this fear more deeply, call upon the energy of your inner child and inner adolescent. It might help you to close your eyes and visualise these inner family members; to feel their essence or hear their voice. Ask them to take you back to your past and find a fear from your formative years, one that feels familiar to the adult fear you are examining today. Allow yourself to emotionally get in touch with your core fear.

Once you have a recollection of your childhood fear, ask yourself the following questions and respond, writing with your *non-dominant hand.*

1. When did this fear originally occur and what happened?

Four years old

Gordon from next door came over

Me playing tea party under big tree

Gordon picked me up and put me in branch high in tree

Wouldn't let me down

I cry

Gordon called me cry baby and laughed

I afraid and want my mum

2. What effect did this fear have on me as a child?

Afraid of men

Helpless

Can't let them see me cry

I play alone

I safe

3. What was it that I truly wanted when this incident occurred?

I wanted him to like me and be my friend

Take a deep breath and **change and write with your dominant hand.** Look upon this situation as an adult. Allow yourself to realise you may have been a victim of the situation when you were a child. Now ask yourself:

4. What effect has this fear had on me as an adult?

I've been single for nine years and would like to be in a committed relationship with a man, but I am afraid of being hurt.

I don't know how to have intimacy with others.

At times I've felt intense pain from loneliness.

5. Specifically, how am I different today than when this fear originally occurred?

I'm physically bigger and can often perceive if someone is going to harm me. As an adult, I can speak up for myself and not allow men to emotionally abuse me.

6. Do I still want to allow this fear to control me? Why?

No. I'm really sick and tired of feeling intimidated by men and I don't want to be alone any more.

7. What Steps can I take so I don't have to continue to react in this fearful way?

I can feel a sense of power by exercising positive self-control in my life. I will take a course in assertiveness training.

I can take classes in self defence so I can feel secure in protecting myself physically.

Step Three

Before proceeding with Step Three, it is helpful to share what you've written in Steps One and Two of this process with a counsellor, a non-shaming friend or perhaps a support person from a self help group. This will help you to connect with the reality of the situation in a more realistic way.

As you look back upon the original incident from your adult perspective, it is easy to acknowledge that you have more wisdom, resources and experience than when the fear originally occurred. Although you have a mental understanding and know what steps you can take to conquer this fear, when a situation arises that generates the fear, you may find you are still holding the emotional reaction you felt in childhood. At this point in life, the fear may be deeply embedded because you have had many re-enactments of the original fear. Therefore every time you are faced with it, the fear that you cannot conquer it comes to you. The next steps will help to change that.

CLOSED EYE GUIDED PROCESS

Take a deep breath - relax - and call upon your inner parent. Visualise yourself as the Discoverer. What resources are available today that you didn't have when this fear originally occurred? Step into your body and allow it to become *apparent to you*. Feel, see and hear your parent aspect. Recall some of the resources you listed when you were playing with your adult. (Examples: You may be more articulate, assertive, relaxed. What strengths, talents and abilities are available for you to utilise?) Respond to the following questions using your dominant hand.

1. List the resources you feel you can use today when dealing with this fear.

> My support group.
>
> My counsellor.
>
> I will find a committed listener and unload so I have the experience of being heard.
>
> I can say 'no' when I want to.

2. If faced with this fear again, how am I going to handle it?

> I can close my mouth and breathe, rather than react in a sarcastic way.
>
> The next time I am raging in my head, I will stop and check with myself to see if I am using this behaviour to cover a fear. 167

3. What specific actions am I going to take to free myself?

I will talk to people in my support group and get suggestions about appropriate behaviour.

I will use my 'committed listener' to discharge overwhelming emotions rather than react to them.

If I think my boss is being abusive towards me, I will ask him to re-state his last comment rather than use sarcasm or internal raging to cover up my fear.

Uncover the core fear or bottom line in each fear you explore. As you continue to find the core fears, you will be aware of them showing up in your adult life and be able to stop before you react. You won't do this perfectly, rather, two steps forward and one step back. If you persist, you will actively eliminate current adult fears and their attendant dramas.

Seeing the benefit, value and positive intent in your reactive fears will help you to pinpoint the core fears within you. As you continue to do this process, you will become aware that you have many core fears. This is a good sign! Only when you learn to embrace the core fears, will you be able to break free from reacting to your current fears. Embracing fear is an essential key to attaining balance in your life.

LET'S GET PHYSICAL

Of our four realities - intellectual, emotional, physical and spiritual - the physical is the most evident to us. Our bodies may be regarded as vehicles of expression for our thoughts, feelings and spirits. In this sense, the body is the outward manifestation of these inter-related aspects of us.

Our physical reality becomes distorted and imbalanced by addictive behaviour. Although we don't know it, we *need* our addictions to relieve stress and pain. However, instead of regarding our bodies as instruments to be relieved of stress and pain, we *can* look to them as instruments through which to feel and express energy, pleasure and optimum health.

In defining good health, a major shift has taken place in recent years. The old concept of good health was the absence of disease, whereas today's view increasingly is that good health is our natural birthright and is experienced as a state of well-being.

This modern view of good health is shifting the emphasis from curative medicine towards prevention of illness. In its wake, the holistic approach to healing and health continues to gain wide recognition and acknowledgement.

In the holistic approach, self-help factors such as nutrition, regular exercise and personal preventive health-care measures are all essential steps to take to avoid illness. To regain our physical equilibrium, we need to develop (but not to over-indulge in) daily priorities - such as slowing our pace of living, getting regular exercise, routinely eating healthy foods and getting plenty of rest. Without taking this approach to our physical self-care, we risk the onset of progressively deteriorating health. Usually this is signalled by minor problems such as skin complaints, headaches, allergies, intestinal problems and other minor aches and pains for which doctors can never find a reason. A colleague of mine who is a doctor used to say to me, "Shirley, about 80% of the patients have the aches and pains of life. There is nothing medically wrong with them". Today he spends most of his professional time counselling and facilitating therapy groups, helping his patients to heal their aches and pains and have a great quality of life.

In this holistic approach, it is also important for us to take an active part in establishing the cause of any ill health. As children, many of us were shamed for asking questions. Frequently we were expected to regard our authority figures as omnipotent. In our society, doctors rank high on the totem pole of authority figures because they deal with life and death issues and as a result many people feel they don't have a right to question, discuss or make suggestions to their doctor during a consultation. When it comes to our physical healing, it is paramount that we take responsibility for it, in partnership with our health practitioners. If you're currently receiving treatment from someone who is not open to this approach, I would suggest that you find another health practitioner.

There is also a growing body of scientific research which shows the relationship between an individual's psychological outlook, ability to cope with stress and the onset of cancer. Dr Carl Simonton, a physician specialising in the holistic treatment of cancer, believes there is also a 'cancer' personality. The most dominant characteristics are a very poor self-image, a tendency towards self-pity and holding resentment, a marked inability to forgive and little ability to build and sustain meaningful, long-term relationships. Note the marked similarity to the co-dependent personality.

Dr Simonton's work emphasises that chronic stress suppresses the immune system - the infrastructure which kills or holds off the cancerous cells present in the body. He states: "The problem is not the cancer cells, but the breakdown of the body's ability to deal with them and rid itself of disease".

The late, eminent Australian psychiatrist Dr Ainslie Meares strongly contended that the immune system determined whether cancer would develop or not and he also believed that the immune system could be influenced by mental and psychological processes.

It is commonly accepted that nervous, anxious, depressed and over-stressed people who are unable to handle the stresses and tensions in their lives, have increased pressure on their entire physical systems. This pressure can lead to heart attacks, strokes, cancer, AIDS and other ailments caused by a lowered immune system.

Dr Deepak Chopra, MD, a respected New England endocrinologist, makes a fascinating intellectual journey of discovery into the realms of the mind-body connection in his book *Quantum Healing*. Dr Chopra shows that the human body is controlled by a network of intelligence and that tapping into this potential produces what he calls quantum healing. He writes: "Quantum healing moves away from external, high-technology methods towards the deepest core of the mind-body system. This core is where healing begins... A minute fraction, far less than 1%, of all patients who contract an incurable disease manage to cure themselves. A larger fraction, but still under 5%, live much longer than average...These findings are not restricted to incurable diseases...

"Apparently the successful patients have learned to motivate their own healing, and the most successful have gone much further than that. They have found the secret of quantum healing. They are the geniuses of the mind-body connection. Modern science cannot even begin to duplicate their cures, because no cure that relies on drugs or surgery is so precisely timed, so beautifully coordinated, so benign and free of side-effects, so effortless as theirs."

Quantum Healing, Deepak Chopra, reprinted with permission by Bantam books, New York.

Many health professionals claim that if co-dependency is not treated, it will result in physical illness. I believe this to be true, but I don't see it as an indictment on the co-dependent. Rather, I view such knowledge as an opportunity to address the inherent source of illness and to attain good health and a longer life.

WHICH LIZARD ARE YOU?

Sometimes we feel physically out of balance or 'stuck' and usually this manifests in one of two ways - hyperactivity or physical apathy. I've heard many people share in my workshops that they know only two speeds - flat out like a lizard drinking or flat on their backs. Either of these states causes us stress and problems and takes the joy out of doing things we want to do.

When you feel stuck, 'the way to is the way through'. The key to move into a balanced state is through incorporating movement and beauty in your life. The next time you feel repressed, lethargic, reactive or hyperactive, START MOVING! It's important to find a type of movement that resonates with you and to surround yourself with beauty as you are moving. As the blocked energy is released through movement, you'll find yourself clear in mind, naturally creative and motivated in spirit. When this happens, your cravings and compulsive behaviour will begin to fall away from you.

MOVIN' AND CHOOSIN'

When you feel speedy or you're having a strong reaction to something or someone, do NOT try to absorb any more mental data. In other words, don't try to figure it out or ask someone for advice. Your brain will short circuit and you won't be able to take anything in. Alternatively, if you feel lethargic or sluggish and unable to get up and get off the couch, you don't have to succumb to escapism or 'analysis paralysis'.

Instead, it's time to get moving - whether you jog, jump on a trampoline, go for a walk, play tennis, beat a pillow, exercise or go for a swim. Your activity may take as little as 10 minutes or longer than an hour. Listen to your body! It has its own intelligence system and will let you know when you've had enough. This physical activity is not an end in itself, not a 'fix'. I am recommending only that you use your physical reality as a means to get you started on the path to balance.

It's not appropriate for you to use physical activity to distract yourself from dealing with the cause of your problems. Physical movement is a tool to get your blocked energy moving so that you can resolve your problems and increase your sense of freedom. Once you've started moving the blocked energy, realisations may come to you, which will allow you to make better choices. It may be that you need to embrace a fear, talk to an inner family member or deal with some carried shame.

Action diminishes fear. Sometimes your problems and concerns are much smaller than they've appeared through your distorted reality. Once you start moving, you often receive the clarity to realise that this is the case.

BEAUTY RESTORES BALANCE

We all have our own individual perceptions of what is beautiful and we are all capable of creating beauty about us, no matter what means we have at our disposal.

We can create beauty in our own rooms, homes, offices, and gardens. Beauty inspires us and lifts our spirits. It can be experienced on three levels - visual, auditory and kinaesthetic. Visual beauty is what you see. Some people's ideal of a beautiful scene is the forest, others prefer the beach or the bright city lights. Surround yourself with your preferred colours - on your walls, in your clothes or the even the car you drive. Auditory beauty is sound that you hear. For some, it may be listening to rock and roll, for others, it may be gentle classical music. Or you may like both types at different times. Some people find silence golden; others enjoy the buzz of the city. Kinaesthetic beauty encompasses what you're feeling, externally and internally. Styling your hair or dressing in colours and styles that you like, instead of following fashion's dictates, can give you a good feeling inside. Asking for a hug or taking a long, warm, luxurious bubble bath can make you feel beautiful.

As I write this section, two of my former clients who were in the same therapy group, come to mind. They were both hairdressers, working in the same salon. One day when the salon was totally booked out, they both arrived at work feeling upset. One had had a fight with her husband the night before and was hopping with anxious energy and the other was feeling apathetic and overwhelmed by life in general. They shared their feelings with one another and as they had half an hour before their first clients arrived, they decided to use movement and beauty to snap themselves out of it. They went into a private room, put their walkmans on and started moving to their favourite music. The lethargic one did graceful, Thai-Chi style movements to soft, flowing music; the anxious woman put on a disco tape and did some aerobic movements. Both of them felt the stuck energy 'pop', then they concluded with a few minutes of quiet reflection. They each reported that they went on to have a great, productive day.

As we refine our ability to tune into our bodies and our physical environment, they can become a great resource for us in our quest for balance.

RECOVERING YOUR SPIRITUALITY

Recovery from co-dependency or any other addiction is spiritually based. The Twelve Step programs, which have the highest success rate of treating addictions and compulsive, addictive behaviour, all have their foundation in spirituality.

I want to draw the distinction between spirituality and religion. Religion is a man-made concept with sets of rules usually based on the Bible or other religious text. Religion is imbued with rituals and ceremony. Sometimes the structure of ritual, ceremony and rules will assist us in having a spiritual experience, but it is not the only means by which we can experience our spirituality. Bill Wilson, one of the co-founders of Alcoholics Anonymous, had a profound spiritual experience in a hospital bed and never had to take another drink.

The foundation of true spirituality is humility. The confusion between humility and humiliation is a major reason why many people struggle with their spirituality. To have humility is to be free from false pride and arrogance. When we have humility, it relieves us of the 'better than/less than' syndrome which is at the heart of co-dependents' lack of self-esteem. The Alcoholics Anonymous book *Twelve Steps and Twelve Traditions* describes humility as "the avenue to true freedom of the human spirit" and "the nourishing ingredient which can give us serenity".

Our healthy shame is the psychological foundation of humility and is a natural human emotion. When we are utilising our healthy shame, we realise that we don't have to have all the answers and that sometimes we need help. Healthy shame gives us permission to be human and allows us to know that we can and will make mistakes. It occurs when we notice our fallibility and allow others to notice it, too. It is in the sharing of who we really are - whether that involves disclosing our healthy shame or showing our strengths and abilities - that we experience our spirituality and feel connected with all of life.

DISCOVERING YOUR HIGHER POWER

Having a degree in philosophy and training in theology, I have explored many spiritual avenues in my life. The Twelve Step programs' gift to addictive people and their families is the support to develop a practical relationship with a higher power. I find this approach to spirituality most freeing because it encourages the development of a relationship with a higher power of each individual's personal understanding. Among recovering people I've encountered a tremendous range of individuals' concepts of a higher power. These include God, Higher Self, Allah, Buddha, Jesus, Mohammed, God-self, Nature, Infinite Power of Love, Good Orderly Direction, Universal Intelligence, Great Spirit, and so on. There are many atheists and agnostics in recovery and they often choose their Twelve Step group as their higher power. It doesn't matter what your concept of a higher power is - but *for recovering addicts and co-dependents it is essential to believe that there is a power greater than you.*

There are several reasons why one's relationship with a higher power may be imbalanced. Some people have had religion forced on them by hypocrites who exhibited little of what God or Good stands for. For others, talking about God against the backdrop of their own guilt and shame makes them very uncomfortable. This is exacerbated by traditional God concepts which state that G-o-d is just, holy, righteous, superior, judgemental or wrathful. How many of us learned of a controlling God - a white-bearded man sitting in prime heavenly real estate watching our every move and keeping a check list on the 'good' and 'bad' things we were doing? Isn't this similar to another white-bearded, paternal figure - the one who 'knows when you've been bad or good so be good for goodness sake?'

Other higher powers we may have known include:

- The Sugar Daddy (give me what I want when I want it),

- The Fireman (necessary in case of all emergencies),

- The Party God (comes out for special occasions - Easter, Christmas...),

- The Sports Fan (found in locker rooms and on the winning team)
- The Gutter God (friend of the down-and-outers and the wallowers in self-pity).

We have known some of these Gods, worshipped at their altars and ultimately became disillusioned with them and found them inadequate to meet our deep, deep needs for healing and recovery.

If we have been living a rather meaningless and pointless existence, it seems a remote possibility that an abstract God would come in and fill up the gaps in our lives. If we have a fear of the future, this can so immobilise us that our minds will be closed to the possibility that anyone or anything could have a hand in controlling or directing our future.

In any case, most of us need to assess our feelings and take a realistic look at our histories, especially our formative years, with regard to God or the concept of a higher power. Dancing with an addiction or having untreated co-dependency cuts us off from the light of the spirit. The Big Book of AA says: *"we are like men who have lost our legs."* Without our spiritual reality available to us, we will be imbalanced and there will be no hope of attaining personal freedom.

FORMING A PARTNERSHIP WITH YOUR HIGHER POWER

In my search for spiritual balance I've learned that my relationship with my higher power has to be treated as a partnership. It's a universal truth that 'faith without works is dead'. I once heard a story that I think is a great metaphor for this concept. There once was a farmer who had a large field. He laboured long hours, ploughing, fertilising and watering the soil to produce a fine crop. One day one of his neighbours came by and remarked to the farmer how wonderful his field looked. The neighbour said: "Look how your crop has flourished. God certainly has been good to you."

"Yeah," the farmer replied dryly. "You should have seen my field when I left it to God by himself!"

The key to balancing your spirituality is learning how to find the balance within your partnership with your higher power. I feel this requires a lifetime of practical application and trial and error. We must learn to tread the fine line between doing our part (taking action and doing the footwork) and allowing the higher power to do its part (letting go and letting God). In other words, we need to learn to be co-creators with God.

Many people try too hard to connect with or form a partnership with their higher power. The key to making this connection is to set your intention and maintain a relaxed focus.

NATURAL CREATIVITY

It is in our spiritual reality that we find our imagination and creativity. Our imagination gives us the power to shape and form our ideas. The spirit within us brings life to our imagination which in turn activates our creativity. Think of a cartoon strip. The artist first imagines pictures of a character or setting. But it is through the artist's creativity that the cartoon comes alive for us. Creativity is imagination in action.

It is as natural for people to be truly creative on a regular basis as it is for the sun to shine. If as children we had been encouraged to have confidence in our own ideas and the ability to carry them out, our creativity today would be in full bloom.

Social programming dictates that only a few of us are truly creative and that the rest of us should find secure jobs and be glad to have them. This message has been absorbed by generations of people who then pass it on to their children, thereby retarding their children's creativity.

I have a theory that as we open up to and use our creativity, our addictions and compulsive behaviour will begin to fall away from us. I've noticed in my own history that each time an area of my creativity was repressed, shortly after that I took up an addiction. Addicts always seem to want *more, now!* For an addict, 'more' equals 'better'. Many recovering addicts willingly acknowledge this and view it as a character defect. I suggest there is a positive intent of this desire for 'more, now'.

In working intimately with people I have discovered that in their hearts, their desire is to expand, become all that they can be and make a contribution. In other words, they want to be *more* of their authentic selves in every moment - e.g. in the *now!* Instead of fulfilling our 'more, now' desire through compulsive addictive behaviour, we can instead choose to fulfil it through using our creativity. Using our creativity will also help to ease the pain we feel when we are in the withdrawal phase of any addiction.

THE DAYS OF WINE AND ROSES

To conclude this section, I would like to share with you a personal story. Some could view my story as an experience of humiliation and being abandoned by God. But for me it was a great lesson in humility. It developed my inner strength and a closer conscious contact with my higher power. It also gave me a clearer understanding of how my partnership with my higher power worked.

It was the early eighties and I had just resigned from my job as a sales manager with a wholesale wine distributor. I did this to fully concentrate on my studies and finish my last semester at school. The sales territory for which I'd been responsible was the most prestigious in the county and I had left my company and customers on good terms, with many of them wishing me well in my future career. A few months after I'd graduated from university, my higher power led me to a new path - of sobriety. In the first few months of my sobriety I found myself letting go of everything, including my new job. I went into treatment and then proceeded to follow a suggestion to go to 90 meetings in 90 days. I ran out of money and urgently needed a job to pay my bills. A friend of mine told me of a woman who wanted to hire 'flower girls' (the women who go from restaurant to restaurant selling single roses from a big basket). I went to see this woman and she hired me on the spot. She trained me for a couple of nights and then assigned me to my territory. Guess where it was? Yes, it was on my old wine sales stomping grounds. In fact, it was the ritziest street in the district!

As I pulled up outside the first restaurant (where only months before I'd designed their wine list), I sat in my car trembling and chain-smoking. My mind was in agony at the humiliating prospect of what I was about to do. I considered going home, but my rent was due. I stood at the turning point and asked for my higher power's protection and care, with complete abandonment. The answer came: *"If you're ever going to learn to love and accept yourself, Shirley, here is a grand opportunity to begin."* So I got out of the car with my basket of roses, pasted a smile on my trembling face and although my legs felt like jelly, I kept moving. As I opened the restaurant door, I spotted the good-looking owner standing across the room. At that point, I felt like my knees would buckle - but somehow they didn't. Once inside the door, I went from table to table and halfway through the owner, who knew me very well, came up to me. He smiled and said: "Hello Shirley. You look lovely this evening. It's nice to see you again." I was flabbergasted! I couldn't believe that he didn't remark on my new position. He'd acted as if I'd been selling roses there for years.

As the evening progressed, I was confronted with the same situation over and over again. Not one person I knew asked me why I was selling flowers. By the end of the evening, I felt I'd released more carried shame than I could have in months of therapy. This event and the way I handled it created a major shift for me in my life. I felt guided and protected by my higher power in a way that I'd never experienced before and my self-esteem took a huge leap!

P.S. I became the top-selling flower girl and always made enough money to pay my bills through this difficult period.

HANDLING YOUR REALITY IN A BALANCED WAY

Instead of trying to juggle all of the different aspects of your life, the way to balance your reality is to get a true sense of yourself intellectually, emotionally, physically and spiritually. Although these four aspects are inter-related, on your journey of self-discovery, you need to confront each one separately and directly.

When you confront your various realities indirectly, you create confusion and imbalance in your life. Let's say you have a desire for emotional security. If you confront this on the physical plane by doing something like buying a new car or house, this will not 'fix' your emotional insecurity. Instead, this will set you on a confusing path where *anything* physical will be perceived as either security or the lack of it. A more effective way to confront your reality is to confront it directly.

First ascertain in which reality your problem resides. In this case, it was the emotional reality. You would then ask yourself: 'What would give me the emotion of security?' and act on that. Perhaps you need to ask for emotional nurturing from your partner, rather than accept physical substitutes.

On the other hand, if you're being evicted from your flat (physical reality) and you've run out of money, don't try to handle the fear of it by asking an intimate friend for emotional support. Rather, you need to find another source of income and look for a new place to live.

In my experience, I've also found that people's imbalanced realities generally occur in two extreme forms. One extreme occurs when you know what your reality is but you won't acknowledge it to anyone else. Perhaps you've been isolating from others and you're feeling lonely; you would really like some attention and companionship, but you can't bring yourself to ask for this.

The second extreme is that you don't know what your reality is. You could experience this as confusion about what you think, feel, want to do or not do. (To gain clarity about this, take the 'shoulds', 'ought to's' and 'have to's' out of the matter.) In order to restore balance to your reality, you must recognise which of these states you're in. Then, you have to go about taking the appropriate actions to restore your reality to balance.

If you know what your reality is, then you need to push yourself to express it to the relevant people - but only when it is your best interests to do so. For example, you may think that your boss has terrible taste in clothes. But it may not be prudent to express this, especially if he or she didn't seek your opinion on this matter.

If you don't know what your reality is, then take a guess at it or make it up. If you guess incorrectly, your body may give you a signal perhaps an adrenalin rush or a palpitating heart. On a deep, unconscious level, we all innately know what our reality is. Another thing you may have to do is to obtain help from a teacher or counsellor that will prompt you to know how to identify, embrace and express your reality.

The only way you're going to learn what your reality is, is to practise taking action. If you discover belatedly that your reality is not what you originally thought it was, then all you have to do is go back and correct it with the appropriate person. This is how you learn to own your reality. Let's say a wife tells her husband that she's feeling angry with him and wants to take a holiday alone. The next day she discovers that actually she is very sad and hurting over their lack of intimacy, especially since they've been married for 10 years. Her perceived anger and desire to distance herself from her husband is really a defence to cover up her sadness and fear of rejection. What she really wants is to be closer to her husband. So in order for her to claim and express her own reality, she tells her husband that she was confused and made a mistake. She then explains what she's really feeling and what she wants.

On the other hand, if you know what your reality is and you refuse to verbalise it, then you will have to discipline yourself to do this. If someone gives you a compliment and in your heart you know it to be true, don't dispute it, say 'thank you'.

As you begin to balance your reality, it is normal for it to feel uncomfortable or that you're doing the wrong thing. Because of this, many people revert to their old dysfunctional behaviour patterns - being steeped in 'confusion' or refusing to communicate their reality. This is why it is imperative for you to have a non-shaming support group and/or a teacher who will validate your feelings and perhaps give suggestions for balanced thinking and behaviour.

DON'T MEDICATE - MEDITATE

I feel that one of the best ways to get in touch with your own internal information system and attain balance is through meditation. I've known many people who started meditating, only to give it up after a short time. Why? Because once they stop medicating themselves (with sex, exercise, drugs, food, busyness, etc), they have to face the 'mud in the bottom of their bucket'. I've found that meditation comes more easily and its rewards are much greater for people after they've begun the process of emptying their buckets.

Meditation quiets the chatter of the mind, enhances your ability to focus, promotes clarity of thought, calms the overwhelming emotions and, by taking you within, puts you in touch with your true feelings. Meditation also releases physical stress, relaxes the entire physical system and improves resistance to stress and disease. Meditation slows you down so that you are able to hear the voice of your higher power. Prayer is about proclaiming, affirming and asking. Meditation is about listening. It is in 'the silence' that we experience the deepest sense of self.

There are many methods of meditation and much information available about these through books, tapes and personal instruction. The important thing is to find the method which best suits you and practise it regularly.

When it comes to liberating your true self, balancing your reality is an essential key - one which will open the door to personal freedom.

CHAPTER 8

DON'T QUIT...
SURRENDER

In our culture, there is a huge misconception about what it takes to quit an addiction. People with addictions are generally considered to be weak, immoral and lacking willpower. The prevailing consensus is that if only these people would harness their willpower and quit using and abusing whatever they're addicted to, then everything would be fine and all their problems would be solved. Although an addictive person may have willpower in some areas of his or her life, they have a disabled will (lack of willpower) when it comes to their particular addiction.

The addicted person may attempt quitting many times to prove they are not addicted. These periods are usually temporary or they may use another substance to replace what was given up. For example, a person quits using alcohol only to begin or increase using marijuana; or someone quits smoking only to begin overeating. We all know the myth that ex-smokers suddenly have their taste buds 'restored' and food tastes so wonderful to them, how could they help but gain 10 kilos!

I have also seen many who have had a drug problem (especially with recreational drugs) quit taking drugs altogether, only to continue drinking alcohol. Alcohol is also a drug, albeit a legal drug, and for the chemically dependent person, continued alcohol consumption allows their chemical dependency to progress.

Another addictive type may quit an addictive relationship only to start using food to 'stuff' the feelings of loneliness and provide a sense of nurturing. Then there are those who gravitate to spiritual and holistic movements and quit their drugs, alcohol, cigarettes, caffeine, sugar and red meat, only to switch addictions becoming seminar junkies, health fanatics, overweight, or enmeshed in co-addicted relationships. In these movements, I've often heard it said: 'Get involved in a project bigger than you are and the problems in your life will clear up in the process'. Could it be that the real attraction of such projects lies in the fact that they enable people to switch the focus off themselves and onto something else?

When an addict quits one addiction, they usually find something else with which to compulsively replace it. The bottom line is: you cannot *quit* addictions, but the associated obsession can be removed by a power greater than yourself, through the act of surrender. It is through this type of spiritual (not religious) experience that hundreds of thousands of people have been set free from the shackles of addiction.

THE TROUBLE WITH SURRENDERING

Unfortunately, surrender has a bad name around town. It is often perceived as defeat. The dictionary defines surrender as 'to give up or to give way to pressure'. On many occasions in our past, our experiences of surrender have been negative. As children, we may have felt that we surrendered our identity and freedom of expression to our caregivers and other authority figures. As adults, perhaps we've surrendered our creativity to our employers. In marriage, we may have surrendered attending to our needs in order to meet those of our spouse. In this context, we experienced or saw surrender ('letting go') as a loss or something we had to give up.

People have a lot of trouble surrendering in their lives because surrender is often confused with submission. The two are definitely not the same. When we surrender, we no longer fight life, but accept it. Surrender is only accomplished when we do it on both the unconscious *and* conscious levels. As surrender takes place on the conscious level, it is similar to making an admission; as surrender occurs on the unconscious level, the unconscious forces of defiance and grandiosity stop functioning and there is an internal 'letting go'.

Submission occurs when we accept life *only* on the unconscious level. With submission, we experience a superficial yielding, but tensions continue. With true surrender, there is a sense of unity and a cessation of inner conflict and struggle.

Our ability to surrender can also be blocked by the state of compliance. To comply is to act in accordance with another's command, request, rule or wish; to be courteous or obedient; to acquiesce. Compliance often masquerades as surrender. In compliance, we are willing to go along with someone or something, but our consent is grudging and not wholehearted. It does not take much to overthrow this kind of willingness.

Betty, a former client, experienced many gifts from learning the process of surrender.

BETTY'S STORY
A CLIENT'S PERSONAL VOYAGE

In 1988, my life was travelling downhill fast with a 20 year marriage that was going nowhere! My husband, a subcontractor, had worked away from home for much of our marriage and I'd been left to raise our three sons, mostly on my own. Then a restructure forced him to come home and, at last, I'd seen his 'just a few beers to unwind' become an unbearable daily grind. Around lunchtime he'd head off to the local pub and wouldn't return until 7 at night, where upon he would eat his meals in a drunken stupor and then fall asleep.

I was sure we had a drinking problem in our home. Yet, when I'd approached my father, a health professional, I was assured that 'when (I) got it right, my husband wouldn't need to drink'. And, you know what? I'd believed him. Although I didn't know it at the time, I had a problem more deceptive than my husband's alcoholism. I had a higher power problem, my father.

When I'd married my husband I knew my father didn't approve. It was probably the first time in my life that I'd really disappointed Dad. But I loved my husband and thought that eventually dad would come around. What happened instead was I became a chronic migraine sufferer. Lasting for three days at a time and sometimes occurring twice a week, the migraines soon had me relying on Pethidine injections and painkillers. Honestly, I don't know how I didn't become addicted, but I didn't. Nevertheless, with three boys under 4, a full time job managing my father's hospital and an absent husband, my life had become incredibly difficult.

*I knew I needed help. I just didn't know where to find it.
I certainly wasn't prepared to speak with any of the professionals
who frequented my father's psychiatric hospital. So, in January
1989, I walked through the doors of my first Al-Anon meeting.
This would be the second time that I would disappoint my father.
An advocate for controlled drinking, he viewed the Twelve Step
program of Alcoholics Anonymous and Al-Anon with contempt.
And, now his eldest daughter was actively seeking them out.*

*I hoped the program would stop my husband from drinking.
In fact, it did. Within three years I had a sober husband. Working
the Al-Anon program gave me enough insight into the family
disease of alcoholism to know that something was very wrong
with me. Now aware of my lack of life memories I, again, knew
I needed help. And, again, I didn't know where to turn. I hadn't
learnt to surrender yet, I had, however, learned to listen to
someone other than my father.*

*An Al-Anon member now told me about Shirley Smith's
work. Although it was a very long drive from where I lived to
get where the programs were being held, I made the decision to
go. Besides, I was sure no one would know me in that part
of town. I attended 'Inner Child' workshops and discovered a
hyper-vigilant, terrified child inside of me. I attended a program
called 'Healing the Wounds of Adolescence' and learned how
much self hate I'd stored, which contributed to low self-esteem.*

*When I started attending regular 'Family of Origin' groups,
I came face to face with an anger I denied and a tendency to
'leave' my body whenever I was afraid, which was much of the
time. My lack of memories and susceptibility to falling into holes
now made sense. With Shirley's encouragement I also attended
Neuro Linguistic Programming workshops and learned to
appreciate my kinaesthetic learning style.*

*By 1995, I was now ready to take up the education I had
forsaken in 1960 when, with a teacher's college scholarship,
I thought the world lay before me. Dad, however, had wanted me
to become his Secretary, so I gave up the scholarship and went to
Technical College to learn shorthand and typing. Now 35 years
later I was ready to try again. Accepted into a Bachelor of Social
Studies Degree I graduated in March 1999, with majors in*

Psychology and Anthropology. Dad responded to my success by saying "We should have done this years ago." In May 1999, he died.

A terrifying rage now filled me. Twelve years earlier Dad had encouraged me to form a friendship with one of his nurses. In doing so, I had recognised that her new son bore a remarkable resemblance to my own sons. When I'd confronted my father, who remained married to my mother until the day he died, he denied everything. Then three months before his death, he'd finally confessed, not because he wanted to clear the air or make amends, but because he wanted me to take charge of the boy and remove him from his alcoholic mother and heroin addicted brothers.

Thankfully, I had healed enough to accept the situation and say 'no'. I also realised that, although I wasn't living with active alcoholism, I needed to return to Al-Anon. Here I began to work the programme one more time. Only now, because of the work I had done over the years I'd spent with Shirley, the program made so much more sense. Finally I could put the three A's to work. Now Aware, it was time to Accept and put into Action the skills and tools I'd learned along the way.

Surrender has not been easy for me. For over fifty years my higher power had been my father and a lot of hard work had been necessary for me to acknowledge that firstly, I couldn't trust him and finally, that he was an untreated adult child from an alcoholic family. His control issues were enormous and so were mine. A new higher power had to be found.

Today, trust occurs on a daily basis, even if I don't always get things right. My newfound faith has come from regularly practicing gratitude and accepting that whatever happens to me today, happens for a reason and happens for my good.

As I practice surrender I've noticed how my world opens up. In accepting an Honours year at University, I not only received first class honours, but also an offer to study for a PhD. At the age of fifty-eight, the prospect was overwhelming. I needed a sign. So, I turned to my new higher power stating that I would know I was meant to accept the offer, if I was awarded a scholarship. I received one.

Now I'm not only studying for a PhD, but I'm also tutoring. Only last week two mature age students thanked me and told 185 *me they considered me a role model. If I could do it, they said, then they were sure that they could do it too. I still struggle at times to see the glass half full, rather than half empty. I don't, however, suffer from migraines and, I rarely fall into holes!*

The anxiety that I used to live with as a constant companion is a distant memory. With the faith I have developed in a spiritual power greater than myself, I feel very willing to accept what ever comes my way. For me that means my life is no longer difficult, in fact it's very different. I could even go so far as to say, 'my life is blessed'.

Another reason we have trouble getting a handle on surrender is that it contains contradictory elements. It can be perceived as:

1. easy and difficult

2. safe and risky

3. highly comforting and fear-producing.

When we perceive surrender as losing something, we neglect to notice what we gain out of it. In doing this we experience surrender fearfully or negatively. This is when it becomes difficult, risky and fear-producing.

It *is* possible to perceive surrender in another way, however. American psychotherapist Ann D. Clark suggests that surrender can be viewed as a means of exchange. She asks us to consider, for example, that we surrender the registration papers of our old car when we trade it in for a new one; that banks surrender cash when we give them a cheque; and a defeated army surrenders in exchange for certain promises of protection and territory.

THE CYCLE OF CONTROL AND RELEASE

A powerful dynamic that keeps us trapped in our compulsive, addictive behaviour is what Fossum and Mason call the 'control/release cycle'. When this first came to my attention, it gave me a clear understanding of why people have so much trouble with surrendering. This cycle commonly displaces surrender, keeps one in denial about one's addictions and occludes any awareness that one may even have a need to surrender.

Control and release are about holding on and letting go. Between control and release there exists a tension which is capable of creating a mood-altering experience. In adulthood, there are many ways in which it is appropriate to control and let go. I experience this in my public speaking. In preparing a speech, I construct a detailed outline and list my thoughts in logical sequence. Once I've gone over the outline several times, I feel so familiar with the material (in control) that I relax during the delivery of the speech and enjoy the high from my natural creativity and spontaneity as I speak extemporaneously (release). This is a healthy example of control/release, devoid of shame.

When shame is present in the control/release cycle, it intensifies the whole dynamic. Because shame necessitates a cover-up, it activates intense, controlling behaviour. A person will try to control themselves and the responses of others. The more intensely they control, the more they feel the need for the balance of release. I've seen this cycle in action when people oscillate between binge eating and fasting, spending out of control and penny pinching, overworking and then being 'out to lunch' for weeks.

When we're in the control phase, we are compulsive, attempting to get control over our lives or some part of it and are often labelled 'hard to live with'. Our behaviour at this time can take various forms such as perfectionism, dieting, cleaning, being overly critical, people pleasing, super-achieving, self-righteousness and self-improvement campaigns. When we're in the release phase, we are seeking freedom from oppressive rules and the tension of control. In letting go of control, we are seeking relaxation and escape from our conscious will. One of the drawbacks to letting go in this way is that we often simultaneously experience the terror of the loss of control. No matter what form the release behaviour takes - sex, drinking, gambling, eating, spending, abusing others, raging, self-centeredness, dropping out, obsessing about others - it is followed by feelings of guilt, remorse and shame.

Fossum and Mason, in their book '*Facing Shame*' state: 'The more the individual attempts to control, the more demanding is the need for release. The more one escapes into the release phase, the more uncontrolled one will feel and thus the more one will attempt to compensate with more control.'

And so the cycle goes on and on... until we create such harmful consequences or feel such pain in our lives that we 'bottom out'. Hitting bottom means reaching a feeling of personal helplessness. It is at this point that surrender may seem desirable, but because of reasons previously mentioned, it is not always affected. Hitting bottom serves no good purpose if it is not followed by surrender. This is the point at which people are ready to commence Step 1 in a Twelve Step program.

THE BENEFITS OF SURRENDER

Surrender is a bridge to acceptance and acceptance is one of the major benefits of surrender. Acceptance is the key to serenity and peace of mind.

The dictionary defines acceptance as 'a willingness to receive something that's offered or 'taking what's given'. When someone is in a state of acceptance, they stop resisting, are receptive, able to absorb things and to cooperate.

Pinpointing *reasons* for specific, compulsive behaviour is one of the pitfalls to attaining true acceptance. Acceptance is a step beyond recognising and analysing your reasons. The experience of complete acceptance comes when we surrender and admit our powerlessness over something that is controlling us, and ask for help from our Higher Power.

Through the act of surrender a heightened, conscious contact with our Higher Power is realised. As a result of surrender, a new honesty and awareness surface automatically and spontaneously. It's as if someone had taken off our blinkers. We feel relief from stress; we sometimes receive answers on what actions to take and frequently problems clear up without our taking any action at all.

Surrender represents a deep unconscious shift in attitude and behaviour and as such is a vital key to freedom. Shelagh's story is one of someone who found many insights and true freedom through the process of surrender.

SHELAGH'S STORY
A CLIENT'S PERSONAL VOYAGE

Have you ever felt hit by a lightening bolt? That describes exactly how I felt when at 28 years old, I recognised the truth about my mother. My treasured middle-class upbringing was turned on its ear by the realisation that I had been raised in an alcoholic home. I remember that day as clearly as if it was yesterday. I was attending my first counselling session with Shirley Smith. Life for me had become a roller coaster of such super highs and extreme lows, that I had begun to fantasise about 'ending it all'. After taking some background information from me, Shirley gently explained what being a chemical dependent and an alcoholic meant. 'Alcoholism is a family disease' she said, and described some of the destructive ramifications it can have upon a family. I remember my relief to finally know there was a reason why I felt so 'messed up'.

As the light bulb went on, I began to recall how my mother lived on prescription medications and of course, had to have her sherry every night. Some nights it was a lot of sherry. It always began in such a civilised manner, but as the evening wore on she became very critical and even downright nasty towards us. I also remembered that at times of stress, such as when I was going to have to take a test at school, my mother would suggest I take one of her valium to calm myself down. Is it any wonder that when my sisters became stressed out with one of mum's incessant ravings, that I gave them valium and a little glass of sherry to drown her out. As I am writing this now, it seems amazing to me that before going to see Shirley, it hadn't entered my mind that my mother was an alcoholic and a chemical dependent.

As a grown woman, I was a successful businesswoman married to a man I loved, with two gorgeous young sons; yet I felt desperately angry and confused. In spite of my 'picture perfect' life, I was falling apart and drowning in a wretched sea of 'emptiness'. By day I was achieving amazing results in business - negotiating large corporate contracts. Yet in the quiet of the evening, nagging doubts would plague me. As a calming ritual I would pour myself a glass of wine, and then another and another. Imagine my horror when I discovered that not only had I been raised in an alcoholic home, but that I was one as well. The disease that had destroyed my mother's life and impacted so harshly on our family had its greedy grip on me too!

Initially there was a sense of relief to identify my problem. Then, I immediately felt the sting of shame and disbelief. How could I feel relieved and yet so bad at the same time? I struggled with the impact of this realisation for some time - going on and off to Alcoholics Anonymous meetings. I tried changing my type of drink and I tried controlled drinking. One minute I knew in my heart that I was an alcoholic and the next minute I didn't. This soul-destroying torture went on for a few more years. 189

It took one last terrible binge, a near catastrophe before I finally woke up and realised without a shadow of a doubt that something dramatic had to give! At the time, I was managing my drinking and had been relatively sober for some months. I was feeling great! Finally I had this thing 'beat'! It began with a simple dinner in the company of friends.

Knowing that I wouldn't be drinking, I had planned to drive. When I arrived at the function a 'complimentary' glass of champagne was placed in my hands and I remember thinking, "What can I do? After all I don't want to create a big deal. It's only one!" The next thing I knew I was throwing down vodka shots as fast as they were put in front of me. As the saying goes in AA, 'One drink is too many and one is never enough'. I consumed several before it was time to move on to the nightclub. But of course, I was sober and ok to drive. By this stage I had become quite the 'party girl'- loud and obnoxious. "What the hell do you think you're doing?" I shouted at my friends as a struggle broke out over the keys. I knew what I was capable of and no one was going to spoil my fun - everyone else was just boring!

Have you ever heard the expression, 'somebody up there must be looking after you?' Well, I've lost count of the times that I know someone 'up above' has been looking after me. With all the crazy things I've done whilst drunk, I should have been dead many times over. Thankfully, I was protected again on this night and someone wrestled my keys from me.

At the nightclub I 'rocked'! My friends were tossed by now, I was everyone's girl. I couldn't get enough - I danced, I drank, I partied - yet I distinctly remember feeling nothing was enough, I wanted more! I wasn't happy enough, I wasn't high enough - I needed to get higher. So when the cocaine came around, I insatiably accepted... and that was the last thing I remembered. What happened after that is too horrible to publicly put in print.

When I finally crawled back into AA, I felt for the first time in my life, what true humility was. Although I came close to destroying my life, I felt relieved to know, at last, that I was powerless over my drinking. It was beyond me to save my soul from destruction and I finally made a commitment to follow the AA program - I somehow knew my life depended on it. As scared as I was, I was willing. I remembered Shirley saying, 'take a deep breath and fear forward'. I surrendered my broken life over to God and the program of AA, I allowed my life to heal.

By far the concept of surrender was the most frightening thought of all. This meant I had to admit that I'd failed and then feel the humiliation of that. To make matters worse; I was being asked to hand my life over to God! I remembered a childhood God who heard my crying in the night - and did nothing. A God whom I begged to save me from my hell - and did nothing. A God who they said loved me, yet, while I was being abused - did nothing. Why should I surrender and trust God now?

I was seriously angry with God and I let him know it. I let him have my rage; my years of pain and hurt. Everything I could think of I hurled at him. As I went through this cathartic healing process, I realised I was burying my ' punishing and neglecting' God from my religious upbringing in childhood. I began to feel hope. When I was finally done and had nothing left, I felt empty. Boy, did I want to fill up that dry well, until I remembered a promise I made to myself never to go back. So, I just took another step. And step by step, a day at a time, my life began to change.

I returned to the healing work that I had begun with Shirley. I participated in her intensive workshops, education programs and therapy groups. This time, along with the relief I gained from insight, I followed through with action. At last, I was ready to take personal responsibility for my life; realising that I was the only one who could clean it up.

I realised that I had been drowning out many 'bad' feelings I'd suppressed since childhood. I also learned to weed out negative beliefs like, 'if anything went wrong - I was somehow to blame; that I was the mistake'. I learnt to identify what was a mistake, and distinguish this separately from me, and untangle the jumbled black mess inside.

In a relatively short time I could see changes occurring: I no longer felt desperate and depressed all the time and I no longer suffered from extreme highs and extreme lows in my emotions. I began to feel more centred and more balanced in my life. Once I was able to let out the depth of my aching emptiness, then, slowly, I was able to express myself authentically. Gradually

I shared my childhood story and I felt heard for the first time in my life without manipulation; without ridicule or without being made to feel stupid or wrong. In sharing the blackness, lightness came into my soul.

Today as I write this, ten years have passed and I have been sober for three years. I am not drugged by anything, especially not doped by a resentment of the past, nor a fear of the future. There is a peace within my heart that I had never known before. Though my marriage has endured some very hard times, my husband and I are still together and committed to healing the pain from the past. I can now totally enjoy the love of my two beautiful boys and actually feel bliss. This feeling is a little new to me and I never want to lose this ability to reach such a natural, yet peaceful high.

Just the other day I actually found myself asking for help to manage the 'bliss' I was experiencing. I think the best thing that has happened to me, as funny as this may sound - is that I've gained the gift of gratitude. Today I am actually grateful for all the pain, misery and grief I experienced during my dark years. Because of it, and not in spite of it, I have come on this incredible journey to know me. I now have the most precious thing of all -the deepest knowing within my soul that I am 'all right', just the way I am.

HOW I FOUND THE TWELVE STEP PROGRAM

I was first introduced to a Twelve Step program when I was 19 years old and married with a baby daughter. I was also a flaming co-dependent, running on adrenalin. My husband and I became friendly with our neighbours, Joe and Sarah. One morning Sarah and I were having coffee and I was complaining about feeling depressed and some problems my husband and I were having. Sarah responded by asking me: 'If there was an earthquake and you lost your husband, your daughter, your mother, your father, your sister, your little dog and all your worldly goods, what would you have left?'

I thought for a moment and then replied: 'Nothing'.

'Wrong!' she said. 'You'd have yourself'.

I frowned and thought: 'Well that's nothing'.

So you can see where I was at, at 19. Sarah began to share with me all kinds of ideas and words of wisdom, which I absorbed like a thirsty sponge. When I asked her where she'd learned all these things, she told me that she and her husband were recovering drug addicts and alcoholics who were members of AA and NA (Alcoholics Anonymous and Narcotics Anonymous).

Sarah said that she and Joe became members of the programs due to their alcoholism and drug addiction, but that Twelve Step programs really could benefit everyone. Because their meetings were open, anyone was welcome to attend, so she invited me and my husband to come one night.

(At that time, co-dependency and adult children of alcoholics had not even been clinically identified and there were no Twelve Step programs for them).

Being an arch co-dependent and master at controlling and manipulating people, the next thing I knew, I had my husband sitting with me at an AA meeting. Although I did not drink or take any drugs, I found that I related to all the people there. While I didn't identify with their drinking and drugging stories, I certainly did relate to their emotional dysfunction. This confused me - in one way, I felt I belonged and yet in another way, I felt I didn't. Regardless of that, I definitely felt calmer and happier when I attended meetings and various program functions. The recovery process was rubbing off on me.

I can see now that this early experience with the Twelve Steps was a gift from my Higher Power. Several years later when my second husband and I went to the treatment centre, I had a positive attitude to alcoholism and recovery. Because of my early intervention in the program I didn't encounter the major stumbling block that afflicts so many newcomers to the program - that is, feeling shame about our situation. I already understood alcoholism to be a disease and I was grateful there was help available.

We are fortunate today to have so much recovery information and a variety of Twelve Step programs geared to assist people with problems in specific areas of their lives. Nearly everyone can find a program in which they feel a sense of belonging.

WHAT IS THE TWELVE STEP PROGRAM

The Twelve Step Program provides a path of recovery that is spiritually based, but non-religious. Working the steps of the program and practising the principles in all our affairs is a way of life that can relieve us from suffering, fill up the emptiness we feel inside and help us to discover ourselves and the God within.

The programs are not heavily structured with 'musts' or rules, but they are governed by Twelve Traditions that are a roadmap of guidance for the groups. The Steps are designed to help keep people balanced; the Traditions are designed to keep the program balanced. Each individual follows the program and works the steps at her or his own pace. Honesty, open-mindedness and willingness are the characteristics we need to approach the program and work the steps in a balanced way. We don't take advice or orders from others, yet it is important to listen to other members who have already worked the steps for insights and suggestions on how we might apply them to our own lives.

For newcomers it is especially important to remember that people who attend Twelve Step meetings do not always have all the answers and are seeking to heal their own lives. Hence newcomers should take note of the tradition that states 'principles before personalities'. If a person at a meeting approaches you with firm instructions on how you should handle your life, my advice would be to thank them, disengage and don't allow them to lay their trip on you. Some people are so sick in their compulsive caretaking and self-righteousness and their unconscious need to be needed is so strong, they are out of control and inappropriate with their advice.

There are no membership dues or fees in a Twelve Step Program, you don't have to join any membership rosters, take any oaths or make any pledges. The only requirement for membership is a desire to stop the compulsive behaviour or addiction that you may be experiencing. The program is open to all persons regardless of race, religion, age, gender, colour or social class.

Meetings are not like group therapy sessions, nor are they like social or administrative meetings with minutes and agendas. Members share their own experience, strength and hope by identifying what it was like, what happened and what it's like now. There are different styles of meetings. Some are step study meetings; others pick a topic for the evening; and others are identification meetings (identifying specific symptoms and behaviours of their particular disease - eg alcoholism, drug dependency, eating disorders, sex addiction, etc). The thing these three styles of meetings have in common is that during them members share their personal experiences and insights. The only exception to this occurs in speaker meetings, when there is one main speaker for the evening.

Meetings are held morning, noon and evening on a daily basis in large cities and less frequently in country areas. If there is no meeting in your area at a convenient time, it is not too difficult for you to start one, although some perseverance may be needed. You can write to the Central Service Office of a particular Twelve Step group and ask for information and/or a 'starter packet' to start a meeting. You are not required to attend any specific number of meetings at any specific time, although most committed members attended regularly, three times a week or more.

During meetings, members feel a lot of support, concern and caring as each relays his or her own story. Members are also encouraged to be as honest as they can about themselves and their situations. In doing this, shame is diminished and a spiritual connection is established. However, there is never any outside pressure to reveal more of yourself than you are ready and willing to at that point.

It is suggested that people find a sponsor to help them to work the steps.

In choosing a sponsor, the first thing to do is to ask your Higher Power for guidance. Then look for someone with whom you identify and who embodies qualities you're striving for. It is best to select someone of the same gender who has already worked all of the Twelve Steps. A sponsor is someone from whom you'd be willing to take directions and suggestions and someone who you'd be prepared to trust. However, it's inappropriate for a sponsor to tell you how to run your life. They share with you how to work the steps, which is different. The whole idea behind sponsorship is: 'in order to keep our recovery, we have to give it away'.

A sponsor who understands this principle knows that when they sponsor someone they are not caretaking, rather they are teaching what they themselves need to learn. A good sponsor will often derive more out of the sponsorship process than the person they are sponsoring. If the relationship with your sponsor does not work or if it becomes abusive, it is appropriate for you to 'fire' your sponsor and select another one. A caveat to this is - your issues with authority figures may arise or perhaps your self-will runs riot. In these instances you need to learn how to surrender and be willing to learn how to do things somebody else's way.

The relationships I've had with my sponsors over the years have been one of the most treasured gifts in my recovery. These relationships have helped me to learn to love and accept myself more than any other avenue I've tried. I've heard many men share that the first time they ever felt intimacy with and love for another man was with their sponsors. In Australia, I've noticed that the practice of sponsorship is not as widely adopted as it seems to be in the USA and I've speculated about whether Australians' issues with authority figures is at the heart of this. If this is the case for you, I would like to encourage you to try sponsorship (being sponsored or being a sponsor) so that you may enjoy the exceptional benefits of this process.

The Twelve Step program is the only type of organisation I've encountered which is truly egalitarian. I believe that the Twelve Step program is a great model for world peace. In order to have global peace and cooperation, we must first achieve peace within and working the steps will give us this. As I've attended meetings in other countries, I've found acceptance and an affinity and spiritual connection with people from all walks of life.

THE TWELVE STEPS TO FREEDOM

Many good books have been written instructing people how to work the Twelve Steps, so I don't intend to give lengthy explanations and instructions on them. (Check the bibliography and my website at www.theradiantgroup.com.au for several recommended books about the steps). My intention is to give a generic definition, a personal interpretation and a general understanding of the Twelve Steps because for many people this book may be their first introduction to them.

STEP ONE
'We admitted we were powerless over _____
- that our lives had become unmanageable.'

(Fill in the blank space with the addiction or compulsive behaviour that you are trapped in).

Step One is the foundation for all of the Twelve Steps. In step one, we surrender by admitting that our best thinking and resources got us where we're at right now. Step One is the step about honesty. When we honestly admit and claim our addictions, we drop the masks of our false self. In taking the first step, we are willing to let go of control and stop trying to fix and manage everything and everyone, including ourselves. Instead, we learn to observe our behaviour without judgement and to note the impact it is having in our lives. It's with honesty that we see our unmanageability and how, as we've tried to manage our lives alone, they have become chaotic. When we are experiencing our powerlessness, we have *lost* control. When we are experiencing the unmanageability of our life, it's because we're trying to be *in* control. Step One is the admission that we need help.

The first time we take the first step, we effectively end one phase of our life (in which we relied on our ego and self will to direct it) and begin the phase in which we gradually learn to rely on our Higher Power. Step One brings us toward the humility we need to be open to the spiritual guidance that will open new doors in our lives. To be relieved of our problems, we must first admit that we cannot cope with them alone.

It is imperative that we take the first step seriously and concede our powerlessness and unmanageability to our innermost selves.

STEP TWO

'Came to believe that a power greater than ourselves could restore us to sanity'.

Some people encounter two major blocks to Step Two - the belief in a Higher Power and the admission of insanity. A definition of insanity is: 'doing the same thing over and over and expecting a different result'. Keeping this definition in mind, I don't think there is a person alive who isn't a little insane. Do you? It is also insane behaviour when we act compulsively or obsessively and attempt to control anyone or anything.

Concerning a relationship with a Higher Power, the Step says: *'Came to believe'*. This is about strengthening and renewing our faith. I once heard a woman share something in a meeting that I feel is a good analogy for this. She said: 'First I 'came' to the program. After participating for some time in the program, I emerged from the fog of denial and 'came to'. And as I practised the principles of the program in all my affairs, 'I came to believe'.

Step Two is the 'faith' step. We begin to cultivate our faith, we find we come to believe.

STEP THREE

'Made a decision to turn our will and our lives over to the care of God as we understood Him'.

Having gained awareness from working the first two steps, we are now ready to take affirmative action. Step Three is the step of decision and an act of faith. It represents an opportunity for a new level of surrender, to expand our trust, to let go of more control and to establish a partnership with our Higher Power. Because the third step is about 'making a decision', the key to it lies in our *willingness* to turn our lives over. For so many of us, our self-will has been managing our lives (and the lives of others where we could). This has led us right to where we are now. And most of us are not experiencing life as happy, joyous and free.

Step Three is especially challenging for those who grew up in an alcoholic, violent or other addictive environment. Those who did, probably have issues with trusting authority figures (and let's face it, GOD is the supreme authority), as well as anger towards the God of your childhood for not saving you and stopping the misery and violence.

If we've successfully worked steps one and two, then we're ready for a new manager in our lives, and we're ready to take the third step. The third step contains a prayer (written in the Big Book of Alcoholics Anonymous), which is a powerful way to focus your daily intention to turn your life over to the care of your Higher Power. It reads:

'God, I offer myself to Thee - to build with me and do with me as Thou wilt. Relieve me of the bondage of self, that I may better do Thy will. Take away my difficulties, that victory over them may bear witness to those I would help of Thy Power, Thy Love, and Thy Way of life. May I do Thy Will always.'

STEP FOUR

'Made a searching and fearless moral inventory of ourselves'.

Although many of us have come from dysfunctional families and have experienced various forms of abuse, an inventory is not about our childhood history. Taking inventory involves noting what we have on hand currently in our life. The purpose of this is to help us become non-offensive to ourselves and to people with whom we are in relationships. While we were not responsible for the things that happened to us in childhood, as adults we are responsible for the quality of our lives today. In this step, we take an inventory of how, as adults, we have offended other adults and children. In this inventory, we also note our offensive attitudes and judgements. It is important to be as thorough as possible because the material in our fourth step will be the basis for some of the following steps. Step Four helps us to come out of the denial, which has been a major survival technique for us. Although denial has helped us to survive, it also has made us incapable of self-awareness.

Because this step confronts shame directly in the face, many find themselves procrastinating or making excuses for why they aren't doing the step. If this is the case, then - *'fear forward'* because action diminishes fear.

Step Four is the step of courage. In the serenity prayer, we ask to be granted the courage to change the things that we can. We do not have the power to change others, but we can change ourselves. The awareness that comes by taking a fearless and searching moral inventory is the forerunner to change and to change takes courage.

STEP FIVE

'Admitted to God, to ourselves and to another human being the exact nature of our wrongs'.

Step Five is the step of integrity and offers us restoration. It's been said: 'We're only as sick as our secrets'. Having clearly faced ourselves and our defects of character in the fourth step, we are now ready to free ourselves from the loneliness and isolation of our secrets and shame. Step Five serves to reduce our toxic shame and takes us from humiliation to humility.

STEP SIX

'Were entirely ready to have God remove all these defects of character.'

Having worked the first five steps, we have now developed a new level of trust in a power greater than ourselves. This bodes well for having our character defects removed. Practically everyone wants to get rid of their most glaring defects of character, but not everyone is 'entirely ready' to have this take place. Step Six is the step of willingness: being entirely ready means being willing. And let's face it, we are very attached to some of our character defects. Character defects essentially are self-defence mechanisms. When we understand them in this way, it is not surprising that there would be fear and hesitancy in asking God to remove them all. Being entirely ready means knowing that you will not be the same after taking this step. Step Six is necessary if we are to proceed along our path of spiritual growth and serenity.

STEP SEVEN

'Humbly asked him to remove our shortcomings'.

Step Seven is the step of humility. It asks us to address our willingness to try humility in asking our Higher Power to remove our shortcomings. Without some measure of humility, no one can sustain recovery from his or her addictions. Developing more humility brings us to happiness and without it we would not be able to summon the faith that we need to meet emergencies or crisis. The basic ingredient of humility is the desire to seek and do God's will. As long as we continue to depend on ourselves first, we cannot genuinely come to depend upon a Higher Power. Humility frees us from pride and arrogance and is the avenue to true freedom of the human spirit. However, we must be willing to do our bit towards removing our shortcomings. In doing this footwork, we demonstrate our complete willingness on an ongoing basis. If we're not willing to change our behaviour, then we are still unconsciously hanging on and unwilling to let go.

As we take this step in partnership with our Higher Power, many of us use the Seven Step prayer from the big book of Alcoholics Anonymous:

'My Creator, I am now willing that you should have all of me, good and bad. I pray that you now remove from me every single defect of character which stands in the way of my usefulness to you and my fellows. Grant me strength, as I go out from here, to do your bidding. Amen.'

STEP EIGHT

'Made a list of all persons we had harmed and became willing to make amends to them all'.

Where Steps Four and Seven are designed to help us retain our right relationship with our Higher Power, Steps Eight and Nine do the same thing with our relationships with others. In Steps Four and Five, we did a personal housecleaning, in Steps Eight and Nine, we undertake a social housecleaning. We rid ourselves of the guilt caused by knowing that we have harmed others. But before we take Step Nine and actually make amends, we must first become focused and clear about who we owe amends to (by making a list) and then ask our Higher Power to help us attain the willingness to do it. Step Eight is the step of brotherly love and again we can see that willingness is a key in moving us on to Step Nine. If we are feeling stuck at Step Eight, we may need to go back and rework Steps Four to Seven. Perhaps our inventory was not thorough enough.

STEP NINE

'Made direct amends to such people wherever possible, except when to do so would injure them or others'.

We do not make amends so that others can forgive us, or to relieve our guilt. We make amends to correct our past wrongdoings and clean up our side of the street. In making amends, we will receive the due rewards for ourselves. In this sense, Step Nine is the step of justice. Making an amends is not the same as saying we're sorry. 'Sorry' only gets 'sorry-er'. Although we may feel sorrow for some of our past behaviour, when we are working Step Nine, it is not a time to wallow in humiliation and self-pity.

Making amends with humility requires great courage because we face the shame of our past behaviours and the fear of rejection. It is important to use reasonable caution when making amends. Some people use the amends process as a way to unconsciously punish themselves. For this reason, it is wise to at least begin the process of self forgiveness before making amends to others. Although we don't wish to procrastinate, sometimes we have to be patient and allow our amends to happen on God's clock.

This brings to mind an experience I had with making amends in my early days of recovery. I had ended an addicted relationship with a man, but he refused to let go and followed me around in a harassing manner. His offensive behaviour infuriated and upset me. As I was whinging about this to my sponsor, she said that whenever we're so reactive to another person, we probably owe *them* an amends. Initially I couldn't believe that I owed *him* an amends, but could think of a long list of counts on which he owed me amends. My sponsor suggested

I go home and contemplate this. When I did, I discovered that she was right. Grudgingly, I prepared myself to find him and make amends so that I could be relieved of the guilt I felt.

I then made several attempts to contact him, but he was suddenly nowhere to be found. It was as if he'd disappeared into thin air! This was hard on me, for even though I was angry with him, I was still obsessed with him and feeling the pain of withdrawal. Several months passed and one evening when I was in a laundromat with a girlfriend, he walked by the window with a girl on his arm. I hid behind the laundromat door with my heart pounding. My girlfriend smiled and asked: 'Are you going to face him or are you going to hide?' Remembering the amends that I owed him, I decided to fear forward and walked to the parking lot to find him. As I stepped out of the door, he was there alone (having said goodnight to his date), waiting for me. We awkwardly exchanged greetings and then I told him I was glad to see him and that I'd been looking for him because there was an amends I owed him and wished to make. As I made the amends to him, tears welled up in his eyes and he asked if he could hug me. When he hugged me, I was amazed to feel my entire former obsession and attraction to him drop away.

I felt like a free woman, and after our exchange that evening, I never saw or heard from him again.

THE PROMISES

After we complete Step Nine, the program offers us promises (benefits or rewards) for the housecleaning we've done. The Promises were originally printed in the Big Book of Alcoholics Anonymous (Page 83). As a result of working Steps One to Nine, I have experienced them all time and time again.

'The Promises' are as follows:

'If we are painstaking about this phase of our development, we will be amazed before we are half way through. We are going to know a new freedom and a new happiness. We will not regret the past nor wish to shut the door on it. We will comprehend the word 'serenity' and we will know peace. No matter how far down the scale we have gone, we will see how our experience can benefit others. That feeling of uselessness and self-pity will disappear. We will lose interest in selfish things and gain interest in our fellows. Self-seeking will slip away.

Our whole attitude and outlook upon life will change. Fear of people and of economic insecurity will leave us. We will intuitively know how to handle situations which used to baffle us. We will suddenly realise that God is doing for us what we could not do for ourselves.'

STEP TEN

'Continued to take personal inventory and when we were wrong promptly admitted it'.

Step Ten is the step of perseverance. Once we've cleaned up the wreckage of our pasts, to maintain our newfound spiritual freedom, we rely on Step Ten. By continuing to take personal inventory, we continue to set right any new mistakes along our way. This unfolds throughout our lives, a day at a time. As we walk this path, it is important to watch for selfishness, dishonesty, resentment and fear. When these arise, we ask our Higher Power to remove them at once. We make amends immediately with people whom we have offended. Exercising our willpower along these lines and resisting the temptation to rest on our laurels constitutes the proper use of human will.

STEP ELEVEN

'Sought through prayer and meditation to improve our conscious contact with God as we understood Him, praying only for knowledge of His will for us and the power to carry that out.'

Step Eleven is the spiritual step. It is through this step that we enrich and expand our spirituality and our conscious contact with our Higher Power. Prayer is about affirming, asking and proclaiming, while meditation is about becoming quiet, listening and going within for our answers. Some say that when they pray, they talk to God and when they meditate, God answers them. As we progress in our recovery, our prayers usually become more humble and simple.

STEP TWELVE

'Having had a spiritual awakening as the result of these steps, we tried to carry this message to others, and to practice these principles in all our affairs.'

Spiritual awakenings are not always signified by 'a burning bush'. This step suggests that through the process of working all of the steps we awaken spiritually. As we reach the Twelfth Step, we are ready to spread our wings and work the principles of the program in every area of our lives.

The Twelfth Step is about service. By the time we've reached this step, we are in a stronger position. We are therefore able to effectively carry the message, rather than to pass on the dis-ease. The whole premise of this step is that in order to keep what we have (our recovery), we have to give it away. But in order to give something away, we first have to have it.

Through working the Twelve Steps, we receive the benefit of healing the wreckage of our past and the subsequent self-transformation. The Twelve Step groups provide a way in which we can join with others for support without having to feel dependent on them.

A WORD ABOUT THERAPY

Although working the Twelve Steps is a healing process, it does not take the place of therapy. Neither does therapy take the place of working the steps and attending Twelve Step meetings. Many clinicians and lay people who've done both agree that they complement each other.

A person in therapy for co-dependency takes an active role (a partnership with their therapist). The therapist may use techniques to help uncover disassociated information about the client's childhood history, although sometimes it has to be allowed to surface in a natural way. It's a process of trust, patience and allowing. The client is instructed to identify their childhood roles and the abuse that took place to them or siblings in their formative years. We do this to understand the impact the abuse has, seeing our caregivers as accountable (not to blame) for the origin of our adult symptoms of co-dependency.

Then the therapist will facilitate process work to help clients confront their distorted thinking; their carried and frozen feelings; their destructive behaviours and their inability to connect with themselves, others and a higher power. Because some people are more damaged than others, the length of therapy will vary from one person to another.

My suggestion for those of you who decide to seek therapy is to do it in a group setting, which facilitates family-of-origin issues, especially historical feeling work (John Bradshaw calls this 'original pain' work). There are several reasons to do group work in place of one on one counselling sessions. Co-dependents and addicts need the other group member's validation for the purpose of shame-reduction and grieving childhood losses and the ramifications it has had on their adult life. Although we don't realise how strong our denial is, witnessing another's process facilitated in group, often penetrates our denial and releases the pressures driving our dis-ease.

In order to have lasting healing, it is important to simultaneously work on arresting our present addictive behaviour and historical issues of abuse, neglect and mistaken identity from our formative years.

When selecting a therapist, it is important for you to remember that you have rights and that you are willing to be accountable for your healing process. I suggest you interview your intended therapist and ask if they have had specialised training in treating co-dependency and addictions, as well as feeling work (particularly fear and shame). A therapist is not God and does not have all of your answers, but a good one is skilled at treating distorted reality. Pick someone you feel you are willing to trust and be willing to take suggestions from, someone who will help you to find your own answers. Your therapist will begin the process of 're-parenting' you until you learn the *apparent* steps to take in new situations.

Usually the people who can't justify spending money on therapy are so shame-based; unconsciously they feel they don't deserve the help. There are always excuses of 'not enough money', 'not enough time', 'I should be able to figure this out myself', 'I'm just going through a bad time', etc. To such people, I would reply: The best investment you can make is in your own mental, emotional, physical and spiritual health - building a solid foundation for living. If you don't have that, then what have you got?

BUILDING HEALTHY
RELATIONSHIPS

The main reason so many of us have difficulties building healthy relationships with others is that we haven't built one with ourselves first (co-dependency recovery). Only when we've begun to do this, are we ready to start building healthy relationships with others.

Like Henry the grasshopper, we need to find and cultivate our own path in life. When we want to have a relationship, rather than hopping onto the other person's path, we need to build, in partnership with them, a common path. This common path becomes our relationship and it is important to regard it as a separate entity with a life of its own. When we are 'path-hoppers', we create enmeshed relationships with all their attendant confusion and pain.

Another way we get enmeshed in our relationships is by being unfocused. In order to be focused in our relationships, we have to do two things:

1. Identify our needs, wants and desires in regard to the relationship.

2. Decide what we are willing to put into the relationship.

Staying focused in the above manner eliminates being enmeshed and confused. When we become unfocused in our relationships, we will place unconscious expectations on them. These unconscious expectations keep us in confusion. And without focus, our relationships will become chaotic. When they do become chaotic, we generally respond by placing even more unconscious expectations and judgements - usually on ourselves. This stimulates our doubts and breeds fear. Rather than face our doubts and deal with our fears, we're inclined to cast them into our relationship, yet they aren't really part of it at all. So you can see how we create relationship 'monsters'. No wonder so many of us want to run away from them.

On the other hand, if we rely on our relationships to meet our needs and give us our identity, rather than look to see *what we can give* to our relationships, it will also lead to chaos and confusion. In the same way, if we take our value (what we're worth) from our relationships, rather than *give* value to our relationships, we will perceive that we have only as much value as the relationships have. This is why people feel that they are a No Thing (nothing) or have diminished value when a relationship ends.

TO OPEN A NEW DOOR... CLOSE THE OLD ONE

Many of my clients seeking happy relationships seem to think that these are bestowed on some - but not others - by some random, magical process. 'Some people are just lucky,' they tell me.

I tell them that one of the reasons many of us don't have the types of relationships we want is that we haven't learned how to complete our past relationships. The most important relationships in our past that we need to complete are those with our mother, father and siblings. Total healing and freedom comes from completing our relationship with our family of origin. By the time we're adults, we usually have several other incomplete relationships which are partly re-enactments from our formative years.

By completing a relationship, I don't necessarily mean finishing it. Rather I mean that you accept and come to terms with the past so that you can close the door on it. This process allows many new doors to be opened.

Sometimes when we complete a past relationship, we say goodbye to the other person and go our separate ways. But it is also possible to create a new beginning in an ongoing relationship by completing the *past* relationship you shared with that person. This happens often to couples in recovery. When their recovery process is underway, they begin to see the addictive and dis-eased aspects of their relationship. Once they complete and heal that, many doors to new possibilities begin to open for them. It's a process of letting the old relationship die so a new one can be born.

This seems a straightforward process, yet it's one that people seem to struggle with a lot. Why? Reasons people give include: 'I'll feel guilty',

'It'll hurt too much', 'I owe it to them to stay', 'It's easier to forget about it and just go on'.

I once heard a very wise saying about this: 'My pain comes from leaving my fingers in doors that are closing'. If it seems there are no opportunities in your life either for new relationships or for improving the quality of your existing relationships, you might like to look at which doors you have your fingers in! Once you identify which doors (relationships) your fingers are stuck in and you're tired of the pain, you then can pull them out and close the door(s). When we complete the past in this way, *we release* it rather than *relive* it.

The following is a written process for completing relationships. Although this process probably will not be sufficient for the work most people need to do on releasing their parents, it will make a substantial impact in this regard. This process can apply to anyone you've had or are having a relationship with (parents, children, siblings, friends, lovers, spouses, colleagues, employers, etc).

COMPLETING RELATIONSHIPS PROCESS

This is a letter-writing process. Find a private place where you can be alone and allow yourself plenty of time. Select the person with whom you wish to complete your relationship. You will be writing six different letters to that person. These letters are not meant to ever be sent or seen by anyone else (unless you're sharing them with a therapist or sponsor).

First, set your intention to be complete. The power of your intention is the most important element in this process. Before you start writing, I suggest that you ask your Higher Power to help you to do this authentically and thoroughly, to the best of your ability.

Letter Number 1: In this letter, you are to express all of your feelings of anger and hatred towards this person - no holds barred! Do not edit or censor what you write. Allow it to be a cathartic process and simply 'pour' your emotions onto the page.

Letter Number 2: In this letter, you are to express your feelings of hurt and pain. Allow your emotions to flow. Many people cry and sometimes even sob. In your letter, include ways in which you felt betrayed, offended and violated.

Letter Number 3: In this letter, communicate your fears about completing the relationship and your fears about relationships in general. For example: 'I'm afraid that I'll become bitter', 'I'm afraid I'll put up walls and never be able to trust again', 'I'm afraid I'll never achieve intimacy', 'I'm afraid I'll never be able to get you out of my mind', 'I'm afraid I can't change', 'I'm afraid you won't change', 'I'm afraid I'll see you with another lover', 'I'm afraid I'll run into you and get caught off guard', etc. Be as thorough as possible in listing your fears. By acknowledging them, you take a lot of the 'charge' out of them. Should any of these things occur, you wouldn't have such a strong emotional reaction. Once you've acknowledged them, you can use the process of embracing fears (chapter seven).

Letter Number 4: In this letter, you acknowledge and account for your own involvement and participation in the dysfunction of the relationship. Acknowledge the bad choices you made, identify where you sold out in pursuit of instant gratification and where your reality was distorted and you assigned your particular meaning to things (eg. 'he introduced me to his mother, therefore he wants to marry me' or 'now that we're married, I don't have to be so particular about my appearance').

Letter Number 5: In this letter, write what your needs, wants and desires are regarding the relationship - in other words, how you would like it to be. Obviously if it's someone with whom you intend to remain in contact, it is important to be very specific and to take time and care with this letter. Perhaps this person is someone you don't desire to have a friendship with, but whom you'd respond pleasantly to if your paths crossed. Then again, if it's someone you don't intend to see again, you might wish him or her peace and love on their path, but state that you wish no further contact with them.

Letter Number 6: This is a letter of love and appreciation. In this letter, you look for the 'good purpose' of the relationship, as well as the knowledge and wisdom you gained from it. The intention in this letter is to complete the relationship, so that you finally can close the door on the past (accept and release it) and move forward to create a healthy relationship - either with or without them.

Don't underestimate the power of this simple process. It has worked wonders for many of my clients who report having experienced radical shifts and miracles in their lives as a direct result of it. Sometimes the letter writing process highlights the fact that there is something outstanding which needs to be communicated. If this is the case, you will now be clear to write another letter (and post it) that says what you really need to say, without being offensive or dumping on them.

TREATING LOVE ADDICTION

Much of what I learned about treating love addiction came from training with Pia Mellody. My training with Pia took place before the first edition *Set Yourself Free* and her ground-breaking book *Facing Love Addiction* was released. I am indebted to Pia for her model because it is simple, clear and easy to follow. The following information on love addiction is mostly taken from her work.

If you have identified yourself as being a love addict, your first step in recovery is to arrest the addiction. This will immediately put you into the withdrawal process. Although withdrawal can be intense and confusing, it is also helps you treat your underlying co-dependency and build intimacy with yourself. In Al-Anon, they have a saying that gives three simple steps to use to take you through the withdrawal process.

1. 'Get off their back' (this is about detachment).

2. 'Get out of their way' (this is about building boundaries)

3. 'Turn and go on with your life' (this is about co-dependency recovery)

While you're in the withdrawal process, it is necessary to establish boundaries as soon as possible. This will help to stabilise the emotional fluctuations that make you feel like you're on a roller coaster. Many love addicts have to begin their recovery by detaching and using what Pia calls a 'wall of pleasant'. A 'wall of pleasant' is smiling, being polite and mannerly and communicating on a surface level. This is not the time to share any profound realisations or deep feelings. This mode of behaviour takes the toxic energy out of communicating with the people to whom you're addicted.

Rage, desolation, carried pain, fear and shame, as well as panic attacks, feelings of betrayal and jealousy are all commonly experienced during withdrawal from love addiction. In fact, withdrawal from love addiction is the most painful withdrawal of any addiction (more painful even than heroin). Understanding the various stages of withdrawal is important for two reasons. Most people have no idea of the intensity that accompanies withdrawal and think something is seriously wrong with them when they are in it. This causes extreme reactive behaviour and leads to decisions made from desperation. Secondly, when you are educated about the process of withdrawal, you know what to expect and you also know there's an end to it.

The reason the pain of withdrawal is so overwhelming, is that it stimulates deep abandonment pain, not only from the person you've been addicted to, but from childhood abandonment issues. Although this is an intensely painful process, it is one which will lead you to an experience of profound transformation as it allows a part of you which has been trying to surface for a long time, to do so. Going through withdrawal helps you become a whole person; to know and have an intimate relationship with yourself. Withdrawal holds the beginnings of your own personal healing and wholeness. And its end effect, which makes the process worthwhile, is that addictive sexual and emotional behaviour, on a daily basis, stops.

STAGES OF WITHDRAWAL

Stage 1
Fear, Pain and sometimes Panic. Usually triggered by rejection or abandonment from the one you're addicted to. In this stage it is very common to have suicidal and/or homicidal thoughts. They are nothing more than desperate thoughts, looking for a way out of the pain. The way out of this, which gives lasting freedom, is to *go through it.* Don't get stuck wallowing in stage one - keep going!

Stage 2
Obsession. This is where the love addict starts mentally obsessing and fantasising about a plan of action to get the other person back. Although most people don't realise it, mental obsession is an effective way to mood alter. This mental obsessing takes the love addict out of their intense feelings and puts them into their heads, which relieves their panic and pain. This also installs a false sense of hope that everything can be ironed out with a quick solution.

Stage 3
Compulsion. This is the stage where the love addict acts out their obsession to get attention or a reaction out of the person they're addicted to. This stage usually carries lots of high drama and intensity, which gives the love addict relief for a short while. Because love addicts have a deep, underlying fear of intimacy, they learn to connect through intensity and are confused about the difference between the two.

Repeating stages 1, 2, and 3 of the withdrawal process can take you into another addictive cycle that will keep you stuck in misery. *The place to intervene is in the obsession stage.* It is OK for you to go ahead and obsess, but close your mouth and breathe and don't act out the plan. Say to yourself: 'Who he/she is, is none of my business'. Once you've done this, the fear and panic will increase. Now is the time to use a mantra or pray. Some people use the serenity prayer or you might say: I have warm, personal regard for all people at all times' or 'Everyone has a right to be in this world the way they are'. This will serve to calm you down and centre you.

Another thing you can do is to make an appointment to obsess about them at another time. For example, if you're at work and you can't stop thinking about your relationship, make an appointment and put it in your diary - to totally indulge and obsess about it at, say 6pm. You'll often find that if you do this, by 6pm it might not be such a big deal any more. You may even be able to see some humour in it. Once you stop obsessing:

- Ask for what you want from the other person.
- Close your mouth and breathe.
- Notice what you get.
- Celebrate the 'no'.

If, after a while you notice that you're not getting what you want from the relationship, you'll know it's time to move on. However, once you close your mouth and breathe and notice what you get, you often find that you're getting a lot more than you may have noticed previously.

Now you're ready to write an inventory of your love addiction with more honesty and clarity. First, write about how you assign too much time, attention and value to the other person. Second, write about how you expect too much unconditional, positive regard from the other person. Third, write an inventory of how your partner seduces you and gets a rise out of you (which keeps you hooked in the intensity of the relationship).

Once you've done this thoroughly, you'll get new insights into where your reality is distorted. This is where you begin to decide on the proper course of action to help you to restore your self-esteem, build boundaries, balance your reality, meet your own needs and live your life in moderation. This is what co-dependency recovery entails.

WRITING AN INVENTORY

The following written exercise will help you identify and inventory your addictive behaviour patterns regarding issues of abandonment and engulfment.

1. Select a past or current relationship that has caused you discomfort, confusion or intense pain.

2. Using either your dominant or non-dominant hand (or alternate them) write about, in journal form:

   How did/do you avoid:

   • spending time with

   • paying attention to

   • acknowledging and valuing the other person?

3. Specifically how did/do you think or feel that you were 'better than' and/or more powerful than your partner?

4. What thoughts or behaviours did/do you use to distance yourself from your partner and control the relationship?

5. How did/do you assign:

   • too much time

   • too much attention

   • too much value

   • to another before your own self care?

6. How did/do you think that you were 'less than' and/or

   • less powerful than your partner?

7. What thoughts or behaviours did/do you use to engulf your partner and control the relationship?

8. What are some of your unrealistic expectations? What specific ways do you expect too much unconditional positive regard? (List as many as possible).

9. What specific needs and wants do you feel shame and fear about? These may be ones where you experience difficulty

in receiving or in asking for them to be met? (List as many as possible).

10. How have you allowed another to seduce or influence you to do something you really do not want to do?

11. How have you seduced or influenced another to get your way?

12. How do you use anger and/or sex to create intensity and give you the illusion of being connected? (list specific incidences).

13. How are your behaviours diminishing your choices and how do they affect other areas of your life? (i.e. career, parenting, friendships, physical vitality, spirituality, mental clarity, emotional well-being, sexuality).

At this point, it would be useful for you to share what you have written with a counsellor, sponsor, or another non-shaming support person. Once you've done this, then continue with the following. These are there to support you to take action - to do things differently.

1. The behaviours I am willing to change and work with now are:

2. The new steps I will take are: (Generate 3 steps or different options for each desired change).

3. How specifically are you going to support yourself to move through the grief as you go through this time of change?

BOUNDARIES, THE KEY TO SELF-PROTECTION

Boundaries are an essential key in the achievement of healthy relationships. Pia Mellody defines boundaries as: 'a system of limit-setting that enhances a person's ability to have a sense of self and to control the impact of reality on the self and others.' The purpose of having boundaries is to protect and contain your reality and to keep you from offending and violating others.

Having boundaries helps to give you a sense of your own identity. They allow you to know where you end and someone else begins. With boundaries, you can detach from others in a healthy way, without isolating. Only when you can do that, can you begin to have intimacy with yourself. You can't have intimate relationships with anyone unless you first have an intimate relationship with yourself.

Boundaries keep you from being enmeshed and fused in your relationships. When you're fused, you're usually become confused, which makes matters appear difficult and overwhelming. Then, it's almost impossible to define and separate yourself from another in a healthy way. You'll begin to feel engulfed, as if you don't have your own privacy, causing you to put up walls and isolate from others as a seeming solution.

Sometimes we use walls of fear, anger, talking, smiling, etc to shut people out and to protect ourselves. Operating in this manner is dysfunctional because when you're behind those walls, intimacy cannot occur and, after a while, it becomes very lonely and empty behind those walls. This can bring up your fear of abandonment. So after a while, you may say to yourself: 'I'm going to start to trust again. Maybe I'll get into a relationship. Maybe intimacy isn't such a bad thing after all.' But because most of us haven't learned how to build boundaries, we collapse our walls and become totally open with no protection, which usually allows us to get hurt. Co-dependents generally vacillate from one extreme to the other. We're either open with no protection and being hurt or we're isolated and lonely.

These lines from a poem by Kent Dixon called '*These Walls*' illustrate the pain of isolation we feel when we have walls rather than boundaries.

'These walls are tall to break my fall
These walls are inside so I can hide
These walls are real so I won't feel
They rise high above so I won't love
These walls are near so I won't fear
These walls impair so I won't care
These walls are high so I won't cry
These walls won't leave so I might believe
That in the space beyond the stone I'm not alone'

Boundaries are not rigid like walls. Rather, they are flexible, acting as a block and filter to offences, intrusions and abuse. Boundaries help you to define, contain and separate your reality from another's. These realities are:

Physical - how you observe and behave in your environment;

Intellectual - how you assign meaning to the things you observe and do in your environment;

Emotional - the feelings that are generated by thoughts and behaviour;

Spiritual - the connection you have with yourself, others, the earth, animals and a power greater than you.

Reality is a matter of perception and each of us is responsible for our own reality. There is not another person on this earth whose reality is the same as yours, because no one has walked in your shoes. If you're co-dependent, you have unconsciously learned to take on other people's thoughts, feelings and behaviour patterns and thereby not had much freedom of conscious choice. Boundaries help us to attain freedom because they act as a container for our reality, thereby enabling us to ascertain what our needs, wants and desires are. In this way, they also help us to give ourselves permission to get them fulfilled. Without boundaries to protect and contain your reality, you will be a victim or an offender or both.

In building boundaries, you are working on your identity and if you've been raised in a functional family, you've been dealing with this from puberty onwards. The more that you are able to build and maintain healthy boundaries, the more you will be able to let go of control in your relationships. People in co-addicted relationships have impaired boundaries, which leads to elements of control and manipulation. However, it wouldn't be appropriate to let go of control without some sort of protection. The degree to which you can protect yourself in a functional way with boundaries is the degree to which you can finally relax, let go and begin to trust (yourself and others) because you feel that your boundary system is intact. Boundaries are imperative in learning how to let go and trust, particularly in our intimate relationships. A former client, Zara, gained a lot more than protection, once she established boundaries.

ZARA'S STORY
A CLIENT'S PERSONAL VOYAGE

I was at work staring at the gum trees outside, feeling the familiar weight of my own misery. The voice popped into my head 'you are alone, you will always be alone, no one wants you'. Instead of ignoring it, I found my hands trembling, I was sweating and short of breath. This had happened many times before, but never at work.

I had sought help after my divorce four years earlier, however the therapist's happy wedding portraits seemed to mock me while I poured out my relationship failings, so I stopped going. In reality, it was just too much hard work.

Instead, I spent the next few years living a double life. Nights spent partying, one-night stands, drinking, then crying myself to sleep only to wake at 4:00 am with the unshakeable belief that I was all alone. During the day, I would glide through my work, confident and capable. As a senior manager, interacting with many high-powered men, I was revered for keeping everyone and everything under control.

My trembling hands told me I had to try again. I found a new therapist who I learned to trust and respect. She told me I was suffering from acute anxiety, one of the five most severe cases she had seen. I was also severely depressed, and had been for a long time. Our work together helped me tremendously in my job, yet I still could not seem to shake the anxiety, obsession and pain about my personal life - particularly my lovelife. My therapist referred me to Shirley Smith.

*After reading **Set Yourself Free** and attending a couple of counselling sessions with Shirley, I was surprised to learn that my impaired emotional state, along with my double life pattern, stemmed from my childhood. At home I was anxious about being overweight, anxious about my dad's moods and drinking and my parent's fights. At school I achieved good marks, and was proud of my ability to make people laugh. This also had its benefits at home, where I could use this skill to break the tension.*

My older sister and I both have strong memories of this tension. My dad was often in a bad mood. We knew by the sound of his footsteps on the path, and how he opened the door if it was going to be a good night, or a bad one. He got worse with alcohol, so I hated their parties. The arguments slowly got worse and at the age of eight I started to intervene. At first, calling out or simply appearing in the doorway was enough to stop them, but slowly that lost its impact.

By the age of eleven I was 'fixing things'. I would stop my dad from what ever he was doing to mum - taunting, punching, choking -and get her to a safe place, often the car. I would pour dad's drink down the drain, sit him down while he cried his remorse then I would seek out my sister's hiding place so I could comfort her. I would always go to school the next day as if nothing had happened. As an adult, I would recreate this role in many different ways, with my family always expecting me to fix things. I became the 'responsible one' and the 'caretaker' not only for my family - but for everyone!

Both my parents were sexy and good looking - my mother especially so. The attention they sought from people outside the marriage lead to jealousy and mistrust. I learned much later that heightened tension in the house often coincided with one of them having an affair. The bad fights were usually followed by a separation. Desperate for things to be normal again, I was always relieved when dad came back.

Funnily enough, I grew up thinking that these events gave me strength of character, that I could cope with anything. I eventually lost the weight I carried as a child, but inside I was still the tense, overweight child seeking approval.

So imagine my joy at the age of 19 when I started dating the most popular boy from high school. I thought he was nothing like my father because he didn't drink. He was, however, smart, charismatic, very good looking, and needed the constant attention of other women.

Over the next 10 years his real or imagined affairs became my obsession. I would search for evidence while I lie awake imagining that I'd find him with someone else. Feeling like a private detective, I'd examine photos of his women 'friends' that he had hidden, and then anguish over my shortcomings. I rode this merry-go-round of intensity for years feeling the hurt and pain.

We fought, broke up and reconciled over and over. I slowly became numb, losing all of my feelings for him and our façade of a marriage. Finally it took the shock of my own parent's divorce for me to wake up and find the courage to leave him.

During Group Work with Shirley Smith I learned how I had recreated the familiar feelings of my childhood in my marriage. I was hyper-vigilant and had become addicted to intensity and to him. My obsession kept me numb to the deep abandonment pain buried in the pit of my stomach. I thought he was proof of my worth, and if I lost him, I would be nothing.

Throughout almost two years of different group activities, 'weekend intensives' and sometimes just watching and listening to others, I learned slowly how to grieve for my childhood and adult losses. I learned to feel anger toward my parents, feel the fear I hid as a child, and the betrayal that while I looked after everyone, no one was there to look after me.

It took a number of group sessions before I truly let go and went into the pain. I learned how to stop being the 'grown up' for my parents and sister - to set some boundaries, by saying 'no'. In hindsight this seems a very simple thing to do, but I assure you it was one of the hardest things I've ever done. My value was tied up in those family roles and it literally felt like I would lose all of my worth if I changed my behaviour with them.

I also learned to distinguish love from love addiction. I set an intention to have a loving, caring relationship. I then 'let it go' and decided to live my life to the fullest, and enjoy myself - whatever happened.

Now, six years after that day staring in panic at the gum trees, I no longer lead a double life and I have a much better relationship with my parents.

I met a wonderful man and for the first time, I am truly in love and loved in return by my husband. At the age of 39, I am expecting my first baby. I feel happiness, contentment and a joy in living that I never thought possible. Sometimes I struggle with my weight a bit, but I know when I apply the principle of surrender and let go, I don't really have a problem. More importantly, I have stopped the cycle of fear and abuse suffered by me, my sister and my parents and I can give my son a happy and safe childhood, free of fear and anxiety and full of fun and an abundance of love.

TYPES OF BOUNDARIES

There are basically three types of boundary systems - internal, external and spiritual. Within these, there are four components.

The external components are physical and sexual; they function outside of the body and control distance and touch with others and (for others) with ourselves. Physical touching is about nurturing whereas sexual touching is about arousal or lust. Many co-addicts confuse the two.

For the co-dependent, the internal boundaries are the most damaged. The internal components are emotional and intellectual. Internal boundaries act like a filter, letting things in and out. I often suggest to clients to imagine they are like fly screens - they let the fresh air in and keep the bugs out. Protecting your thinking and feeling realities, internal boundaries allow you to jettison things that are not true for you. For example, if someone accuses you of hurting them, with a healthy internal boundary you would be able to take that information in, think about it, have some feelings about it and easily decide if it were true or not - without being defensive. Perhaps you didn't offend that person and they're 'hurt' because their attempted manipulation of you failed. (eg. Your mother whines that you're hurting her feelings because you won't visit her for tea on Sunday).

An internal boundary will facilitate you to allow others to have their own reality, even when it conflicts with yours. This occurs in two forms:

1. Say that someone gives an appraisal of you that you feel is not true. You don't have to defend yourself or argue with them. You can simply allow them their opinion of you without it affecting your own opinion of yourself - as long as it's not a statement of offence (such as 'you're stupid' vs 'I don't think you have the capabilities for this job').

2. Say you and another person have differing opinions about something ('the movie was wonderful' vs 'the movie was lousy'). With healthy internal boundaries, you can agree to disagree.

If another's reality conflicts with yours and you wish to stand firm in yours, you can do this by closing your mouth and saying it silently to yourself. Doing this, helps you take ownership of your own reality and value yourself. You cannot do this if you lack good, internal boundaries because without them, you can't get enough separation from another to resist owning their reality - even when it doesn't sit well with you. Exceptions to this are therapists, sponsors and other people who you have invited to comment and assist you in clarifying your reality.

A spiritual boundary occurs when two people are being intimate with one another while both of them are using their external and internal boundaries. This allows them to expand and experience spirituality, the essence of their wholeness, together.

HOW TO SET BOUNDARIES
PHYSICAL BOUNDARIES

The first thing to do is to visualise yourself as being protected (perhaps in a white light, or a large glass jar like a bell or being enveloped by a series of gold rings from head to toe). This physical boundary is flexible and moves according to who you're with - it may contract when you hug someone and expand to provide extra protection when you're in a crowd.

In setting this boundary, there is one statement to memorise:

'I have the right to determine when, where, how and with whom I want to be touched, and how close I'll allow you to stand next to me. And you have the right to do the same with me.'

SEXUAL BOUNDARIES

The sexual boundary is similar to the physical boundary, but it is important to note that even when you're being sexual with someone, you still maintain a boundary... on your skin.

The statement to memorise here is:

'I have the right to determine with whom, where, when and how I'm going to be sexual. And you have the right to do the same with me.' This means that if you want to negotiate being sexual with someone and they decline, that's the end of it. A sexual boundary allows you to be sexually appropriate and protective of yourself.

EMOTIONAL AND INTELLECTUAL BOUNDARIES

You cannot set these internal boundaries until you have set your external ones. When you visualise the internal boundaries, picture something that acts like a filter.

The statement to memorise here is:

'I create what I think and feel and I am in control of what I do or don't do. The same is true for you.'

You can also add: *'My reality is derived more from my history than from what you are saying or doing in front of me. And the same is true for you.'*

The caveat to this is that although you are not responsible for another's responses, you must note the impact of your behaviour on the other. If you offend another, you are accountable for that and owe them an amends. Let's say someone is giving you the silent treatment and obviously ignoring you. You let them know that you are feeling hurt about their behaviour towards you, and then they respond by telling you that you've created your own reality (this is a favourite cop-out among New Agers). It's important to clearly make distinctions here. If a person is in the act of offending or abusing someone physically, sexually, mentally, emotionally or spiritually, they are responsible for that.

It is only through developing healthy boundaries that you will be able to honour another's boundaries and thereby build healthy relationships.

KEYS TO INTERDEPENDENCY

If you know you are overly dependent in certain areas of your life or if you know you are a completely dependent type, the following keys will assist you to become less dependent and to work towards interdependence.

- The first thing to do is to make a decision that you are capable of being independent and then sit down and write your own 'Declaration of Independence'. Combining your intention and writing makes a very powerful therapeutic tool. Begin to think of what you will allow and what you will not allow in your life and list the specific areas - career, your body, with your partner, parents, children, finances, sex, etc. In your declaration, spell out for yourself how you want to function in all relationships. Stay open to negotiation and compromise, but eliminate any manipulation. Write it in the first person eg: 'I, Shirley, in order to have more balance and freedom in my life, now declare...'

- Talk to each person you feel psychologically dependent on in some way. When you do this, state your aim to function independently and explain how you feel when you do things out of a sense of sacrifice and obligation. You might wish to explain you'd like to have more intimacy in your relationship and that dependency destroys intimacy. (We usually give out of obligation because we have a hidden agenda - unconscious expectations or unspoken expectations). When you're honest about this type of behaviour, you are owning your dependency - which then allows it to shift. This is an excellent strategy for getting started, because others may not even be aware that you feel dependent.

- Experiment with how you handle the dominant people in your life. These are the people you have difficulty saying 'no' to. Try saying: 'No, I don't want to' without giving any reason, and test the other person's reaction. When you tell yourself you're doing this as an experiment, it will help you to start saying 'no' when you mean no and 'yes' when you mean yes. Giving people 223 reasons is a way to keep you hooked in your dependency and is a waste of energy. Basically, we are all motivated by our needs, wants and desires - not reasons. We take action or refrain from taking action because we want to. Full stop. You're the one who will face the consequences of all your decisions and behaviour as an adult, so you have the right to do what you want to do.

- Arrange a planning session with your dominant partner at a time when neither of you is feeling highly charged or over reactive, especially when you're not feeling threatened. During this session, state how you sometimes feel manipulated and submissive. Explain that you would like to agree on a non-verbal signal whenever you're feeling dependent on that person, but you don't want to discuss it at the time (eg. tugging an ear or tapping two fingers on your heart).

- The moment you feel shoved around psychologically, stop and state how you feel. Then, even do something different to interrupt the pattern and act the way you'd like to behave. ('Fake-it-till-you-make-it' is sometimes the only way that you can begin to change your dependency patterns).

- Frequently remind yourself that your parents, spouses, friends, bosses, children and others will often disapprove of your behaviour, but this has nothing to do with who you are. It is a given fact in any relationship that you will incur some disapproval. If you learn to expect this disapproval, then you won't be surprised by it. In this way, you can break free of many of the dependency ties that enslave you emotionally.

- By deliberately avoiding dominant people, you are still allowing yourself to be controlled by them if you experience emotional immobilisation because of them.

- If you feel obligated to visit or spend time with certain people, ask yourself if you would want others to do the same with you simply because they felt required to do so. If this is the case, talk about it with them, explaining the fears behind your obligated behaviour.

- Make a firm decision to get out of your dependency role by doing volunteer work, reading, getting child care, getting a job (even if you don't financially need one) because the remuneration of your own money in any creative way that you can devise is important to your independence.

- Recognise your desire and need for privacy and stop feeling as though you need to share everything you feel and experience with someone. You are a unique and special individual. If you think you must share everything, then you are without a choice, and of course, dependent.

GUIDELINES FOR COUPLES IN RECOVERY

It is possible to recover from a co-addicted relationship without ending the relationship. Although a great challenge, it also provides a tremendous opportunity for personal growth and intimacy building. However, both parties must be willing to follow these guidelines in order for them to work effectively.

It is best to make a mutual co-existence pact, which works like a contract. There is usually a time limit of one year on the pact in which each of the parties agrees not to end the relationship. For example, you may agree to continue living together and have 'time out' occasionally. 'Time out' (a few days to a week apart) can be called by either person for the purpose of self-care and well-being. You may agree not to have sex for a designated period of time (especially if one or both partners are sex addicts). If you're living together, you may have a special room which you declare 'off limits' to the other person. You can make any types of agreements that you want, as long as you both agree and as long as your contract incorporates at least the following specific rules:

1. Don't assign blame when you're in a conflict.

2. Do not keep score on your partner.

3. Do not threaten abandonment when you're in conflict.

4. Do not argue or debate about facts or perceptions, so you can be right.

5. Do not lecture, counsel or instruct your partner unless you were asked for your advice or suggestions.

6. If you have an upset, you can usually communicate it in four sentences, which are statements, not questions. It is important to stay with your own awareness, using 'I' statements. First, say to yourself: 'What is it that I:

   - See and hear

   - Interpret

- Feel
- Want

For example: 'I heard you slam the door. I gather from that that you're angry about something or maybe you're angry with me. I feel frightened of your anger and I'm afraid you might leave me. I would like you to tell me what's going on.'

When we communicate in this manner, we may be surprised to find that, metaphorically speaking, it was only the wind that slammed the door.

Once you've set up this type of contract and begun following these rules, there will be a lot less talking and emptiness in your relationship. This stage of recovery often features a great amount of fear and panic because the addictive part (the pseudo-intimacy which is really a false connection established through fighting and intensity) has stopped. This is when you'll confront whether you do have enough between you to continue the relationship. This is also the time to reapproach your partner about what your needs, wants and desires are. After some time has passed, write an inventory of what healthy needs, wants and desires are being met in your relationship.

The key to building a healthy, intimate relationship with your current partner (even if it's been addictive) lies in the willingness of you both to take the necessary steps to participate in your recovery.

I believe the most effective way to treat couples in co-addictive relationships (marriage counselling) is to have them set up a mutual co-existence pact as outlined above, and then initially to detach emotionally by using a 'wall of pleasant'. Then I treat them individually, working on their family of origin issues, their current symptoms of co-dependency and/or treat any prevailing addictions. Next, I suggest that in tandem with their therapy, they attend relevant Twelve Step meetings. It is ideal if they can attend separate meetings. After they have some solid recovery under their belts (this is very individual and could range from six months to two years), they are then ready to go back into therapy together to learn to utilise the tools and skills for balanced relationships. In short, for most couples, especially co-dependents, marriage counselling does not work!

SEVEN STEPS TO BUILD HEALTHY RELATIONSHIPS

Healthy relationships aren't 'made in heaven'. They take work, time and are built progressively, a step at a time. To those in pursuit of the 'quick fix', this may sound like a drag, but actually there is a lot of adventure, fun, laughter and personal insights to be enjoyed along the way.

Below are seven steps to build a healthy relationship:

Step 1
Picture the relationship that you want. Visualise this relationship as a separate entity, a common path and ask yourself what you are willing to give to it. Then ask yourself: 'What will I allow and what will I not allow within this relationship?' It is important to be focused on this, so write it down. You may also desire to write out an ideal scene for this relationship, incorporating in it your needs, wants and desires as well as what you will give to the common path. Many times we experience an undesirable situation in our relationships, not because we wanted it, but because we didn't take the time to specify what we *didn't* want. Clarity in the latter is as imperative as clarity in the former.

Step 2
Consider the steps you'll take to begin the formation of the relationship (eg. be more social, take more risks when you fear rejection, take a course which helps you express yourself better).

Ask yourself what type of person you desire to join with and in which manner (lover, friend, etc). A word of caution: this step is to come from your desires, not from your fears. If you choose to join with someone out of fear, what you may do is allow yourself to join with someone for fear of not having anyone. If you already have a partner in your life, you may join together to decide the steps that you'll take on your common path.

Step 3
This step is about control and cooperation. Look at how you control emotionally and how you allow yourself to be controlled emotionally. It is important for each of us to learn how to control ourselves positively and to remain in control of our own reality. We need to learn how to cooperate without giving ourselves away. Often, we give our power away by not controlling ourselves and we unconsciously send out a message that we need to be controlled. If this is going on in your relationship, this is unbalanced cooperation. You must decide and discuss with your partner where you both are willing to cooperate and where you are not.

Step 4

Define how you want to join with them in terms of how close or how separate you wish to be. Determine what is appropriate for you at this time. This step involves practising being separate (containing your own reality) while you share a common path with another - without taking on their fears, anger, pain, judgements, etc. Boundaries will help you with this step.

Step 5

Ask yourself how you can best place your talents, abilities and actions to cause this to happen. Look at how you can harmonise your needs, wants and desires within the relationship. Work out your own balanced recipe.

Step 6

Examine your past and draw from your knowledge to give you insights so that you won't repeat the same dysfunctional patterns. Remember that all mistakes are opportunities for the beginning of new creations, so draw strength and wisdom from your past mistakes. However, as you reflect on the past, do not dwell upon it. Rather, accept it, embrace it and use it as a tool to help you in your life today. Your fears are held in the past. In order to create a healthy, balanced relationship, you may at this time want to release any fears that are standing in the way of achieving this. I recommend using the process on embracing fear (Chapter Six).

Step 7

This last step encompasses looking at the past, present and future. When you look at your relationships from this overall perspective, you are looking into all possibilities. Perhaps there are things that you have not experienced in your relationships yet, but you'd like to. To open yourself up through assuming this overview on your life may stir your imagination and bring about new desires. However, it may also bring forward more of your fears. In order to have truly satisfying relationships and fulfil your hearts' desires, you must be willing to release your fears and know in the core of your being that you deserve these relationships. If you feel blocked with this step, perhaps you need to go within and discover the core fear behind realising and having what you really want. Perhaps, deep down you feel unworthy of having a balanced, loving, giving, healthy relationship. Perhaps if you did achieve such a relationship, your life would be devoid of drama and high intensity. How would you know if you were *really alive* then?

If you take these seven steps in the order they are given and build your relationships in that way, they will be balanced, healthy relationships. When you come together too fast with another, it creates chaos. When you come together slowly, a step at a time, it will create the balance and intimacy that you desire.

To develop intimacy with another requires years of shared time. Intimacy grows from two people building a history together. You can't have intimacy without a shared history. Intimacy with another is impossible if you don't first have intimacy with yourself. In an intimate relationship, each person is able to share an internal experience with the other who can listen, receive and acknowledge the communication.

Our addictive relationships have been built using the above steps - in the reverse order, starting with step seven and ending with step one. For the love addict, the scenario goes something like this:

Step 7
You sit down and write out your laundry list for your ideal mate, allowing your imagination to run riot with your desires and referring to your past to remember to exclude what you *don't* want. You open yourself to all possibilities - now! And then, whammo! You meet him or her.

Step 6
Once you've met him or her, you're on red alert to ensure that this is the right relationship. Because your coming together was so explosive, the honeymoon period is over quickly and in the fall-out familiar fears from the past begin to emerge.

Step 5
You feel out of balance and chaotic at this point and thus you haven't got a clue about what talents and abilities of your own to apply in the relationship. So you begin to focus on your partner to discover their recipe for balance, hoping it will rub off on you.

Step 4
At this point, because the relationship was forged so quickly and is now doing so much for you, you begin to lose your own identity and you become enmeshed. You lose sight of where you and they begin and end.

Step 3
By now, you're in so deep, you start controlling everything and everyone, including yourself because you're afraid you won't get what you want.

You have no idea of how to negotiate and cooperate and sometimes you allow yourself to be controlled because you feel inadequate.

Step 2

You realise that the person you're with isn't anything like the one on your original laundry list and you can see that you joined with them out of fear rather than desire. You decide to take some steps! You look for a self-help book or a course to take. You may go into therapy or drag your partner into couple counselling. Or perhaps, you're just looking for a quick fix and you consider dumping them in favour of someone 'better'.

Step 1

You're really addicted at this point, so your fear of abandonment will be great, so great in fact that it obscures your clarity about what you will allow and what you will not allow in your relationship. You probably don't even have a clue about what you want, how to get your needs met or what your desires are.

Sound familiar?

I've included this information for the purpose of self-observation, not self-indictment. All I'm really saying here is: Don't beat yourself up. Instead, the next time you do the 'love dance', make sure you learn your steps in the right order!

ONE MEAL YOU CAN DO WITHOUT

In considering ways to build healthy relationships, by now it goes without saying that we need to take into account the relationships we have with our families. When individual family members don't have their own healthy boundaries and realities, the family unit ends up with one big boundary around it and everyone inside becomes enmeshed.

Let me give you a story to illustrate this:

Dad comes home from work one day deeply troubled as he's afraid he's going to lose his job. But because his father taught him that real men 'shouldn't be afraid', he can't share his fear with his wife or children. So he takes his fear and mentally dumps it in the family 'porridge'. Then he sits down and cuts off from his family by reading the paper.

Mum's upset because he's shutting her out and angry because he never talks anything over with her. But her mother told her that it wasn't nice for ladies to be angry and it should be avoided at all costs. So rather than express her anger, she dumps it into the 'porridge', too and goes off to do the washing.

A while later, their son comes home from school, runs into his bedroom and shuts the door. He made a mistake in maths class and the teacher shamed him in front of all his peers. But he doesn't tell anyone at home what happened because he's picked up dad's 'message' that boys aren't sissies and they don't reveal their insecurities. So he puts on a brave face, takes his shame and dumps it in the 'porridge', then goes out to play.

His sister is feeling especially sad and lonely because mum is always busy doing the washing and dad is constantly immersed in his newspaper and doesn't want to be disturbed. She tries to tell her mother how she feels and her mother screeches: 'Lonely? What have you got to be lonely about? Your father and I are always here and you have a big brother, a dog, a cat and a bird and the televisions always going. You have no reason to be lonely'. So the daughter shamefully leaves the room and takes her loneliness and shame and throws them into the 'porridge'.

The next morning at breakfast, the whole family sits down together and eats the porridge.

This classically illustrates family enmeshment. The way to prevent this is by building boundaries and having regular family meetings.

FAMILY MEETINGS... A MEANS TO CO-OPERATION

It is essential for families to have regular family meetings if they want to evolve and remain open. A family meeting is a tool designed to promote meaningful communication within the family. It allows a dysfunctional family to learn to function in a balanced way.

Family meetings provide a safe place to talk about your thoughts and feelings. You listen as each person 'owns' their feelings. You express *your feelings* only, not your opinions as to why another person acted in a certain way, nor your judgements and criticisms. Using the word 'feel' or 'feeling' does not always constitute a true feeling. (eg 'I feel you were mean not to let me go to the disco' or 'I feel you let me down when you failed your maths exam'). In a family meeting, it is important to relinquish the parent-child relationship. When it comes to sharing feelings, everyone is equal.

Family meetings are not for the purpose of problem solving, nor are they the time to issue ultimatums or give out expectations for change in another's behaviour. They should not become a group process. If therapy is needed, seek help from qualified persons who are not members of the family.

Family meetings provide a place to 'own your own reality', so you don't get caught in the unconscious practice of taking on roles to balance the family system or to feel that you matter. They will help a family to function as a nurturing unit.

GUIDELINES FOR FUNCTIONAL FAMILIES

1. Do no keep score. It is not helpful to justify our past behaviour.

2. Do not assign blame.

3. Do not lecture. Instead, share your perceptions and feelings.

4. Do not judge the feelings and perceptions of others. Allow them without comment.

5. Be honest without being blunt or hurtful.

6. Always differentiate between one's behaviour and being.

7. No matter what happens - hang in there. Do not give up.

8. Treat your family members with unconditional positive regard.

BEYOND COPING... A NEW WAY OF RELATING

The purpose of a family meeting is to promote self-disclosure and the art of listening. It also provides a forum in which family members can feel nurtured, loved and worthwhile within the family unit.

Format:

1. Select a 'sacred time' agreeable to all family members. It is essential that the 'sacred time' be honoured above any other activity or event. This demonstrates the fact that the family members hold the family unit as something of great importance.

2. The family meeting will be held once a week at the agreed upon 'sacred time'.

3. Each week, a different member of the family will lead the meeting.

4. The leader will begin the meeting by sharing his or her reality with the other family members. This self-disclosure is designed to include all feelings, for example:

'I feel happy about...'

'I feel disappointed about...'

'I feel pain when...'

'I feel ashamed about...'

'I feel afraid when...'

'I feel guilty for having done...'

'I feel proud of myself for...'

'I become sad when...'

It is extremely important that the person sharing tell only of their feelings.

During this sharing, this is not the time to talk about others, nor is this the time to lecture, preach or complain. No one is allowed to interrupt the one who is sharing. There is no cross-talk. The other family members must listen until it is their turn to share. Each family member takes a turn and this process of sharing continues until everyone has shared.

5. Once all family members have shared, a discussion period may be held for points of clarification, so there is no misunderstanding. It is important to keep this time free from advice, argument and problem solving. This discussion time is for clarification only.

6. In the event of a disagreement or fight, ***no one is allowed to leave*** the room until an agreement satisfactory to all family members has been reached. The reason for this is to show that difficulties can be solved by verbal communication.

7. Do NOT justify your behaviour when someone expresses their feelings about something you have done. This amounts to shoving those feelings back into their faces and, in essence, saying: 'You're wrong for the way you feel'. Example:

Child: Mum, I felt angry when you yelled at me because I came home late.

Mum: (when it's her turn) I understand you were angry, but I will not tolerate you being late and I've already told you several times how it upsets me when you're late. If you would come home on time, I wouldn't have to yell at you.

The More Effective Way:

> Mum: I felt very angry when you came home late the other day, especially after I'd asked you so many times before to be on time. I felt worthless and unimportant having to repeat myself again.

Sometimes we think it is rude or cheeky for a child to tell us how they feel, especially if it has to do with the discipline we have instigated. The important thing to consider here is that children DO have these feelings and it really doesn't matter what caused them. They have a right to own their feelings and express them appropriately.

RULES FOR FAIR FIGHTING

The following rules for 'fair fighting' may be helpful in the development of meaningful communication.

1. Never attack - keep the focus on yourself using 'I' statements. For example: 'I feel', 'I sense', 'I believe', 'I think', 'I will', 'I hear', 'I see'.

2. Repeat everything you think you hear to the person who said it.

3. Take everything that is said seriously. Don't discount another person's reality.

4. If someone is hostile, don't take it personally. Rather determine the direction of the hostility by asking yourself: 'Who is this person really angry with?'

5. Encourage the person with whom you're in conflict to deal with you as one with whom they can share ALL of their emotions.

Fighting is not necessarily bad. If the fighting is fair, communication continues. The real enemy of communication and relating is silence.

I learned and adapted the above process while interning at The Meadows Treatment Centre in Wickenburg, Arizona. It's a powerful process. Try it several times before you make a judgement about its effectiveness. This process can also be adapted for couples or at marriage meetings.

CHAPTER 10

TOWARDS FORGIVENESS
THE BALANCED
APPLICATION OF LOVE

A CUP OF TEA, A BEX AND A GOOD LIE DOWN!

Having digested all of the information in this chapter, you may be considering taking time out to have the proverbial 'cup of tea, Bex and a good lie down'. Instead, what you really need now is time, patience and plenty of practice. These qualities are fundamental to building healthy relationships. Additionally, there are two essential keys. One is having a non-shaming support group where you can get your reality validated. The other is to love and respect yourself for having the courage to strive for healthy relationships in a society which offers few role models in this area.

In or to be in a healthy loving relationship in this day and age, I believe we have to have a pioneering spirit. The old ways of relating do not work any longer. I challenge you to break your multi-generational moulds and let yourselves discover new ways to love.

'Hold no one prisoner .
Release instead of bind,
For thus are you made free.'

from 'A Course in Miracles'

235

In my early days of recovery, I repeatedly was told: 'You've got to forgive your parents'; 'You've got to forgive yourself'. I didn't realise what an impossibility that was for me at that time, but I was willing to try anything, so...

I took instructions and suggestions from counsellors and others in recovery. I dutifully wrote my forgiveness affirmations - seventy times seven ('I forgive my mother for...', 'I forgive my father for...'). I said them aloud to the mirror and I prayed, asking my Higher Power to help me develop the willingness to forgive. I thought if only I could master the act of forgiveness, then I would be a good person and somehow the forgiving would set me free and restore everything.

However, I can see only too clearly now that I didn't have the capacity for complete forgiveness at that stage in my recovery. Like any other co-dependent, I was so bottled up with carried feelings, frozen childhood feelings and distorted thinking, that the first order of business for me was to begin to 'empty my bucket' and to start discovering what *my* reality really was (What did *I* think?, How did *I* feel?, and What did want to do or not do?)

Since that time, many clients have come to me with similar experiences about forgiveness. Some of them are religious zealots (from 'New Agers' to 'Born Agains') who claim they've already forgiven their parents or major caregivers. They just can't understand why they're trapped in a love-addicted relationship or why they have an eating disorder. Others feel shameful, guilty and have judged themselves harshly for retaining feelings of anger, loneliness, fear and pain towards their major caregivers and others. They are confused and questioning. 'Why are these feelings of anger and resentment still coming up when I forgave my parents years ago?' they ask. (Denial). Or they might say: 'I know my parents did the best they could do. After all, they came from a dysfunctional family, too.' (Minimisation).

In other words, their illusion of forgiveness has actually been a block to their recovery and the attainment of inner freedom because they still don't know that *they have the right* to have and express their feelings of anger, loneliness, fear and pain about their childhood history, especially when 'mum and dad did the best they could'!

The reason I titled this chapter 'Towards Forgiveness, the Balanced Application of Love' is that complete forgiveness is something towards which we gradually move in stages. *Complete forgiveness* cannot even be realised until we are in the *final* stages of healing our family of origin issues and our adult symptoms of co-dependency. In fact, forgiveness cannot be realised until we have completed the grieving process. I suggest that if you are in early stages of recovery, you *do not* practise forgiveness at all. Especially with those who you share a history or with those you strongly react to. At this point, it would be better practise forgiving the butcher who apologised to you for snapping at you the week before.

Being a practical person, I like to have ways to demonstrate a concept in my life rather than just conceptualise. So, in this chapter, I will talk about forgiveness as an action that expands our capacity to love. Many people rightly consider forgiveness to be a great idea, but they want to know exactly *how* to go about forgiving - beyond writing hundreds of affirmations until they have writer's cramp.

By keeping in mind that we're moving towards forgiveness, before I go any further, I first want to talk about the process and stages of recovery as outlined by Pia Mellody.

MOVING THROUGH RECOVERY - WHAT CAN I EXPECT?

As you journey forward, you may come across many unknown fears. Remember, you will be travelling in unmarked territory (the future) and you want to participate differently so you won't end up in the same miserable place. I always appreciate being informed of what to expect, even if it's exactly what I want to hear at the time, at least it allows me to make better choices in challenging times. Remember, you are in a *process* and it is vital to allow yourself to move through it - a step at a time.

The first and foremost thing to keep in mind is that co-dependency is a dis-ease of immaturity. The reason you are powerless within the self is that you do not have the maturity to be functional. When you criticise, ignore or indulge your wounded inner child and adolescent, you will remain in a state of immaturity and experience harmful consequences as a result. Recovery from co-dependency allows the process of maturity to take place. The wounded child and adolescent within us are immature because their stages of development were impaired due to growing up in dysfunctional environments that were less than nurturing.

Recovery from co-dependency involves treating two things:

1. Our history and family of origin issues and
2. Our disease process.

In the initial phase, we begin by literally growing up (the maturing process). How we do this is by healing our five primary symptoms of co-dependency which are:

1. Self-esteem issues

2. Boundary issues

3. Reality issues

4. Dependency issues

5. Moderation issues

The first thing my clients ask me when I explain this is: 'How long does it take?' I tell them that this is an on-going process and they will experience benefits along the way. The time it takes to heal these issues varies according to two major factors:

1. the extent to which the person has been 'damaged'

2. the degree to which they are committed to their recovery in terms of the time and energy they are willing to put in - eg. Are they working the Twelve Steps? Do they have a sponsor? Do they attend Twelve Step meetings regularly? Are they seeing a therapist, if needed? In other words, is recovery a priority in their life?

If you had cancer, wouldn't you go to the doctor to be properly treated and wouldn't you regard that treatment as a priority in your life? Or if you were a severe diabetic needing a daily injection of insulin, wouldn't you make sure you took all the necessary steps to get it? The only difference with this dis-ease is that although it is life-threatening, there is usually more *long-term suffering* involved before you die from it.

Now, getting back to the healing time involved, I can give you some guidelines as to how long it takes, but you must remember that these are only averages and they vary according to the factors I've just mentioned.

1. Self-esteem issues (better than/less than) - three years

2. Boundary issues (protection) - two weeks to six months (emotional boundary takes longer)

3. Reality issues (thoughts, feelings, behaviour) - three years (greatly improves in six to 18 months)

4. Dependency issues (needs, wants and desires) - three to five years

5. Moderation issues (tone down or tune up thinking/feeling reality and behaviour) - three to five years.

The process of healing your five primary symptoms will trigger a number of other processes which facilitate self-development. For a start, you'll begin to face your reality on two levels:

1. You'll face who you are and how your false self and adapted behaviour has made an impact on you and others.

2. You'll face the current reality of the dysfunctional people involved in your life. This usually precipitates a significant degree of discomfort (ie. you begin to see the dis-ease of co-dependency and addictions in your partner, friends, family, colleagues... even the butcher does not escape your scrutiny). At this point, the facing of your reality, especially with yourself and loved ones, will make you feel worse than you did before. It's normal to feel worse for the first six to eighteen months - that's because you're moving out of your misery and into your pain. When you allow yourself to drop into your pain, you are finally in a position where healing is possible.

In this phase of facing your reality, the key is to keep it simple. Here's what to do:

1. Suit Up and Show Up (at your job, meetings, appointments, etc)

2. Stay Present (learn to listen and observe)

3. Tell the Truth (as quickly and rigorously as possible)

4. Let Go of Outcomes (accept what you get and trust that it's enough).

STAGES OF RECOVERY

On the following page I've made a chart showing the stages of recovery. The five stages of recovery apply both to our histories and our dis-ease process.

OUR HISTORY	OUR DISEASE

STAGE 1 - DENIAL

In this stage, we either minimise the events of our childhood or deny them. E.g. 'I was not abused' or 'I came from a very normal family'.	'I'm not a co-dependent!' 'I don't have an eating disorder, 'I'm just a little overweight.' 'I may have a bit of a drinking problem but I'm not an alcoholic.' etc.

STAGE 2 - BLAME

In this stage, we blame our parents for the way our lives turned out. Some people never move beyond being professional victims.	We blame ourselves for how awful we've been in offending our mates and children. We feel shame and that we are not good enough.

STAGE 3 - ACCOUNTABILITY

In this stage, we begin to hold our major caregivers accountable for their impact on us and our personal development. Grieving starts in this stage	We hold ourselves accountable for our impact on others and for our symptoms. We take responsibility for our behaviour and for recovering from our symptoms.

STAGE 4 - SURVIVORSHIP

In this stage we've released enough toxic energy to start feeling joy again. We may even begin to see the humorous aspects of our dysfunctional families.	We begin to feel balanced and centred and to feel a sense of personal power and hope through the grieving process.

STAGE 5 - INTEGRATION

In this stage, we are grateful for who we've become, despite and because of our dysfunctional histories. We forgive our offenders.	We are grateful for our path of recovery and can see that we've gained depth of character amid the chaos. We forgive ourselves.

*Any trauma in adult life will knock a person back to stages one or two.

If we know this, we can avoid judging or blaming ourselves for any perceived lack of progress. In the event of a trauma, simply be aware of the process, acknowledge it and continue to take the necessary steps on your path of recovery, knowing that you have not lost the ground previously gained.

Forgiveness begins in the third stage of recovery and is well-established in stage five. By the fifth stage, a person has healed to the point where they no longer desire to see their major caregivers punished or victimised.

GRIEF, THE CRUCIAL STEP TOWARDS FORGIVENESS

Grieving starts in the Third Stage of the recovery process. Grief is a normal and natural response to any loss and although it is a process in itself, it's a topic most people know very little about. This is because the majority of people are in denial about what constitutes a loss. We are taught how to acquire and hold onto things rather than how to let go of things. We also experience loss whenever we make a change. With each change we make, no matter how small, there is a completion or an end to the previous experience. It doesn't matter if the change is good, bad or indifferent. Whether we desired the change or not, there is pain in letting go of the familiar. The pain is often accompanied by feelings of disorientation and confusion because in new beginnings, we are also entering the unknown.

Grieving generally involves moving through intense emotions and is a big taboo in our society. Because our society has placed negative judgements on expressing our intense emotions, the grieving process is usually expressed in private, hidden from us and therefore remains a mystery. As you recall, one of the ways the child and adolescent learn to express is by mimicking the behaviour of adults. In other words, the reason many of us don't know how to grieve, or will not give ourselves permission to, is because we haven't been able to witness much of it.

Therefore, as we grew up, we learned how to suppress our grief. Because of this, most of us have massive unresolved reserves of it inside us. (Lots of mud in the bottom of our bucket.) Intuitively, we feel that letting go could be overwhelming. It is part of the human condition to fear emotionally letting go, yet this is exactly what we need to do if we are to thoroughly empty our bucket.

Grieving is a healing process that cannot be done alone. We move through grief and heal, when we give ourselves enough time and find a non-shaming support group or person who can validate our experience. Validating someone is not the same as giving advice or a personal opinion. Rather it's being present for someone and really listening as they debrief their experience. Then, saying things such as: 'I can see by the tears in your eyes that you're sad' or 'I can hear by the tone in your voice that you're angry' and 'You have a right to express your sadness and anger.' This reflects back the reality of the experience. When our experience is validated we are finally able to have resolution about our losses and then move on. Grieving helps us to be complete with a past situation so we may be fully present in a new situation.

Bucket Emptying vs Cesspool Wading

Grieving is very different from wallowing in our feelings. In working with many clients, I've discovered there is a cesspool of feelings swirling in the bottom of our bucket. Sometimes people mistakenly think they are letting go and grieving, when all they've really done is sunk to the bottom of their bucket and are wading in their cesspool. When you empty your bucket, the mud is moving up and out rather than you sinking down into it. Sinking is similar to wallowing in self-pity rather than expressing grief. It's important to understand the difference between bucket emptying and cesspool wading so you don't drown as you move through your grief.

For many, the authentic self is lost and sometimes drowning in the bottom of the cesspool. The grieving process not only lightens the load, it helps to uncover the authentic self.

STAGES OF GRIEF

The grieving process actually has stages you can identify and track as you move through it, although they do not always follow the order below. This lets you measure your healing and gives you a light at the end of the tunnel that isn't the front end of a train.

John Bradshaw outlines the stages of grief in his book, '*Homecoming, Reclaiming and Championing Your Inner Child*'. The following is my adaptation of his work.

Stage One	Shock, Fear and Depression
Stage Two	Denial
Stage Three	Anger
Stage Four	Pain, Sadness and Hurt
Stage Five	Remorse
Stage Six	Shame
Stage Seven	Loneliness
Stage Eight	Joy

STAGE ONE - SHOCK, FEAR AND DEPRESSION

The first stage of grief incorporates shock, fear and depression. Shock occurs at the very beginning of grief, following a change or loss. If the change or loss is small there may be no recognition that we are in shock. If the loss is larger such as an end to a primary relationship; abrupt, such as being fired; or a big change, such as a move to a new country rather than a new house, then your degree of shock may be greater. The period of shock can last from a few minutes to several months, depending on your degree of loss or change and the abruptness of it.

Once we come out of shock, we experience fear. We may only feel the fear for a fleeting moment and then repress it. If we repress the fear rather than embrace it, then we will experience a state of depression. Depression acts as a lid on our fear as well as on our other feelings. In order to lift the lid on our depression and gain more positive control of our lives, it is important to learn how to embrace (accept, encompass, take up willingly) our fear. As we do this, we learn wisdom from our fear rather than allowing it to control our lives. In fact, embracing fear is a significant part of bucket emptying.

For example, let's say your primary relationship ends abruptly. Once the shock wears off, you may become depressed, stay indoors and hide under the covers. After a time, your best friend may drag you out of bed and encourage you to get on with living. Once you get back into the swing of life, then you're probably ready to identify your fear. In a situation like this, you may have fears about being unable to pay your bills on your own, fear of what people are saying about you, or even fear of being alone the rest of your life. Once you've identified your fear, then you have the choice to embrace it - or let it control you.

Current fears might be connected with impending loss or change because you are already projecting those events into the future. Maybe you've heard rumours that someone is going to be fired from your company and you fear it's going to be you. Or perhaps your fear doesn't seem to be connected with an adult loss or change, but as you examine it further, you may discover it is a *re-enactment of an original fear,* which was generated from a loss or change in childhood. For example, the fear of losing control may have originated when you were seven years old and fell off your bicycle. Perhaps you *felt fear* when you *lost* your balance. Whether you're experiencing a current fear in your life today, or fear generated from your past, it needs to be embraced. This gives you more freedom of choice and the ability to score your goals and win in the game of your life.

STAGE TWO - DENIAL

The second stage of grief is denial. Denial is a defence. A state of being that protects us from experiencing the shock, fear, pain and anger of loss and change from our childhood, as well as from our adult life. As we have seen with the Embracing Fear exercise, losses in adult life are frequently generated from childhood re-enactments. Some examples of adult losses to be grieved are lack of intimacy in relationships, lack of self-respect and low self-esteem. There are losses with money; job opportunities, homes, friends, spouses, children, health, etc.

Denial often comes in the form of bargaining. This is a more subtle way of defending and holding onto our cherished, illusionary pictures from childhood. When growing up we denied and often still deny the reality of how it really was in our families, schools and religious organisations. Rather than acknowledge this, we learned to repress our feelings and deny the abuse and lack of nurturing we experienced as children. Childhood losses also consist of opportunities missed because of our family situation. These include not getting the time and attention we needed, as well as missed opportunities around education, material items, social activities, sports, trips and friendships.

Having denial is not necessarily a bad thing. Denial works for us until we realise the repetition of behaviour patterns that are undesirable to us. Denial has protected many of us and allowed us to exist in situations where perhaps we otherwise may not have been able to. We often didn't have the power, resources, permission or knowledge of how to change things. But once we acquire this, we no longer need denial.

Once you come out of denial of your losses, you will be able to talk about what happened and begin to experience how you really felt about it then and how you feel about it now. This will help you continue to move through the grieving process. It is essential to grieve your losses in order to heal and stop re-enacting undesirable or destructive situations.

STAGE THREE - ANGER

After our denial begins to diminish, the next feeling that usually comes up in our grieving process is 'anger'. Anger is a very powerful energising emotion and a legitimate response to our painful losses. It's an active emotion that has an outward expression. The problem most of us have with expressing anger is - we haven't been shown how to do it appropriately.

Anger is a natural reaction to mistreatment. People often gloss over or rationalise hurtful treatment from others if they have been taught to repress their anger. If you've been violated or offended in any way, the expression of your healthy anger will restore your dignity.

Anger is usually disowned or displaced. Perhaps this is because we were shamed or punished for expressing our anger. Shame bound anger goes underground and often hides out in the body. This can manifest as high blood pressure, rashes, headaches, heart disease and even cancer.

Feeling and expressing our anger is not about blaming or being a victim. Recycling anger over and over in our head is internal raging and not the healthy expression of anger. This keeps us feeling victimised. To restore ourselves to wholeness through the grieving process, we must own all parts of ourselves. The part of us that is angry deserves its place. Learning the appropriate expression of your anger is vital to your healing process.

The following is a checklist for hidden anger. Although each symptom can have causes other than anger, the presence of these symptoms often act as a warning sign and are a good reason to look within for hidden anger.

1. Boredom, apathy and loss of interest in things you are usually enthusiastic about.

2. Liking sarcastic or ironic humour.

3. Smiling while you're hurting.

4. Frequent sighing.

5. Clenched jaws, especially while sleeping.

6. Waking up tired, rather than rested and refreshed.

7. Procrastination in the completion of set tasks.

8. Chronically stiff or sore neck.

9. Migraine headaches.

10. Stomach ulcers.

11. Excessive irritability over trivial matters.

12. Difficulty in getting to sleep or sleeping through the night.

13. Frequent disturbing or frightening dreams.

14. Perpetual or habitual lateness.

15. Getting tired more easily than usual.

16. Sarcasm, cynicism or flippancy in conversation.

17. Over-controlled monotone in your speaking voice.

18. Facial ticks, spasmodic foot movements, habitual fist clenching and any other similar physical acts that are done unconsciously, unintentionally and repeatedly.

20. Grinding of teeth, especially when sleeping.

21. Chronic depression with extended periods of feeling down for no reason at all.

22. Getting drowsy at inappropriate times.

23. Over politeness, constant cheerfulness with an attitude of 'Grin-and-Bear-it.'

24. Slowing down of movements.

25. Whining tone in voice.

STAGE FOUR - HURT, SADNESS AND PAIN

After you've begun to feel and express some anger, you will then realise how much you've been hurt. This leads to the expression of sadness and pain. If you were victimised in your childhood, you will begin to feel as though you've been betrayed. As you allow yourself to recall the feelings of victimisation and betrayal, you may feel vulnerable and needy. This experience often comes from un-met childhood developmental needs. Memories of deprivation begin to surface. Feeling and expressing the pain of this, is an essential part of the grieving process.

Most people feel ashamed of this deep pain and attempt to hide it. If there is shame attached to the pain, people will usually end up wading in their cesspool rather than emptying their bucket. To support you through this stage of grief, it's important to select people and situations that give you the feeling of safety.

STAGE FIVE - REMORSE

The feeling of remorse often follows sadness and the recollection of betrayal. In the case of the death of a loved one, we often feel remorse for things left unsaid. Perhaps we feel remorse about some of our actions or wish we had spent more time with the deceased. We may also feel remorse over changes we've made and losses we've had in our adult life.

Dealing with our losses from childhood is different. We didn't have the power to prevent the losses from happening. Often children who have been victims of physical abuse end up feeling guilty. They feel responsible for their caregivers' abuse of them. When grieving childhood losses, we must understand there was nothing we could have done differently. We were not at fault. Our pain is about what happened to us, not about us. Remorse and false guilt is not useful when grieving childhood losses.

STAGE SIX - TOXIC SHAME

Moving into the last stages of grief gives us the opportunity to heal at our deepest level. 'Healing Shame' has become a widely recognised subject and a key to personal development in the past few years. There are several aspects of healing shame and many good books have been written about the subject. In this stage, we will be addressing shame from the perspective of grieving loss and change.

Shame is commonly misidentified as guilt. When we feel guilty, our conscience is troubled and we regret having behaved in a way that violates our personal values. Guilt does not reflect directly upon our identity, nor diminish our sense of personal worth. A person with guilt might say: 'I feel terribly sorry about the consequences of my behaviour.' In doing so, they reaffirm their personal values. With guilt, the possibility of repair exists and learning and growth are promoted. (This is what you did when you wrote your amends letter to yourself earlier.) But shame is a painful feeling about one's self as a person. A shameful person sees no possibility of repair because shame pervades their very identity. No growth or learning is derived from the experience because it only confirms one's negative feelings about one's self. There isn't any remorse to shame because it's not about something we did wrong. It's about *being* wrong. Simply stated: guilt says, 'I *made* a mistake,' shame says, 'I *am* a mistake.

Feeling shame in this way is toxic and always necessitates a cover up. Our shame core has been hidden with the denial and defences we have been moving through in our grieving process. When we feel our shame it immobilises us and keeps us from taking the steps we want to take, even if our intentions are strong. Toxic shame makes us feel flawed and defective as human beings. It causes us to feel bad, stupid and not good enough. When we feel this way on the inside it often drives us to look to externals for our self-esteem and validation. Therefore, when we reach this stage in our grieving process, it is common to distract ourselves. This is the point where we usually run. If this happens we miss our chance to complete the grieving process and to give ourselves the freedom to choose what we really want. In order to discover our needs, wants and desires, we must embrace our shame.

STAGE SEVEN - LONELINESS

At the centre of our shame-core is our authentic self. Our true essence and ability to grow and expand has been covered up and retarded by our shame. Once we begin diminishing our toxic shame, we can discover who we really are and what we want in a very intimate way. This is an exciting time and it is also a time when we experience the depth of our loneliness. Healing shame leads to loneliness, which is the next stage of our grieving process.

Perhaps this is the most challenging stage of the grieving process and usually the stage when people give up. Why? Because it's the stage when we feel the pain of abandonment - and we finally understand how we have abandoned ourselves.

Once we've emptied our bucket and uncovered our authentic self, we feel more space, emptiness and a void. It can be tempting to distract ourselves and fill the void so we can continue to hide and isolate. Even though we've seen the harmful consequences of shame and isolation, it is still a familiar feeling. If we wish to connect with others and have intimacy in our relationships, we must give ourselves this time and space to develop, expand and grow. Only when we have an intimate relationship with ourselves can we move to intimate relationships with others.

There are two precious gifts in this stage of grief. The first is having the quietness and space to discover more about yourself. The second is to reach out. When you are feeling lonely, the pain of abandonment can motivate you to become actively involved in life. It can nudge you to reach out and find others to join with. Reaching out and joining with others is not the same as using people to fill up the emptiness and soothe your pain of abandonment. To truly join with others, you must be more vulnerable.

At this stage of grief you will be feeling your vulnerability at a deep level. Although this can be a bit risky, you needn't be concerned because many of the exercises you've been playing with have allowed you to experience the *power* of your vulnerability. Even though it may feel somewhat unfamiliar, you are probably more authentic than ever before.

The key to moving through this stage of grief is to balance quiet time and discovery of yourself, with reaching out and joining with others.

STAGE EIGHT - JOY

As we embrace the last stage of grief, we begin to celebrate and en-joy more vitality and enthusiasm. This gives us more energy and motivation to play in the game of our life.

In the process of emptying our bucket, we have become willing to look at the lessons in our life and examine the situations that have caused us fear, pain, anger and shame. In doing this we've sometimes judged ourselves harshly. We can also tend to analyse and focus on all the things we've done wrong.

As we empty our bucket, it's important to examine the mud as it comes up and out extracting the wisdom from it, without focusing on it. Whatever we focus on and place our attention to will manifest.

Why is it that we cannot focus more on joy by examining it and gaining understanding of how we attained it? This may be a new way to continue our growth process and a foundation on which we can play in the game of our life.

SELF CARE DURING THE GRIEVING PROCESS

Although it is 'good' and healthy for you to grieve, most people don't know how to take good care of themselves during the grieving process. The following suggestions for good self care during the time will help you get through the experience with more ease and self control. This is how you will have an experience I call *'good grief'*.

1. **Pay attention to what your body is telling you.** If you need to sleep then do so. If you need to cry, cry. Freely express your emotions with people who will listen with compassion and have been in similar situations. Most importantly, honour all of your emotions and go with the flow.

2. **Lower expectations of yourself.** You can't expect to run at full capacity when you are in this healing process, so give yourself a break and don't expect to perform as well as you normally do. Let others know that it may take a bit of time before your performance is back to normal.

3. **Communicate your needs.** Don't expect others to know what you need. Communicate to your family and friends and let them know how they can support you. Give feedback to people who are meeting your needs, so that they will continue to do what is working.

4. **Take time to do the things you need to do for yourself.** Engage in activities that are healing and nurturing to your soul. Spend extra time caring for your needs.

5. **Pamper yourself.** Treat yourself extra well at this time. Without breaking your budget, do things for yourself that are helpful. Being with people who are nurturing to you, taking hot baths, extra time in the shower, massage, long walks at the beach or any other inexpensive activity will help to nurture your soul and protect your bank balance while you are indulging in this down time.

6. **Keep a personal journal.** Writing down your thoughts and feelings can help you to validate your losses. Journaling is a powerful way to pour out your grief, often bringing clarity and resolution.

7. **Eat properly and get plenty of sleep.** Maintaining a healthy diet and getting proper sleep is essential for functioning as well as you can. If you are having difficulty, get a check-up from your doctor, naturopath or wholistic practitioner.

8. **Get physical exercise.** If you exercised prior to this time, try to maintain the same routine. If you weren't exercising... start! Moving your body helps to move the feelings out. It will also help you to sleep and maintain physical balance which is essential to feeling grounded. Of course, if you are overweight or have health problems, visit your doctor before embarking on a physical exercise routine.

9. **Be aware of others' reactions.** Many people will not know how to react appropriately to your grief. Some are more comfortable than others in responding to people who are in an emotive state. Be true to yourself and let others know if they say something inappropriate.

10. **If you need extra support, such as individual counselling or coaching... get it.** Get all the support you need. Once you have

opened up to the grieving process you can go through it quite quickly with a skilled counsellor, coach or facilitator. Making this investment can save you a lot of heartache and get you back on your feet more quickly. It is normal for feelings of hopelessness or even suicidal thoughts to surface at this time. Don't hesitate to contact a professional and talk about these feelings and thoughts so they may pass and you don't feel crazy.

GRIEF AND RECOVERY

Participating in your recovery by focusing on the five core symptoms of co-dependency, facing your reality in your current situation and parenting yourself will bring you out of denial of the many losses you have incurred in your life. These include the losses of childhood, such as not getting the attention and time you needed and opportunities missed because of your dysfunctional environments (e.g. education, family, social activities, sports, trips,) etc.

You will also need to grieve the losses in your adult life related to your co-dependency and addictions, (e.g. intimacy in relationships, lack of self-respect, job opportunities, friends, spouses, children, health, etc). Once you come out of denial of these losses, you will begin to be able to talk about what happened and how you really feel about it. All of these types of feelings and realisations constitute grief. Grieving contributes enormously to the healing process in recovery. It is essential to grieve these losses in order to heal them. You cannot grieve alone. This must be done in the presence of others who will offer non-shaming support and validate your feelings.

You can never go back and make up for what you lost in childhood or for what you've lost in your adult dis-ease process of co-dependency. All you can do is grieve this and then make the changes in your life that will put a halt to any self-victimising behaviour.

OPENING THE DOORS TO FORGIVENESS

Once the grieving process is underway, it opens the door to forgiveness. In some cases, grieving automatically triggers complete forgiveness. I had a profound experience of this some years ago while watching a John Bradshaw lecture video. He was discussing dysfunctional family systems and referring to Alice Miller's work on Hitler. I grew increasingly uncomfortable listening to this material and soon realised I was feeling very angry. Bradshaw was discussing the totalitarian nature of German fathers in Hitler's era. As he described some of the family 'rules', I became extremely emotionally upset. I felt as if he was talking about me and my family. (My father's father had emigrated to the USA from Germany. He was an alcoholic and died when my father was seven.) I began to cry uncontrollably and in the depths of my grief, doubled over in a near-foetal position. The intensity of my pain frightened me so much that I telephoned my sponsor. Between my choking sobs, I told her what was happening and she was wise enough to explain to me that I was experiencing deep grief and that this was a natural part my deep healing occurring in me. She told me to allow myself to go deeply into it and to be gentle with myself. I hung up the phone and continued to cry about the losses of my childhood.

After a while I began to cry for my father. (I was releasing the pain that I had carried for my father for so many years). A few hours after I had finished crying and moved through the deep pain of my grief, I felt uplifted and a wave of forgiveness for my father washed over and through me. I became centred and clear and wanted to talk to my father. When I phoned him, I told him that I'd realised how hard it must have been for him as a small boy without a father, a mother who was always working and three domineering older sisters. I also realised that he'd never had any support or functional role models for how to be a parent. I told him that I forgave him for being so strict and rigid with me and that I loved him.

This deep feeling of forgiveness came only after I allowed myself to acknowledge my feelings of anger, resentment and pain for all that I had lost in my childhood.

WHAT IS FORGIVENESS

'Nothing in boundless love could need forgiveness'

from A Course in Miracles

Volumes have been written about forgiveness, countless sermons have been preached about it and many lessons taught. I would like to focus on the practicalities of forgiveness and to explain how it can be applied as a balanced action to bring about positive change in our lives.

For a start, everyone has their own perception of what forgiveness really is. What does forgiveness look like to you? Perhaps you see it as a duty or obligation to forgive or perhaps you feel superior when you forgive. Some people feel like a peace-at-any-price doormat when they forgive. Maybe you've encountered the loving, righteous martyr types who completely deny their anger and 'numb' their pain by being constantly loving and forgiving. Take a moment now to focus on your perceptions of forgiveness.

When I contemplate forgiveness, I think of it as a balanced action that we can understand from three different perspectives:

1. Relinquishing Judgement

2. Exercising Our Capacity to Give

3. Expanding Our Capacity to Love.

FORGIVENESS AS THE RELINQUISHING OF JUDGEMENT

A Course in Miracles, the text says that in complete forgiveness, we recognise there is nothing to forgive. Initially this may seem a difficult, if not impossible concept to grasp, but try thinking of it in the following way.

In looking at issues of individual reality, we've already seen that no two people have the same reality because no two people have had identical life histories. We also know that co-dependents have dichotometrical thinking. They see things as either good or bad, right or wrong, black or white, etc.

People almost always feel that their own perceptions are 'right'. On an individual level, we perceive as 'wrong' those things which go against our personal values. Yet there are different values for other individuals, as well as the government, the church and society in general. Values also vary incredibly in different societies, countries and cultures. When we consider this, I think it's fair to ask if 'right' and 'wrong' are valid concepts. And if they're not, why do we need to forgive at all? In our dualistic thinking, when we forgive, what we are really doing, therefore, is judging who is 'right' and who is 'wrong'. I'm not suggesting that we ought to agree with something that we feel is wrong, as we each have the right to think and feel the way we want. But we also don't need to adopt a superior position by casting a judgement on someone else and then forgiving them. Forgiveness, then, in this context, is about relinquishing judgement.

When we forgive in this way, we are exercising our capacity to forget and let go of the past. You may think of it this way: When a creditor forgives a debt, it is written off the books and the slate is wiped clean. When we relinquish judgement, we usually have resolved and let go of the unpleasant feelings of our past. This is what happened for me when I acknowledged and let go of the uncomfortable feelings I had towards my father - the judgements automatically dropped away too.

FORGIVENESS - EXERCISING OUR CAPACITY TO GIVE

Forgiveness provides an opportunity for us to exercise our capacity for giving. Think of it in the following manner: To 'for-give' can also mean to 'give before'. This 'giving before' basically entails taking the initiative and acting assertively. To forgive in this manner, you use your intuition and your feeling reality to anticipate and intercept future events or behaviours. By seeing clearly the potential situation, you give yourself forewarning. In other words, before something occurs that you don't want to happen, you can make clear to someone that you will not allow it.

On the other hand, if someone says they are sorry (expecting your forgiveness), sorry is not enough. Sorry only gets sorry-er. Instead, ask them what they will do to make certain that this does not happen again. What steps will they take to change? (This is how to make a true amends). If you simply forgive them with no provision for change, then what you are effectively saying is: 'You are allowed to do this to me until you are tired of doing it!' To forgive in this manner will make you confused and unfocused. When this happens, you become 'invisible' and your ability to create what you want in your life is hampered by everything outside of you. Also, this lack of focus significantly reduces your ability to observe.

Why do we repeatedly forgive the people who always profess their sorry-ness, but never seem to change? Could it be that we feel powerless to change them? Although this is true - we really can't change another person - what we can do is speak up and give them a direct understanding of what we will allow and what we won't allow.

FORGIVENESS - EXPANDING OUR CAPACITY TO LOVE

Each time that we perceive forgiveness is required, that situation holds potentially wonderful growth and wisdom for us. Whenever we feel forgiveness is needed, we are being given the opportunity to view the person, situation or event as something to be embraced in love. By that I mean we can look - and find - the value and good purpose that *very* situation or person holds for us.

In practical terms, forgiveness takes place through the energy of love. In everyday life, we use the energy of love to clearly define and distinguish between ourselves and others and to determine how close we will allow others to interact with us. When we do this, we are protected by our boundaries, we are preventing someone or something from controlling us and/or we are not allowing their offensive behaviour to affect us. Therefore there is no need for forgiveness. By protecting and containing our reality in this way, we avoid being confused and enmeshed with others. This is the essence of true forgiveness in that we are giving out (to give before) to others a clearer statement of who we are. When we for-give in this manner, we are expanding our capacity to love.

I saw a very clear demonstration of this in the lives of two women friends of mine, Leanne and Rachel. Both women were friends and business associates of Sam, a high-powered businessman. Sam is a very charismatic, but domineering man who is often offensive towards people who appear to be kind, giving and loving. He sees them as 'easy touches' and tends to bully and abuse them. Leanne and Rachel are both loving and giving women, but while Rachel exemplifies forgiveness as the expansion of her capacity to love, Leanne often does not use the energy of love to define her boundaries and protect herself from being controlled and offended by others. Some years ago, Rachel was doing freelance work for Sam's company and he wanted her to come on his full-time staff. She declined because she intuitively foresaw a potentially disastrous situation in which Sam would have abused her and tried to control her. When he asked her why she wouldn't join his staff, she laughingly replied: 'Are you kidding? And let you be a monster to me like you do to your secretary?' She realised that working for Sam full-time would have jeopardised their friendship. She had always known when to expand or contract her boundaries with him and their professional and personal relationship had survived and thrived as a result.

Leanne was also aware of Sam's character defects as she had seen him attack and criticise others, but when he offered her a full-time position, she not only accepted, but in her caretaking manner, she gave her time, attention and counsel in the hope of transforming him. In doing this, she failed to protect and contain her own reality by *not* giving out to Sam a clear statement of who she was. She allowed him to perceive her and her loving, giving manner as an easy touch, rather than expanding her capacity to love by using her boundaries. Consequently, Sam made her the scapegoat for anything that went wrong in his office. And Leanne 255 ultimately resigned. Now she has to relinquish her judgements of Sam in the process of forgiving him, while Rachel continues to love and appreciate Sam without allowing his character defects to impinge on her.

If an opinion poll were taken on both women, I would lay long odds on Leanne being voted the more loving and giving of the two. Rachel's behaviour almost certainly would be viewed as cheeky, distant and self-serving. Whereas, in fact, Rachel is no less loving than Leanne. She was expanding her capacity to love through forgiveness.

When we learn to become more of our authentic selves and maintain balance, we expand our capacity to love. The action of forgiveness in this manner *is* the balanced application of love.

Once you have set yourself free from your unfinished family business; your unresolved losses and destructive compulsive/addictive behaviour (yours or anothers), forgiveness and expanding your capacity to love is as natural as breathing.

AFTERWORD

Socrates said: "The unexamined life is not worth living". I can certainly attest to this as I've walked a path of recovery for the past twenty years.

When I began taking steps on my path towards personal freedom, I felt frightened, inadequate, lonely and trapped. I was sick and tired of pain, confusion and *trying* so hard at everything I did. This emotional bottom brought me to a point where I was willing to go to any lengths to experience true happiness, inner peace and personal freedom. At the time, I had no idea of the adventure I was about to embark on.

As I've continued to walk on my path of self-discovery and healing I've learned two things that have given me the greatest sense of personal freedom. The first was to surrender (to let go and give up the fight). At times this was easy and a great relief. But there were other times when I was fighting and kicking all the way before I let go. Out of much trial and error, I finally learned how to surrender without being a doormat or allowing others to offend me. Secondly, I've developed a practical working partnership with my Higher Power that is available to me in every moment (not just in church, meditation or on a mountain top). From this I discovered that I had rights and choices in my life, and that I could give myself permission to do some of the things I wanted to do.

Today my life is very different than when I first began. My security and fulfilment are generated from within me rather than by people and material possessions. I first arrived in Australia in 1988 because my daughter was getting married, and my son-in-law-to-be lived in

Australia. My decision to immigrate was a choice - a choice I couldn't have made had I not known I was free to choose. When I left my home in San Diego, California, I had several functional relationships with friends and colleagues. Because of my recovery, it was the first time in my life that I left a situation where I felt safe and supported rather than escaping a situation that I wanted to be free from. Moving half way around the world has been one of the most liberating experiences of my life. I now know that I can go anywhere and still feel at home. This would not be possible without my recovery.

My intention for writing this book was to help you to set yourself free. Because we teach what we need to learn, I have gained a lot in the process of writing this book and for this I am very grateful.

In closing I would like to share with you my favourite passage about recovery. It is from the The Big Book of Alcoholics Anonymous (reprinted with permission of Alcoholics Anonymous World Services Inc., New York, NY) and it reflects the way I feel in my heart.

Abandon yourself to God as you understand God. Admit your faults to Him and to your fellows. Clear away the wreckage of your past. Give freely of what you find and join us. We shall be with you in the Fellowship of the Spirit, and you will surely meet some of us as you trudge the road of happy destiny. May God bless you and keep you until then.

Love,

BIBLIOGRAPHY
AND SUGGESTED READING

A Course In Miracles. New York: Foundation For Inner Peace, 1975.

Alcoholics Anonymous, The Big Book. Third Edition.
New York: Alcoholics Anonymous World Services Inc., 1976.

Beattie, Melody. *Codependent No More.* New York: Harper/Hazelden. 1987.

Bradshaw, John. *Bradshaw On: The Family: A Revolutionary Way Of Self Discovery.* Pompano Beach Fl.: Health Communications, 1988.

Bradshaw, John. *Bradshaw On: Healing The Shame That Binds You.* Deerfield Beach, Fl.:1988.

Bradshaw, John. *HOMECOMING: Reclaiming and Championing Your Inner Child.* USA: Bantam Books, 1990.

Carnes, Patrick. *Out Of The Shadows: Understanding Sexual Addiction.* Minneapolis, Mn.: CompCare,1983.

Carnes, Patrick. *Don't call it love: Recovery from Sexual Addiction.* USA: Bantam Books, 1992.

Firestone, Robert W. *The Fantasy Bond: Effects Of Psychological Defenses On Interpersonal Relations.* New York: Human Sciences Press, Inc., 1987.

Fossum, Merle A. and Mason, Marilyn J. *Facing Shame: Families In Recovery.* New York: W.W. Norton & Company, 1986.

Friel, John and Linda. *Adult Children: The Secrets Of Dysfunctional Families.* Deerfield Beach, Fl.: Health Communications, 1988.

Gibran, Kahil. *The Prophet.* New York: Random House, 1951.

Hay, Louise L. *You Can Heal Your Life.* Concord, NSW Australia: First Australasian Edition,1988.

James, John W. and Cherry, Frank. *The Grief Recovery Handbook: A Step-By Step Program For Moving Beyond Loss.* New York: Harper & Row, 1988.

Lerner, Harriet Goldhor. *The Dance Of Anger: A Woman's Guide To Changing The Pattern Of Intimate Relationships.* New York: Harper & Row, 1989.

Mandino, Og. *The Greatest Miracle In The World.* New York: Bantam 1977.

Mellody, Pia. *Facing Codependence: What It Is, Where It Comes From, How It Sabotages Our Lives.* San Francisco: Harper and Row, 1989.

Mellody, Pia. *Facing Love Addiction: Giving yourself the Power to Change the Way You Love.* Australia: Harper Collins Publishers, 1992.

Miller, Alice. *The Drama Of The Gifted Child.* New York: Basic Books, Inc., 1981.

Norwood, Robin. *Women Who Love Too Much.* Los Angeles: Jeremy Tarcher, Inc., 1985.

Schaef, Anne Wilson. *When Society Becomes An Addict.* San Francisco: Harper and Row, 1987.

Schaef, Anne Wilson. *Escape From Intimacy: Untangling the "Love" Addictions: Sex, Romance, Relationships.* San Francisco: Harper and Row, 1989.

Sex and Love Addicts Anonymous. Boston: The Augustine Fellowship, Sex and Love Addicts Anonymous, Fellowship-Wide Services, Inc.,1986.

Siegel, Bernie S. *Love, Medicine & Miracles: Lessons Learned About Self-Healing From A Surgeon's Experience With Exceptional Patients.* New York: Harper & Row, 1986.

The Twelve Steps For Adult Children Of Alcoholics And Other Dysfunctional Families. San Diego: Recovery Publications, 1987.

The Twelve Steps For Everyone... Who Really Wants Them. Minneapolis, Mn.: CompCare,1975.

Twelve Steps And Twelve Traditions. New York: Alcoholics Anonymous World Services, Inc., 1953.

Wegscheider-Cruse, Sharon. *Choice-Making.* Pompano Beach, Fl.: Health Communications, 1985.

Resources from Shirley Smith

For more information visit our websites:
www.SetYourselfFree.com.au or www.TheRadiantGroup.com.au
Call: +61 2 9953 7000 • Email: info@TheRadiantGroup.com.au

Wholesale rates and quantity discounts are available for practitioners and organisations on The Set Yourself Free *Series (books & audio programs).*

BOOKS BY SHIRLEY SMITH

SET YOURSELF FREE: ANNIVERSARY EDITION
Break the cycle of co-dependency and compulsive addictive behaviour.

ISBN: 9780975102107
Pub: The Radiant Group Pty Ltd

Australia's #1 selling title on co-dependency.
This new edition includes real life, inspiring, Australian stories from those who set themselves free! The book is more relevant today than when first written over a decade ago. Why? Because co-dependency and addictive behavior is a costly and pervasive element of Australian society; increasing significantly since the book was originally released.

A must read for people with addictive personalities ...... and those who love them!

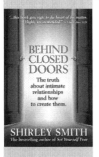

BEHIND CLOSED DOORS
The truth about intimate relationships and how to create them.

ISBN: 978-0-9751021-3-8
Pub: The Radiant Group Pty Ltd

Secrets, lies or what we cover up, are the real betrayals in relationships. When we hide things from our partner or from ourselves we sever our connection - and the love, passion and intimacy we've built starts to break down. This creates loneliness, anxiety, withholding, jealously, distrust, infidelity, depression and lack of confidence. This guide offers vital information and easy to follow exercises to give you the key to find solutions, and learn to create fulfilling relationships and lasting intimacy.

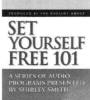

SET YOURSELF FREE 101
A series of audio programs presented by Shirley Smith

This four pack CD includes a series of audio programs developed to help you express your true self in ways that furnish more happiness; cooperation; love; satisfaction and success in your life. CDs include:

CD1: **The importance of a strong personal foundation.**

CD2: **Anchors Away**. *Set yourself free from what anchors you to the past.*

CD3: **Good Grief**. *Grief is as a dynamic healing process of transformation.*

CD4: **Needs, Wants, Desires, Values.** *Learn to identify your needs, wants, desires and values in relationships. Defining the difference makes the difference!*

PODCASTS: *Log on to www.SetYourselfFree.com.au and view our Free Resources. Download Podcasts by Shirley Smith immediately covering Relationships, Family Roles and how to Create Healthy Relationships.*

AUDIO PROGRAMS
BY SHIRLEY SMITH

All Audio Programs are available on CD or downloadable.
Check the website for prices and special package savings.
www.SetYourselfFree.com.au • Shipment is available worldwide.

THE SET YOURSELF FREE SERIES

BREAKING THE FAMILY TRANCE
Single CD: 61 min.

History doesn't have to repeat itself! This audio program will help you unlock unconscious psychological defenses that keep you stuck. These defenses create destructive habits and sabotaging behaviours causing you to recycle the same unfulfilling relationships and circumstances.

SET YOURSELF FREE FROM ADDICTIVE BEHAVIOURS
Single CD: Duration 63 min.

This program teaches the critical distinction between compulsive and addictive behaviour and why the approach to their treatment must be different. You will learn a simple, 3-Step model to treat the 'process addictions' to: work, sex, money (gambling, spending, debting) relationships, raging, rushing, religion, romance, eating, starving, body image, internet, sport or being busy. Learn to have more consistency in your daily life.

This program is a must for people caught in addictive behaviours... and for those who care about them!

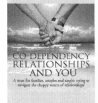

CO-DEPENDENCY RELATIONSHIPS AND YOU
Single CD: 62 min.

This program explains what's required to establish a solid, soulful relationship with yourself first, and then shows you how to expand to form healthy relationships with others. This process is possible whether you are currently in a relationship or not. If you want to learn to make choices that satisfy you and changes that last, then you can't afford not to hear this comprehensive presentation on Co-dependency, Relationships and You!

THE RELATIONSHIPS SERIES

IS IT INTIMACY OR IS IT INTENSITY?
Single CD: 52 min.

Do you swing between highs and lows, causing you to seesaw between intense pleasure and intense pain? This highly informative audio program gives you deep insights into the nature of intimacy and how we use intensity as an addictive substitute. Lack of real intimacy is the source of pain, confusion, loneliness and mistrust in relationships. Discover the true characteristics of intimacy, why it is fundamental to your happiness and how to create it in your relationships today.

THE RELATIONSHIPS SERIES (CONT)

THE ROMANCE TRANCE
Double CD Pack: 83 min.

Learn to stop power struggling and discover how to relate between the paradoxes that are present in all relationships. Gain deeper insights into your patterns of relating, receive guidance and encouragement to express yourself honestly and discover the tools to create healthy, loving relationships built on a spiritual foundation of hope.

THE CO-ADDICTIVE LOVE DANCE
Single CD: 39 min.

This CD is not only reserved for romantic lovers. Many mothers and daughters; mothers and sons; fathers and daughters; fathers and sons... or in fact any two people can dance this dance! Co-addictive relationships are set up from unresolved issues from our formative years. These include neglect, abandonment, abuse, engulfment, extreme control and unmet needs. 'The dance' distracts partners from discovering their real issues, so they don't have to acknowledge the emptiness and loneliness in their relationship or their unresolved childhood wounds.

They are caught in an addictive cycle (a swirling dance) that is an intense replacement for true intimacy and real relating.

If you want to stop dancing and create honest, loving, 'real relationships' ... then this program is for you!

CREATING A FULFILLING LIFE SERIES

IT'S TIME TO SHINE
Single CD: 70 min.

Are you tired of missing the boat and wonder when it's your time to shine? Is there a personal or professional voyage you're ready to take, yet something seems to be anchoring you to the dock?

This audio program explains how to pull up your anchors, discover your passion, get clear on your direction and let the wind fill your sails.

During this program you will learn to set sail and create anything with purpose, passion and pleasure!

BON VOYAGE - CO-CREATING AND MANIFESTING VISION
Double CD Pack: 110 min.

Successful people have a secret. They know the inner workings of what drives them and fuels their passion. Not only do they have a vision, they know specifically how to create their vision in their own unique way. This secret allows them to stay focused, avoid distraction, create structure without rigidity, let go of absolutes and they are prepared to seize opportunities in the moment.

Successful people know how to chart their course by co-creating with the invisible power of the Universe. They not only reach their destination - they enjoy the voyage and sail with spirit!

All programs are available on CD from our website -
www.SetYourselfFree.com.au or by calling +61 2 9953 7000

Made in the USA
San Bernardino, CA
23 February 2013